Readers are invited to view and download
supplementary materials for
Bookkeeping for Nonprofits:
A Step-by-Step Guide to Nonprofit Accounting.

The supplementary materials are available FREE on-line.

If you would like to download and print out an
electronic copy of the supplementary materials,
please visit www.josseybass.com/go/bookkeepingfornonprofits.

Thank you,

Murray Dropkin and James Halpin

Bookkeeping
for
Nonprofits

Previous books by Murray Dropkin include:

The Budget-Building Book for Nonprofits:
A Step-by-Step Guide for Managers and Boards,
Murray Dropkin and Bill LaTouche (1998)

The Cash Flow Management Book for Nonprofits:
A Step-by-Step Guide for Managers, Consultants, and Boards,
Murray Dropkin and Allyson Hayden (2001)

Bookkeeping
for
Nonprofits

A Step-by-Step Guide to Nonprofit Accounting

by
Murray Dropkin
and
James Halpin

JOSSEY-BASS
A Wiley Imprint
www.josseybass.com

Published by Jossey-Bass
A Wiley Imprint
989 Market Street, San Francisco, CA 94103–1741   www.josseybass.com

Jossey-Bass books and products are available through most bookstores. To contact
Jossey-Bass directly, call our Customer Care Department within the U.S. at (800)
956–7739, outside the U.S. at (317) 572–3993, or fax (317) 572–4002.

Jossey-Bass also publishes its books in a variety of electronic formats. Some content
that appears in print may not be available in electronic books.

Library of Congress Cataloging-in-Publication Data

Dropkin, Murray.
  Bookkeeping for nonprofits: a step-by-step guide to nonprofit accounting/
  Murray Dropkin, James Halpin.
      p. cm.
  Includes bibliographical references.
  ISBN-13 978-0-7879-7540-1 (alk. paper)
  ISBN-10 0-7879-7540-0 (alk. paper)
  1. Nonprofit organizations—Accounting. I. Halpin, James, date.
II. Title.
  HF5686.N56D76   2005
  657'.2—dc22
                                                    2005003106

Printed in the United States of America
FIRST EDITION
PB Printing   10 9 8 7 6 5 4 3 2

CONTENTS

PART THREE • PUTTING IT ALL TOGETHER   145

PART FOUR • RESOURCES   195

List of Exhibits and Checklists

DEDICATION

This book is dedicated to the bookkeepers who inspired this book—all those who helped train me as a bookkeeper (on my way to becoming an accountant and CPA)—and to the profession of bookkeeping itself.

Bookkeepers are the backbone of a good nonprofit organization. They keep things going. They pay the staff accurately, they keep vendors happy, and they watch every disbursement to make sure the organization is getting value. They file reports required by funding sources on time. They understand what the organization's mission is.

When you graduate college with an accounting degree, you know a lot of theory but not a lot about bookkeeping. Part of the reason for this phenomenon relates to human beings creating a great number of different ways to record transactions. Each client I visited in the early stages of my career maintained varying quality of records from excellent to nearly non-existent.

The one constant was that the bookkeeper was trying valiantly, sometimes with little or no training or supervision or assistance, to keep the records straight. If the records were not correct, the same vendor could get paid twice—or perhaps not at all—or checks could bounce if the cash records were wrong.

I was sent to a very hot factory one day to do a payroll because the bookkeeper was ill. The payroll was *piece-work payroll,* where the staff is paid a certain amount for each piece of work completed. Virtually the entire shop's staff consisted of non-English-speaking immigrants. Being a neophyte bookkeeper I made several mistakes in calculating the amount of the payroll check due to several workers. Within five minutes of the checks being distributed, three employees came into the bookkeeper's office waving official government payroll tax tables at me to show me I was unable to read a withholding table correctly. My understanding of how difficult it was to be a bookkeeper really increased that day. My respect for bookkeepers went up enormously after that experience. It was very difficult to prepare accurate bookkeeping records, especially under pressure.

Bookkeepers taught me what a recurring journal entry is and what an accrual is and what a reversing entry is. I remember one bookkeeper lecturing me on the importance of making sure that all operations of the organization were properly insured. Time and time again the glue that held the entity together was the bookkeeper, who seemed to know everything about what was going on. The bookkeeper would plot and scheme to conserve cash so a payroll was never missed. A good bookkeeper had the guts to tell the boss *no* if an improper transaction was being contemplated.

I hope this book helps those individuals working as bookkeepers now to understand better their roles within an organization. I hope this book will encourage bookkeepers to learn more and improve their skills so that they can become better bookkeepers and (if they so desire) continue growing in their professional career to achieve the highest possible goals. Based on my experience, by starting in a bookkeeper position it is possible to grow professionally to a more senior career position—all it takes is hard work and perseverance. I sent drafts of this book to eighteen different reviewers for an overall review of its contents. Most of the reviewers were bookkeepers before they became accountants, controllers, treasurers, directors of finance, and CPAs. Bookkeepers and their supervisors, working together, can create outstanding staff development opportunities. I truly hope this book, written for bookkeepers and based on the input of former bookkeepers (wearing their new hats), will be useful to members of that profession as they perform their current job and as they work their way up the organizational and professional ladder. I wish all of you bookkeepers the best of luck in your current and future career.

March 2005   Murray Dropkin
                                                                             Brooklyn, New York

This is dedicated to Janny.

March 2005   James Halpin
                                                                             Edison, New Jersey

PREFACE

We have been working with nonprofit organizations for decades. As far back as 1965, we saw how difficult the financial record-keeping challenge was for a nonprofit organization. In one consulting engagement from that year, the executive director of the organization was a poet and educator. His scholarship had made him a relatively famous individual in literary circles. The organization he headed was a small nonprofit with an annual income under $100,000. He was both executive director and bookkeeper and would ask interesting, complex questions about how best to keep the books. His knowledge of literature far exceeded his bookkeeping skills, and it was a challenge for him to keep the organization's financial records properly and to prepare accurate financial statements and tax filings to satisfy the government and the funding source.

Many nonprofit organizations then and now have intelligent people in charge with little or no financial expertise. While this is also true in the for-profit world, the compliance and administrative burden for a small nonprofit organization is far greater than for a similar sized for-profit company. In some states, a nonprofit organization with $250,000 or less per year in support and revenue is required to file an audit with the state attorney general and to pay a filing fee based on income or net assets. This is seldom a requirement in a for-profit company. Furthermore, the financial statements and tax returns of nonprofit organizations are published, often on the web, for interested parties to see. In fact, Internal Revenue Service regulations require most tax-exempt organizations to make available upon request their application for tax exemption and recent annual information returns filed with the IRS.

Successful financial management of nonprofit organizations has become more and more complicated each year. Every aspect of the nonprofit environment has undergone, and continues to undergo, many changes. The ways in which government, foundations, and individual donors support nonprofits are constantly evolving. Regulation of nonprofits has been intensifying. For example, many states have introduced legislation to expand the role of state government in monitoring these organizations. The current level of oversight for nonprofit organizations above a certain income and asset amount will probably be substantially increased.

Nonprofit organizations are under a great deal of scrutiny at all times, based on their high visibility in the community and their sometimes-controversial activities. This scrutiny often focuses on the organization's finances; funding sources are not immune to public pressure, and they sometimes respond by auditing the nonprofit's books. Quality bookkeeping and accounting techniques, when used by the organization, are the best ways to guard against an adverse result. A solid accounting system helps the nonprofit organization remain in compliance with federal laws, state laws, and funding source covenants and regulations. Violations can result in bad publicity, and the effect is felt beyond the organization itself. Good financial records are very important to the entire nonprofit community.

The need for services has increased, both in quantity and breadth. Recent media attention has created a greater public demand for accountability. For many nonprofits, these issues are further complicated by reductions in government-sponsored social-service programs. All of these circumstances have contributed to the financial and management challenges many organizations now face. Increasingly, nonprofits must develop new strategies to remain effective in meeting the needs of our nation's most vulnerable populations. In many instances organizations have risen to the occasion and have maintained (and even expanded on) the high level of services they offer.

Our goal in writing this book is to offer some practical assistance on bookkeeping for a nonprofit organization. The changes in the operating environment and the added pressures just described have made keeping accurate financial records more difficult. Those who work with and in nonprofits must respond by adopting new perspectives and approaches to continue their services to the community. Organizations have to learn to function at a higher level of efficiency to remain viable, to serve their purposes, and to obtain the resources they need. We believe that three of the most important financial management tools for achieving these objectives are good bookkeeping techniques (which will produce accurate financial records), effective budgeting, and proactive cash flow planning and management.

Improving the quality of financial records via good bookkeeping, using effective budgeting processes and proactive cash flow management helps organizations succeed and therefore accomplish their mission. Financial operations generate important information that nonprofit organizations need to manage their operations properly.

> In addition to the resources in this book, updated information and helpful tips and techniques are available from the Jossey-Bass website: http://www.jossey bass.com/go/bookkeepingfornonprofits.

Organizations must learn to operate as effectively and as efficiently as possible. Operating effectively means that organizations are fulfilling their missions and best serving their clients. Operating efficiently means that organizations are devoting the greatest possible amount of their resources to fulfilling their missions. Ultimately, greater efficiency will mean that organizations will have a greater amount of financial resources with which to increase their impact on society.

This book is written for the bookkeeper of a nonprofit organization. It serves as an introduction to the bookkeeping process, and it describes how bookkeeping in the nonprofit world can differ from keeping the books for a for-profit business. This book is also for nonprofit management and board members, who must understand and enforce procedures and policies. Complete management support of the accounting system will result in information that is timely, accurate, and useful.

In researching literature relating to financial management of nonprofit organizations, we came across a number of texts written to help the controller, Chief Financial Officer, or treasurer of the organization. Missing was a text to help a nonprofit bookkeeper learn and apply techniques designed to create and maintain reliable and accurate financial records. We hope that *Bookkeeping for Nonprofits* will fill this gap and, in doing so, help nonprofit organizations fulfill their missions, which are so vital to our society.

March 2005

Murray Dropkin
Brooklyn, New York

James Halpin
Edison, New Jersey

ACKNOWLEDGMENTS

We would like to thank the following people for their time, effort, and encouragement as we researched, wrote, reviewed, and revised *Bookkeeping for Nonprofits: A Step-by-Step Guide to Nonprofit Accounting.* Eusebio David; Theresa Dominianni, CPA; Eric Havemann; Allyson Hayden; Philip M. Henry, publishing consultant, freelance writer, and editor; Edward Kitrosser, CPA; Everard Digges La Touche; Bill Levis; Mel Nusbaum; and Christine L. Manor.

We also want to express our sincere gratitude to Judy Barmak; Peter Block; Galen W. Booth; Pamela Brause; Randolph Brause; Tom Burgin; Joseph Cappadona; Conrado Caunan; Shirley Dey; Glenn Helfrich; Frances Hesselbein; Susan Keyasko; Wendy Kolb, business manager, Community Legal Aid Society, Inc.; Sylvan Leabman; Michael Leggiero, president and CEO, North Hudson Community Action Corporation; Kurt Lindsay, controller, Northern Manhattan Improvement Corporation; Barbara Lowry, executive director, Northern Manhattan Improvement Corporation; James G. McGiffin, executive director, Community Legal Aid Society, Inc.; Steven Mildener; Vincent Milito, CPA; Danny Mims; Ralph Porter; Barbara Starling, board member, Community Legal Aid Society, Inc.; Stephen Stempinski, CPA; Carolyn Terefenko; Leona Terry; Peter Ventrice; Al Villavecchia; Ronald J. Werthman, vice president of finance, treasurer, and CFO, Johns Hopkins Health System Corporation; Michael Wojciehowski, CPA; and Carol Wolff, executive director, Camden Area Health Education Center.

Dorothy Hearst and Alan Shrader of Jossey-Bass Publishers helped enormously with collaborative professional guidance and suggestions. We also are appreciative of Allison Brunner, associate editor, David Greco, marketing director, Akemi Yamaguchi, assistant marketing manager, and all of the staff at Jossey-Bass Publishers and of Rachel Anderson of Satellite Publishing Services for their help and support in publishing this book.

Finally and most importantly, we thank Goldie Dropkin, Lisa Dropkin, Madeleine Stephan, Louis Stephan, Janette Halpin, James Halpin III, Brian Halpin, Kate Halpin, Jamie Rausch Halpin, Rita Halpin, James Halpin Sr., and Roberta Holmes for their support and assistance.

M.D. and J.H.

THE AUTHORS

Murray Dropkin is president of CMS Systems, Inc., a consulting firm that specializes in improving the operational and financial systems of both nonprofit and for-profit organizations. Dropkin is a certified public accountant in New York, New Jersey, and Wisconsin and is managing partner of Dropkin & Company, Certified Public Accountants. He has over thirty-five years of experience in accounting, auditing, taxation, and management consulting for government, commercial, and nonprofit organizations ranging in size from $250,000 to $2 billion in annual revenue. Dropkin is coauthor of *The Budget-Building Book for Nonprofits* (Jossey-Bass, 1998) and *The Cash Flow Management Book for Nonprofits* (Jossey-Bass, 2001). He is coauthor of the three-volume publication *Guide to Audits of Nonprofit Organizations* (Practitioners Publishing, 1989), coeditor of the monthly newsletter *Nonprofit Report* (Warren, Gorham & Lamont), and author of articles published in professional financial and management-related publications. Dropkin is a member of the American Institute of Certified Public Accountants, the Association of Government Accountants, and the New York and New Jersey State Certified Public Accountants Societies. He has served on the American Institute of Certified Public Accountant's committee on tax-exempt organizations and on the national board of directors of Accountants for the Public Interest. He has also served as a member of the New York State Charities Registration Advisory Committee. Dropkin holds an M.B.A. from New York University and a B.S. from Brooklyn College. He can be reached at murray@dropkin.com.

James Halpin is a software developer, systems consultant, and accountant specializing in cost accounting concepts applied to the long-term health care, legal, transportation, manufacturing, and retail industries. Halpin is a certified public accountant in New Jersey. He has thirty years of experience in accounting, auditing, taxation, management consulting, software development, and computer consulting. He developed a job cost accounting software package that was widely used in the construction industry. He is the coeditor of the monthly newsletter *Nonprofit Report* and author of articles published in professional business and computer magazines. Halpin is a member of the New Jersey Society of Certified Public Accountants. He holds an M.S. in Management Systems Analysis and a B.S. in Management Science from Kean University. He can be reached at jph@jhalpin.com.

Bookkeeping
for
Nonprofits

PART ONE

Understanding the Importance of Good Bookkeeping

Bookkeeping is the foundation of the entire accounting and financial reporting process. The bookkeeper must analyze and record every financial transaction in an organization. The sum of all of those transactions forms the basis for everything that follows: financial reports, tax returns, budgets, cash forecasts, grant proposals, and so on. The three chapters in this part discuss the bookkeeping and accounting system: what needs to be done, how it should be done, and perhaps most importantly, why it should be done.

All staff members need to understand the mission and goals of the nonprofit organization to perform their jobs with maximum efficiency and professionalism. The organization performs more efficiently when the participants understand the operation of the system, the requirements of the system, and the goals of the system. This is particularly true of an accounting system. Each transaction represents an element of information important to staff members, management, board members, funders, donors, volunteers, and community constituents. Timely and accurate information provides stakeholders with feedback about the financial health of the organization.

A good bookkeeping system processes paperwork by adhering to standard written policies and procedures. In well-managed, efficient organizations, the bookkeeper is also charged with "seeing the bigger picture." This book encourages the bookkeeper to take an active role in assisting the organization in a more meaningful and collaborative manner. To facilitate this role, the organization must provide the bookkeeper with timely access to information about issues affecting the nonprofit. The entire organization's operations can be improved by a better understanding of the reasons for performing bookkeeping and accounting tasks using a good set of up-to-date accounting policies and procedures.

The systems, methods, policies, and procedures described in *Bookkeeping for Non-profits* should serve as guidelines for designing and implementing an accounting system in your organization, though some of the policies and procedures described in this book will only be implemented by larger organizations. While not every nonprofit has the human and financial resources to implement every idea, it is important for you to understand the concepts being discussed. Situations change, and organizations grow. The best systems are designed for the future as well as for the present. The first part of this book describes the goals of the accounting system; design your record-keeping methods and procedures for your organization with these goals in mind, and you will have a much better chance of providing the best services to your community.

CHAPTER 1

Overview of the Bookkeeping Function

K eeping the books of an organization is a simple concept to visualize: we can all conjure up the image of an oversized ledger on a desk, and the bookkeeper, wearing a green eyeshade, adding columns of figures. A more modern image is of a worker sitting in front of a computer screen with piles of paper on the desk. But what exactly is bookkeeping?

Bookkeeping is the systematic recording of transactions that affect the financial operations of an organization. While most of these transactions are monetary, nonprofit organizations also receive non-monetary donations (for example, volunteered time) that also must be recorded if they meet certain criteria. Later on, we'll explore what gets recorded, how it gets recorded, and even when it should be recorded; but for now let's examine why bookkeeping is important.

Every organization needs a method of tracking and understanding day-to-day operations. Monetary transactions can take many shapes, but they generally fall into four major categories:

- Cash received

- Cash disbursed

- Cash due to be received (accounts receivable)

- Cash due to be disbursed (accounts payable)

Theoretically, tracking the cash balance of an organization is the bare minimum you need to do to keep the organization going. You could accomplish this by simply putting all incoming cash into a shoebox, and paying all expenses by removing cash from that shoebox. Count up what's left in the box, and you have your current cash balance.

In the real world, this minimum knowledge is not only impractical but also totally inadequate. To manage the organization effectively, to plan future events, budget, to analyze, to file a tax return, more information and more skills are required.

Nonprofit organizations have a large number of different stakeholders: clients, community members, funders, board members, staff members, volunteers, and (in many states) the attorney general. The Internal Revenue Service, after many years of paying little attention to nonprofit organizations, has more aggressively started enforcing the laws and regulations governing nonprofits. Even small nonprofit organizations are in the public eye to a far greater degree than small businesses are. Each stakeholder needs information, and the accounting system is the primary source of that information.

Communication is essential to the management of any organization. While this chapter focuses on the flow of information from the accounting system to stakeholders, it is equally important for information to flow from stakeholders into the accounting department. Transaction details are just one such type of that information. In a well-managed nonprofit, communication helps the bookkeeper anticipate situations and provide management with the information and analyses needed to run the organization effectively.

Users of the Information

Who are the users of a bookkeeping system's information? The bookkeeper uses financial information all day long. Accountants analyze the information the bookkeeping system produces. Managers use the information to assess past results and to plan for the future. Board members use the information to monitor the financial performance of the organization in comparison to its official budgets. Others—the IRS, banks, lenders, funders, government officials, and the general public—all need access to reliable information generated by the bookkeeping system.

Program managers and department heads benefit greatly when they understand why and how to properly record transactions. Their own performance may be reviewed using financial information. They may evaluate personnel and program effectiveness by looking at the numbers, among other factors. When asked to prepare next year's program budget, the manager relies heavily on this year's financials. Applying for a new grant means the manager must analyze, project, and justify financial information that is based on historical bookkeeping data.

Bookkeeping, Accounting, Auditing: Who Does What?

Bookkeeping, accounting, and auditing are three processes that may appear to overlap, especially in a small organization. They accomplish different goals, but they use the same information. There is not a clear line of demarcation between bookkeeping and accounting. Depending on the size of your organization, one person might perform both functions. Based on recent changes in auditing standards, your organization needs to carefully monitor the role you are asking your auditor to play. Certain funding sources and just plain common sense prevent auditors from playing too prominent a role in bookkeeping and accounting services.

Accountants are often employees of the organization who supervise the bookkeeping function in addition to other responsibilities. They normally perform a more analytical function than *bookkeepers,* who primarily deal with the posting of transactions. Accountants begin with the accounting information (ledgers and journals) and analyze the results, looking for causes and effects. They also are responsible for maintaining the accounting information so that it can be used to generate financial statements for anyone who needs them.

Auditing is an attest function; *auditors* examine the books and determine whether the financial statements derived from those books conform to GAAP (generally accepted accounting principles) and accurately reflect the financial position of the organization. GAAP is a set of commonly accepted standards, principles, and procedures promulgated by the Financial Accounting Standards Board (FASB). Auditors must be independent of the organization, and should report to the board of directors with input from the president or executive director. Auditors use GAAS *(generally accepted auditing standards)* promulgated by the Auditing Standards Board of the American Institute of Certified Public Accountants (AICPA) and *Government Audit Standards* from the GAO (Government Accountability Office) and other standards required by funding sources or governmental agencies in auditing nonprofit organizations.

The Nonprofit World

Nonprofit organizations exist to fulfill a mission. In the business world, a for-profit enterprise is ultimately concerned with making a profit in order to provide a return on the owners' investment; if a product or service is not profitable, the for-profit enterprise will shift gears and sell something else. The nonprofit organization is committed to its "product or service"; it focuses on obtaining and allocating resources to get the job done. The goal of the nonprofit organization is to improve society without a profit motive.

There are many types of nonprofits. Some are direct service providers (hospitals, day care facilities); others collect and distribute resources (United Way, funding organizations); and still others are social organizations (local community clubs). Each nonprofit is organized to accomplish a specific mission, and money is one of the main resources used. How the money is collected and spent depends on many factors:

- Community needs
- Current events
- Funding source requirements
- Financial planning
- Budgeting
- Cash flow forecasting

In financial operations, a nonprofit organization is very similar to a for-profit enterprise. All organizations need to be financially healthy to function effectively. For-profit firms seek to maximize their net profits. Nonprofit organizations seek to minimize or eliminate any operating deficits, because they cannot fulfill their mission if they have inadequate resources. In reality, a nonprofit organization uses profits (called *increase in net assets*) to provide resources for future periods.

This is an important point that unfortunately is often misunderstood. Peter F. Drucker has underscored the point that every organization needs to have an economic basis. Many organizations interpret their *nonprofit* status to mean that it is improper to show an excess of income over expenses. That makes no economic sense. Any organization, nonprofit or for-profit, needs reserve funds to handle emergencies. Organizations also need surpluses to fund new and innovative ideas (Drucker calls these *opportunity budgets*). (We will explore this point in more depth in Chapter Thirteen, where we discuss operating budgets.)

Nonprofit organizations apply for tax-exempt status from the Internal Revenue Service. (For more details, see Resource E.)

Terminology

While the terminology used in nonprofit accounting is sometimes different, many of the same accounting concepts apply to both the for-profit and the nonprofit world. As we mentioned, nonprofit organizations can generate a net profit or a net loss, only they call them increases or decreases in net assets. Most accounting terms are the same, and often bookkeepers coming from a for-profit work experience can quickly grasp the differences. We'll explore this topic in more depth throughout the rest of this book.

The Goal of Bookkeeping

Whether nonprofit, or for-profit, the primary goal of bookkeeping is the same:

> To capture each transaction one time in a way that is fully documented, completely traceable, and fully usable by every person within and outside the organization who has a stake in the organization.

Let's break that goal down into its components.

Capture Each Transaction. As we mentioned earlier, bookkeeping is about recording monetary transactions. As the bookkeeper, you need a system in place that not only records a transaction; you need a system that helps you record every transaction. A missing transaction is a bigger problem than an incorrectly recorded transaction.

One Time. Ideally, you should deal with a transaction just one time, recording everything you need right then. Remember that there are many potential users of the information you are gathering; your bookkeeping system should be designed with each of those potential users in mind.

Fully Documented. Each transaction should be backed up by appropriate information. The organization's internal control system will specify the details of the documentation, but you should be satisfied that someone looking at the transaction at a later date could see what happened, how it happened, and when it happened without relying on anyone's recollection.

Completely Traceable. As transactions are recorded, either manually or electronically, you need a method to find your way back to the originating entry. Every total in the general ledger and every amount on a financial statement means something. The total usually represents a number of transactions; you need to be able to dig down and examine the individual transactions that make up the total.

Fully Usable. This is the complex part about designing a bookkeeping system. You need to stand back and take a look at the organization: who funds it, who runs it, who oversees it, and so on. Your system has to provide information to a wide variety of users in a form that they require. Here is a brief example:

Your organization employs a driver. The driver spends approximately one-half of the day working for Program A; approximately one-quarter of the day working for Program B; and the remainder of the day working for Program C. As you process the payroll, you'll charge the driver's gross pay to an expense category called *Driver Wages.* This satisfies some reporting requirements; it might be enough information to provide a financial statement to a bank or to file a payroll tax form.

Without capturing more information, how can you report to the funding source for Program C? How will the program managers plan their operations; how will they prepare future budgets?

Of course, if acceptable to a funding source, you might be allowed to estimate an allocation of the driver's gross pay, and in some cases the result would be the same. You'll make a judgment about when to capture details and when to allocate, but for items such as gross pay it is generally better to capture the details. Work schedules change; employees come and go; rates of pay change throughout the year.

If your organization receives money from federal, state, county, or city governments, some very detailed cost-definition and cost-allocation rules exist. (See Resource G for more information.)

The Bookkeeper As Information User

The bookkeeper represents the most basic user of an accounting system's information. Having up-to-date balance information—whether petty cash, cash in a checking account, cash in a savings account, accounts receivable, accounts payable, loan balances, lines of credit, or other balances—is essential to the bookkeeper's role in the organization. You'll constantly be checking these balances and reconciling them to more detailed sources (such as the accounts receivable detail report) or documents prepared by third parties (such as the monthly bank statement).

Management relies on the bookkeeper to summarize certain information and to provide frequent snapshots of balance statuses. A very useful report that many bookkeepers produce for management has the information shown in Exhibit 1.1.

EXHIBIT 1.1	Snapshot Report from Bookkeeper to Management

Date	
Cash in Bank	
Total Accounts Receivable Balance	
A/R Current (Less than 30 Days)	
A/R Between 30 and 60 Days	
A/R Over 60 Days	
Total Accounts Payable Balance	
A/P Due in 15 Days	
A/P Due Beyond 15 Days	

Using today's computer software, producing this type of snapshot report takes only a few minutes if your books are properly set up. The information is gathered from various accounting reports, such as the Trial Balance, the Aged Accounts Receivable (A/R) Report, and the Aged Accounts Payable (A/P) Report. Tasks that used to take a bookkeeper hours to do, such as adding up vendor ledger cards to produce the Accounts Payable Aged Invoice report, are now accomplished by the software with a few mouse clicks. This gives the bookkeeper time to investigate the anomalies: the very old vendor invoice or the accounts receivable balance that is now 120 days past due.

Other Information Users

As we mentioned earlier, the organization's managers will frequently be using the information from the accounting system.

Cash Flow Management. This is an essential function, and management needs accurate information about cash, A/R, and A/P in order to do it properly. Most enterprises that fail, both nonprofit and for-profit, do so because of a lack of adequate cash flow. Even when the organization is generating a surplus of revenues over expenses, inadequate cash flow can result. Timing is the key to good cash flow management. Payroll is often disbursed every two weeks; some vendors have very short payment terms (such as seven days); yet some funding sources only send in their checks every few months. Without adequate cash flow management, the organization could run out of cash, despite a financial statement (prepared on an accrual basis of accounting) showing an increase in net assets. This is a very important topic. (Chapter Fourteen discusses the concept in much greater detail.)

Budgeting. All nonprofit organizations should prepare accurate and complete budgets. The more successful nonprofits prepare budgets for every aspect of the organization.

Budgeting is a means of financial planning, and, with a proper reporting system, it is a means of evaluating results. We devote an entire chapter (Chapter Thirteen) to the topic.

Pricing Services. Without quality cost information, management would not be able to price services accurately. As in any organization, you want to price the services you offer at a point that covers all of your costs. There is no room for the old joke, "We lose money on each sale, but we hope to make it up with volume." (Since nonprofit organizations meeting specific IRS guidelines can solicit and accept donations and grants, necessary but unprofitable services can be subsidized.) The nonprofit typically tries to price services at a point where the targeted clientele can afford them. Frequently, nonprofit organizations adopt a sliding scale for services to accommodate clients on an ability-to-pay basis. So the price must be not too high, nor too low. A careful ongoing analysis of the accounting information helps management to determine what to charge.

Fundraising. The fundraising effort requires the use of quality accounting information. Fundraising costs are a major factor, but so is accurate information about prior funding performance, pledge collections, and program results. Showing a funding source the financial results from a program they previously funded, combined with an impact study showing the program's efficacy, often goes a long way toward securing future grants. The IRS and the Attorneys General of many states have become very interested in organizations accurately identifying fundraising costs.

Organization Planning. Organizations need to focus on what they do best. A careful analysis of the financial results for each program and department in the organization helps the board of directors and senior management to steer the nonprofit into areas where it can do the most good.

Financial Reporting. At the program level, at the department level, and the organization level, financial reports drive planning, budgeting, and operations. As we mentioned earlier, the staff accountants start with the information recorded by the bookkeeper and produce interim and year-end financial statements. They typically also provide budget-versus-actual (variance) reports to program managers and department heads on a regular basis. The auditors examine the year-end financials and issue a report to the Board of Directors and management. The auditors also prepare annual reporting forms (depending on the organization's IRS classification and size). This financial reporting all begins with the bookkeeper's work.

Staying Organized

A well-planned and implemented accounting system will include an accounting manual with properly designed internal controls, standard operating procedures, and financial policies. The fundamental role of the bookkeeper is to record the monetary transactions according to the internal controls following the accounting manual and to stay organized.

What does staying organized mean? For the bookkeeper, it means you must do the following:

- Be accurate

- Keep up to date

- Obtain documentation

- Ensure traceability

- Check authorization

- Check budget for availability of funds

- Obtain proper approvals

- Enforce policies and procedures

Let's examine each of these guidelines in detail:

Accuracy. This is the most highly prized attribute you can find in a bookkeeper. As the transactions multiply and accumulate, accuracy is essential. The bookkeeper has to take the time to understand the transaction being recorded—what it represents, where it should be entered (in terms of program, department, and overall classification), and who the responsible party is. Over time, the bookkeeper's knowledge about these details will make the accounting information extremely accurate; it will also allow the bookkeeper to become a valued contributor to the process of running the organization.

Timeliness. Information is the most valuable when it is current. Last week's cash balance doesn't tell you enough when you need to know the current balance. In the normal course of operations, no one is capable of being completely up-to-date in all areas, so the bookkeeper (working with management) can assign priority levels to various tasks. The bookkeeper also has a responsibility to inform management if certain tasks start to fall through the cracks due to an excessive workload.

Documentation. Bookkeepers must make sure that all documentation for a transaction is as complete and understandable as possible. Memories fade over time, so if it isn't written down, it will be lost eventually. Certain transactions naturally lend themselves to proper documentation; in other cases, the documentation is only complete if you take the time to request it. A typical example is the purchase of goods: there should be an authorized purchase order, the vendor's packing slip, a receiving document, and a vendor invoice (with proper approvals). Depending on the organization and on the purchase, some of this documentation might not be available. Look for guidance in the accounting manual. When in doubt, try to obtain full documentation.

Traceability. There should be no magic numbers in your accounting information. Every balance, every total is made up of real events; you should be able to work your way back from the total to the individual transactions. For everyday transactions, this is seldom an issue. The unusual event, if not documented properly, often leads to an inability to trace what happened. What seems obvious when you post it can become a "where-did-that-number-come-from?" item in a few short weeks.

Authorization. The bookkeeper should have a written list of individuals who can authorize the various transactions that occur in the organization. Several types of transactions must be authorized prior to the event; a basic knowledge of the authorization process and of the parties involved will aid the bookkeeper in understanding and recording the transaction. Including the bookkeeper in staff meetings will help the bookkeeper to understand everyone's role.

Budget Availability. Nonprofit organizations use budgets in the traditional sense, as a planning tool; but budgets also control cost reimbursement from various funding sources. It is important to check the budget to make sure there is room for the transaction. The bookkeeper, a program manager, or another staff member takes an active part in the process, depending on the size of the organization.

Approvals. Many transactions typically involving the disbursement of funds require written approval. Distinct from an authorization, an approval says that the transaction is correct and complete. In the case of a purchase of goods, the approval says that we received the correct items, that the items were satisfactory, that the item count is correct, that the unit price is as anticipated, and that the vendor's invoice can be paid in a timely manner.

Enforcement. The bookkeeper plays a pivotal role in the enforcement of internal controls, the policies and procedures designed to safeguard the organization's assets. An effective bookkeeper must be able to insist on adherence to the rules specified in the accounting manual by *every* member of the organization, regardless of the person's position. When fraud occurs, a common contributing factor is the inability of the accounting department to "stand up to" the boss and insist on compliance with the rules.

Common Bookkeeping Functions

We'll be covering the most common bookkeeping functions in more depth in later chapters. To complete this overview, here is a brief description of several common bookkeeping functions.

Cash Disbursements. The typical organization disburses funds on a weekly cycle through a check-writing process, with the occasional single disbursement occurring between check runs.

Posting Vendor Invoices. Vendor invoices are posted to the accounts payable system throughout the month.

Billing for Services. Billing for services includes creating and posting client or customer invoices to the accounts receivable system. Depending on the organization and on the service, this invoicing is done as the service is rendered or on a periodic billing cycle.

Recording Cash Receipts. Recording cash receipts includes crediting open accounts receivable items for payments received from customers or clients, as well as recording miscellaneous cash receipts. These transactions are typically posted every day.

Bank Reconciliations. This task involves analyzing the difference between the balance on a bank statement and the general ledger balance for a cash account. This is typically done once per month.

Account Analysis. As the name implies, account analysis means analyzing certain general ledger account balances to ensure that they are correct or to explain the details that make up the account balances. This is typically done once per month.

Petty Cash Reimbursement. Petty cash reimbursement involves adding up the vouchers and the remaining cash in the petty cash box, making sure the total matches the imprest (standard, unchanging) amount, then classifying and recording the transactions on each voucher into the correct general ledger account and writing a check to replenish the petty cash balance. This activity is done as necessary.

Summary

This chapter has presented you with an overview of the bookkeeping function. Every organization is unique, but they all have one thing in common: the need for a well-designed, accurately maintained accounting information system.

The Accounting Equation

How are transactions recorded? In this chapter, we'll discuss bookkeeping basics. Depending on your experience, you might choose to skim this material, concentrating on the topics unique to the nonprofit world. If you are new to the bookkeeping function, this chapter is a place to obtain a better understanding of bookkeeping; we recommend you also turn to the bibliography for other sources of information.

Two Views

As we mentioned in Chapter One, a bookkeeper records transactions. A basic accounting system is set up to provide two views of the transactions of an organization. The accounting system has to be able to produce a snapshot of the current state of the organization's finances. That same accounting system must also provide a detailed history of how the organization's finances ended up in the present state.

In Chapter One we mentioned that, theoretically, a bookkeeper could put all the organization's receipts in a shoebox and go from there. But a shoebox approach fails to provide either view. If we look into the shoebox and determine our current cash balance, we still don't know anything about other things we own, and we have no information about amounts we owe to vendors or to the bank. The snapshot of the current state of our finances is incomplete, so the first view is unavailable. In addition, the shoebox doesn't tell us anything about past transactions; receipts might be missing, and nothing has been categorized. The view showing us the financial history is also unavailable.

To create the views we need, we replace the shoebox with *accounts.* Each account represents something. By creating accounts to track our transactions, we develop the structure of our accounting system. In Chapter Three, we will describe the chart of accounts in more detail. A chart of accounts is the complete list of all accounts that make up our accounting system. For now, keep in mind that we post transactions to accounts for two primary reasons:

1. To create a snapshot of our current finances

2. To develop a financial history

Posting Transactions

Whether we use a hand-written ledger or computer software to record our transactions, we *post* our entries to individual accounts. In a hand-written ledger, there is a single account per page. *Posting a transaction* is the act of recording the transaction amount from a source document onto a ledger page. In addition to the transaction amount, we also always provide a posting reference that tells us the exact source of the posting. This reference provides us with the information we need to trace an entry from the ledger back to the source, just as the source tells us where the entry was posted.

Today's technology makes it easy to implement a computerized accounting system, so hand-written ledgers are becoming relics of an earlier time. As we will describe in later chapters, it is important to know the fundamental elements of a well-constructed accounting system when you select your accounting software. Think of the computer program as a power tool; it accomplishes the same objectives as the old hand tool, provided the craftsperson is skilled in its use.

Debits and Credits

In days gone by, when bookkeepers actually kept "books," debits were posted in the left column, and credits were posted in the right column. With today's computer software, debits are simply the positive numbers and credits are the negative numbers; your software handles the placement of entries on the page.

Without exception, every transaction in an accounting system is made up of debits and credits, and these debits and credits must always equal each other in total. The books must always be *in balance,* which means the total of the debits equals the total of the credits. In computer terms, the sum of every transaction equals zero, and the sum of all account balances equals zero. This is enforced by the underlying methodology of double-entry accounting.

Double-Entry Accounting

Every financial transaction, without exception, is recording at least two pieces of information. If we receive cash, there are reasons we received the cash:

- We collected money owed to us (such as a pledge).
- We sold a product or service.
- We borrowed funds.
- Or we received the cash for some other reason (such as a refund on a previous overcharge).

Similarly, we write checks for several reasons:

- To pay a supplier who performed work for us
- To purchase products
- To repay a loan
- To meet other obligations that require our payment (such as a security deposit on an office we rented)

Double-entry accounting is the distillation of a financial transaction into a set of debits and credits that, when added together, equal zero. Accountants view the organization's books as a closed system; no matter how many transactions are posted, no matter how large the amounts involved, the net effect on our books is zero. Every transaction we post changes individual account balances, but the net effect on all of the accounts in total is zero.

Types of Accounts

We talked earlier about replacing a single shoebox with accounts, and we also mentioned the two views we expect our accounting system to provide. To develop a snapshot of our organization's finances, we need accounts that provide details about things we have, things we own, and amounts we owe. To develop a historical record of how we got to our present financial condition, we need accounts that provide details about money we received and money we spent. Accounting has various types of accounts to meet these needs. We'll discuss each of these types in greater detail later in the book, but for now it is important to have an overview of each account type.

The *Financial Accounting Standards Board* (FASB) is the organization responsible for developing standards for financial accounting and reporting in the United States for non-publicly traded entities. In this chapter, we will use definitions published in the FASB's *Statement of Financial Accounting Concepts No. 6* (Financial Accounting Standards Board of the Financial Accounting Foundation, December 1985) to describe the types of accounts in the accounting system. The actual definitions in *FASB Concept Statement No. 6* are more complete than the versions used here. You are encouraged to read the entire Concept Statement for more details; it is available on the FASB web site (http://www.fasb.org).

Assets

According to the *FASB Concept Statement No. 6,* an *asset* is something we have or control that can provide some future economic benefit. Our nonprofit organization has cash in the bank; the cash is an asset. We own a van; the van is an asset. We prepaid our insurance premium for next year; the prepaid amount is an asset. Notice that assets not only include things that we own, but (in the case of the insurance premium) things that provide a future benefit. Everything owned by a nonprofit organization is an asset, but assets are not limited to things owned in the literal sense.

Asset accounts provide vital information for a part of the snapshot view that we need. The organization's assets are things we own; the value of an asset on the books is not affected by the fact that it may have been acquired with the help of some financing (as you will see, that financing is another part of the transaction that results in a liability being recorded on the books).

It is important to note that not everything we own is classified as an asset; as a practical matter, we charge low-cost items and items that will be consumed in the current business cycle directly to an expense category. Normally we record the acquisition of the asset in one transaction, and then we record the consumption of the asset in another transaction. Since the future economic benefit is delivered, and the thing is used up in a short period of time, for certain assets we combine the two transactions into one, recording the expense at the time of acquisition. We will discuss this later as we explore the concept of materiality in more depth.

Liabilities

The *FASB Concept Statement No. 6* states that a *liability* is the probable future sacrifice of an economic benefit arising from a present obligation. Amounts we owe are liabilities; monies received for services we are required to perform in the future (that is, advances) are also liabilities. Our nonprofit organization purchases goods and services on credit; the amount due is a liability and is regarded as accounts payable. We borrow money from the bank; the loan balance is a liability. We receive money for a service we will provide next year; the amount we have not yet earned is a liability. Notice that liabilities not only include amounts we owe but also include amounts we would owe if we ceased operations today. (For example, any vacation pay owed to a staff member is a liability.) Everything owed by the nonprofit organization is a liability, but liabilities are not limited to amounts owed in the literal sense. For example, an advance payment for the coming year that is received during the last week of this year creates a liability until the new year begins or until we earn the money.

Liability accounts provide vital information for another part of the snapshot view that we need. The organization's liabilities tell us how much of our assets are not fully paid for.

Revenue

The *FASB Concept Statement No. 6* states that *revenues* are amounts generated from activities that constitute the organization's ongoing major or central operation. Revenues can increase assets (for example, we receive cash or we add to our accounts receivable), and revenues can decrease liabilities (for example, we earn the money we received in an earlier period by performing services today). Revenues increase net assets, and revenue accounts provide a part of the historical view that we need.

The nomenclature used in nonprofit organizations for Revenues can be a little confusing. Monies donated to the nonprofit are called *support;* money earned by a nonprofit by performing services are called *revenues.* We'll have more on this subject in Chapter Four.

Expenses

The *FASB Concept Statement No. 6* states that *expenses* are amounts consumed by activities that constitute the organization's ongoing major or central operation. Expenses can increase liabilities (for example, we purchase supplies that we will pay for in a future period), and expenses can decrease assets (for example, we pay cash for supplies). Expenses decrease net assets, and expense accounts provide a part of the historical view that we need.

The Accounting Equation

Here it is:

assets = liabilities + net assets

This can be rewritten this way:

assets – liabilities = net assets

This equation ties everything together: debits, credits, double-entry accounting. It simply states that things we have in our possession minus the amount we owe equal the amount of our net worth (our net assets). For our snapshot view, we can define *net assets* as total assets minus liabilities.

The snapshot view can be taken and presented in a financial statement at any time. The most common presentation of the snapshot view occurs at the end of an accounting period.

Since our net asset total is calculated from our asset and liability totals, it might at first glance appear to be an arbitrary value. This is not true. Revenues increase our net assets; expenses decrease our net assets. When we describe each transaction being distilled into a series of debits and credits in our double-entry accounting methodology, we are analyzing the transaction to determine the effect it has on net assets. We have another equation that allows us to double-check our net asset balance:

net assets = previous net assets balance + revenues – expenses

Combining the two equations gives us this single equation:

assets – liabilities = (previous net assets balance + revenues – expenses)

One source of continual confusion arises from the fact that these equations ignore the labels of *positive, negative, debit,* and *credit.* By definition, a set of books is balanced when the sum of the total of all accounts equals zero. In order for this to be possible, some accounts will have a debit (positive) balance and others will have a credit (negative) balance. To make sense of the accounting equation when analyzing a ledger, you need to know which accounts normally have a debit balance and which accounts normally have a credit balance.

Let's look again at the basic equation:

assets = liabilities + net assets

The equation itself gives us the answer:

- Assets normally have a debit balance.
- Liabilities normally have a credit balance.
- Net assets normally have a credit balance.

The total debits in our asset accounts will equal the total credits in our liability and net asset accounts. The sum of the account totals will equal zero.

Because revenues increase net assets and expenses decrease net assets, we know two things for sure:

1. Revenues normally have a credit balance.

2. Expenses normally have a debit balance.

The total credits in our revenue accounts will increase the credit balance in our net asset accounts; the total debits in our expense accounts will decrease the credit balance in our net asset accounts.

A simple example should help to illustrate this idea. Our organization provides a service for which we are paid $1,000. To record the transaction, we will make a two-line entry:

1. Debit the cash account for $1,000.

2. Credit the revenue account (services) for $1,000.

First, notice that our transaction is a balanced entry made up of two parts. We debit the cash account (an asset, normally a debit), which increases our cash balance. We credit the revenue account (normally a credit), which increases our total revenue. Since the revenue account eventually finds its way into the net assets total (which is normally a credit), we've also increased the net assets balance. The books now reflect the reality: we increased our assets by providing a service, and this transaction had no effect on our liabilities. If our assets increase by $1,000, and our liabilities are unchanged, the snapshot accounting equation tells us that our net assets have also increased by $1,000. Our revenue and expense accounts (our historical view) reflect the $1,000 increase.

Confusing Terminology

People who don't work in the accounting field are familiar with the terms *debit* and *credit* primarily from their dealings with banks. A bank will debit your account when the bank withdraws funds, and the bank credits your account when the bank adds funds. When you are introduced to the accounting equation, you learn that you debit the cash account to increase the balance—the exact opposite from the banking experience. Let's review why this is.

When you open a bank account, you deposit funds. On the bank's books, this transaction is posted to two accounts:

1. Debit cash (an asset)

2. Credit customer demand deposits (a liability)

The amount the bank received from you is a liability; they now owe you that amount. They credit your account on their books, increasing their liability, and that credit terminology is on the paperwork they give you. Your personal financial records are the mirror image of the bank's books.

This mirror image exists between organizations of all types. For example, our organization's accounts receivable is other organizations' accounts payable. When seeking to receive payment of an open accounts receivable item, you call and ask to speak to the accounts payable department of the entity that owes you the money.

Expenses and Expenditures

We saw earlier that an *expense* is an amount consumed by the organization's activities. An *expenditure*, in comparison, is an amount the organization disburses. Often these two terms will both apply to a transaction: we spend the money on supplies (the expenditure), and those supplies are consumed by our activities (the expense). Part of our job when analyzing and posting transactions is to distinguish between an expense and expenditure when it is appropriate. For example, we might send a check to a vendor as a refundable deposit; the check is an expenditure (it reduced our cash and increased the amount of refundable deposit being held by the vendor) but not an expense.

Materiality

When analyzing financial results, it is not possible to examine every posted transaction and every account balance. *Materiality* is a threshold amount below which special analysis is not warranted. Amounts above the threshold are important and must be corrected if inaccurate. The concept of materiality applies to the analysis of the financial information, not the posting of the transaction. All transactions, regardless of the dollar amounts involved, must be accurately and completely recorded.

Setting the threshold amount is a challenging concept because a number of factors will influence the amount that is material for your organization, including the organization's total income and cash-flow position. Often different threshold amounts are applied to different types of accounts. For example, you may determine that an amount equal to 3 percent of your organization's total revenue is material for revenue and expense accounts, while $500 is a material amount for any non-cash asset or liability account.

Realization and Matching

Analyzing transactions and recording the amounts by posting them to the proper account codes is the main function of the bookkeeper. Part of that analysis also includes taking a close look at the timing of transactions. Transactions are posted when they show up—when a vendor invoice is dated, for example, or when a check arrives in the mail. These factors are often out of our control.

Realization is the concept of recognizing income in the period in which it is earned.

Matching is the concept of recording expenses incurred in generating revenue in the same period that we record the revenue. We try to match revenue with expenses.

Accruals and Reversals

Since an accounting transaction occurs in one period, and the concepts of realization and matching might require the effect of that transaction to occur in another period, we need a mechanism to shift the financial activity between periods.

An *accrual* is an entry we make to record a transaction in the period it belongs, as opposed to the period in which it naturally occurs. A *reversal* is an entry we make to undo the accrual entry; this reversal entry is made in the period when the underlying transaction actually occurs.

After both periods have passed, the net impact on our books is zero. In the period when we make the accrual, the net impact is the recording of the underlying transaction as posted by the accrual. In the period when we post the reversal, our reversal entry offsets the underlying transaction. Both entries combine to have zero impact on our books. If we fail to reverse our accrual, our books will have the underlying transaction posted twice: once in our accrual and again as the original entry. You always reverse an accrual in the next accounting period.

Nonprofit Net Assets

Net asset accounts in a nonprofit organization are the accounting equivalent of owners' equity accounts in a for-profit company. In a nonprofit organization, a distinction is made among the following categories:

- Permanently restricted net assets

- Temporarily restricted net assets

- Unrestricted net assets

We'll discuss these differences in more detail in Chapter Ten, but it is important to realize that the net assets classification is determined by the underlying character of the transaction, which frequently is related to the intention of the donor. You have to consider the net asset classification when analyzing and posting transactions.

For many of the readers of this book (from smaller organizations), your only net asset classification will be unrestricted net assets. For readers from larger organizations, all three classifications may play a role in your books.

Summary

In the previous chapter, we discussed the reasons why the bookkeeping function is important. In this chapter, we started to explain how you maintain a complete set of accounting records.

The Chart of Accounts

As we discussed in Chapter Two, a chart of accounts is a listing of all of the accounts that make up your accounting system. These accounts provide the framework for recording every transaction in the organization. Careful design of the chart of accounts is important. A good chart of accounts enables us to obtain different snapshot views of our finances, gives us a detailed history of how we got to the current financial position, and provides other valuable information needed by management, board members, and other stakeholders.

Our goal in designing the chart of accounts is to identify all of the information we will ever need from a transaction while only handling and posting the underlying paperwork one time.

Traditional Order

All accounting systems use a chart of accounts. The traditional order of the accounts is dictated by two concepts: (1) the accounting equation; and (2) current versus long-term classification.

Based on the accounting equation, the chart of accounts lists the accounts in the following order:

- Assets

- Liabilities

- Net assets

- Support and revenue

- Expenses

All of our asset accounts come before the first liability account. Within the asset section of the chart, there are many accounts, each representing a real life thing or amount. The order of these individual accounts within the asset section is determined by their *liquidity*; that is, how quickly they are likely to be used up or converted to cash.

Asset accounts are classified as *current* if they are likely to be converted to cash or otherwise used up within the natural business cycle of the organization. With few exceptions, the natural business cycle is one year. The typical organization issues annual financial statements, files an annual tax return, and so on. If there is no other compelling business reason to have a longer or shorter business cycle, the cycle is based on these annual reporting periods. While it is true that nonprofit organizations sometimes have grants or other activities that do not end exactly at the end of an accounting year, this is a reporting issue versus a chart-of-account issue.

In a similar way, all of our liability accounts come before the first net asset account. Within the liability section there are many accounts, each representing an amount owed. Liability accounts are classified as *current* if they are likely to be due or otherwise satisfied within the natural business cycle of the organization (one year).

Accounts that do not meet the current classification guidelines are *long-term* or *non-current*.

This chart of accounts was developed as a result of a great deal of work by a large number of knowledgeable professionals working in the nonprofit sector, including Bill Levis, senior associate at the National Center for Charitable Statistics, and others from the California Society of CPAs, the Urban Institute's National Center on Charitable Statistics, and other organizations. The *Unified Chart of Accounts* (UCOA) is designed to provide a framework that matches the reporting needs of the IRS as well as many other formats. One benefit of adopting the UCOA in your organization is that the UCOA facilitates the filing of IRS Form 990. You can download a copy online. (See Resource I for all of the details.)

As with any standard, the UCOA tries to cover every situation. The typical nonprofit organization will not need every account listed in the UCOA. However, by adopting the standard UCOA, you will know where to position individual accounts in your chart of accounts when the need arises. Another word of caution: Similar to industries that require (in some circumstances) reports to be sent to a regulatory agency, your grant or contract or even applicable legislation may demand that you use a specific chart of accounts or account nomenclature when you report to them. Therefore, you need to understand the environment you are operating in to make sure you do not accidentally violate a regulation or a specific grant procedure. It is good practice to discuss your chart of accounts with senior management, funders, and your auditor before finalizing the design. Switching to a new chart of accounts structure is best accomplished at the beginning of a fiscal year.

We have chosen to list a modified subset of the UCOA. The complete chart is available online. Department, program, and cost centers are represented by a triple asterisk (***) in the UCOA. The account code defines the character of the transaction; a suffix added to the account code specifies to which location, function, or program the transaction belongs. (See Resource H for Web site address.)

Asset Accounts

The asset section of our chart of accounts generally contains the following subsections:

- Current assets
- Plant, property and equipment (fixed assets)
- Other assets

Within each section, there are accounts for each individual asset type in the organization. The asset section of the modified UCOA is presented in Exhibit 3.1.

| EXHIBIT 3.1 | Modified Unified Chart of Accounts—Assets |

1   Assets

1000   Cash:
    1010   Cash in Bank—Operating
    1020   Cash—Payroll Account
    1040   Petty Cash
    1050   Cash—Security Deposits
    1070   Cash—Savings Account

1100   Accounts Receivable:
    1110   Accounts Receivable
    1115   Doubtful Accounts Allowance
    1120   Accounts Receivable—Other

1200   Contributions Receivable:
    1210   Pledges Receivable
    1215   Doubtful Pledges Allowance
    1240   Grants Receivable

1300   Other Receivables:
    1320   Notes/Loans Receivable
    1325   Doubtful Notes/Loans Allowance
    1330   Deposits Receivable

1400   Other Current Assets:
    1410   Inventory
    1420   Inventories for Use
    1450   Prepaid Expenses
    1460   Accrued Revenues

1500   Investments:
    1510   Marketable Securities
    1580   Investments—Other

1600   Fixed Operating Assets:
    1610   Land—Operating
    1620   Buildings—Operating
    1630   Leasehold Improvements
    1640   Furniture, Fixtures, and Equip.
    1650   Vehicles
    1660   Construction in Progress

1700   Accum. Deprec.—Fixed Operating Assets:
    1725   Accum. Deprec.—Building
    1735   Accum. Amort.—Leasehold Improvements
    1745   Accum. Deprec.—Furn., Fix., Equip.
    1755   Accum. Deprec.—Vehicles

    1810   Other Long-Term Assets

    Total Assets

Current Assets

The current assets of an organization include the following types of accounts, organized by their liquidity:

- Cash

- Accounts receivable

- Contributions and grants receivable

- Inventory

- Prepaid expenses

- Other current assets

By definition, cash is a current asset. (It is already cash; there is nothing to convert.) We set up an account for each type of cash account that is separately maintained by the organization. Examples include the following:

- Petty cash (cash on hand)

- Operations checking account

- Payroll checking account

- Client trust funds

- Money market account

Some funding sources demand segregation of their funds in separate cash accounts. Read the grant regulations or guidelines to determine the rules your organization needs to follow.

Client trust fund rules vary. In some jurisdictions, a separate cash account is required for each individual client. In other jurisdictions, a single trust fund account is satisfactory if proper records are kept and if interest income is allocated to each client with funds in the account.

Accounts receivable is an account that represents the balance of support due to the organization, or revenue the organization has earned that it has not yet collected. It follows cash in the chart of accounts because cash always comes first. It comes before inventory in the chart of accounts because accounts receivable balances are generally converted to cash more quickly than inventory is converted to cash. Organizations convert inventory into accounts receivable by invoicing (billing) the customer; at a later time, the receivable is collected and converted into cash.

Subsidiary Books

We've described separate accounts for each real-world item; we have an account for our checking and another account for our money market account. For most assets and liabilities, that is the rule of thumb: one account for each item. The two common exceptions to this are accounts receivable and accounts payable.

Even a small organization might have many accounts receivable items. It would be unwieldy at best (and often impossible) to create a separate chart of accounts number for each different receivable or customer. The method we use to make this situation more manageable is to maintain a *subsidiary* set of records for all of our receivables. The invoice and payment details are recorded by client or customer in the subsidiary accounts receivable records, where each entity that owes us money has its own account. Only the totals are transferred to the accounts receivable account number in the chart of accounts.

Accounting software automatically creates and maintains the subsidiary set of records as well as automatically transferring the totals to the general ledger accounts. The software uses the information entered on the screen to complete both tasks at the same time.

Accounts payable works the same way. Each vendor is assigned a vendor account in the subsidiary set of records, where all vendor invoices and payments are recorded. The totals of these transactions are transferred to the accounts payable account number in the chart of accounts.

It is possible to post every transaction directly to an account in the chart of accounts, but subsidiary records provide several important benefits:

- The chart of accounts can remain relatively stable, without the constant addition of new accounts every time a new source of money or vendor does business with the organization.

- Where a specific source of revenue (for example a special fundraising event) takes place, it is easy to train another person to temporarily help out in bringing records up to date, while still making sure that person cannot perform other functions that would endanger good internal control practices.

- Reporting and aging the amounts due is more easily accomplished when the transactions are posted to a subsidiary set of records. (*Aging* accounts receivable or accounts payable refers to the classification of unpaid items according to how old they are.)

- The subsidiary balance provides a confirmation of the balance in the individual account in the chart of accounts. (They have to agree; if not, we know there was a posting error.)

Additional Current Assets

In addition to cash, accounts receivable, pledges receivable, and inventory, there are other accounts in the chart of accounts that will be converted to cash or used up in one year (the normal business cycle). Prepaid expenses are a good example.

Traditional practice is that we pay for certain expenses before we use the items in question. (For example, insurance premiums are often due before coverage becomes effective.) Recall our description of matching, where we indicated that expenses should be recorded in the same period they are used to generate revenue. The prepaid type of account is a good way to accomplish this.

When we pay an annual insurance premium, we don't want to post the payment to *insurance expense*. While that account is the ultimate destination, posting the entire premium to the expense in a single period violates the matching principle, in which the period when the expense was posted would have all of the expense, and other periods covered by the insurance policy would have zero expense. By posting the premium to a prepaid insurance account, we are classifying the transaction as an amount that will be used up in the normal business cycle (a current asset). For each of the next twelve months, we will make an entry to use up a proportionate amount of the total. We will debit *insurance expense* and credit *prepaid insurance* for one-twelfth of the annual premium. Every month will have the appropriate amount of insurance expense, and the prepaid amount will decrease each month, finally becoming zero as the policy expires. As we'll see later on, most software systems allow the creation of a *recurring journal* entry (also called standard or *memorized*) that would make the monthly posting of such entries easier.

Fixed Assets

Fixed assets, also known as *land, buildings,* and *equipment,* are assets that will be used over many years by the organization. These assets are recorded at their acquisition costs, which include all amounts spent: architects' fees, construction period interest, and title closing costs, among other expenditures. The *acquisition cost* (or *historical cost,* as it is sometimes called) is the value that appears on the financial statements. This amount may be different from the *market value* of the asset, which is the amount the asset would fetch if it were offered for sale.

The chart of accounts has separate accounts for each class of fixed asset. As a non-current asset, these accounts come after the current asset section. As an asset account, a fixed asset normally has a debit balance.

For each fixed asset account in the chart of accounts other than land, there is another individual account in the chart called *accumulated depreciation. Depreciation expense* is an estimated amount recorded in the current period, based on the acquisition cost and estimated useful life of the fixed asset. Land is not depreciated since it has an unlimited useful life.

The accumulated depreciation accounts normally have a credit balance. They are in the asset accounts section of the chart of accounts. They are set up to provide an easy way to record the cumulative write-off of the fixed asset without losing the original acquisition cost details. The cost of a building is recorded as a fixed asset. Each period we record the depreciation expense (a debit) and the accumulated depreciation (a credit). At any point in time, we can compute the net book value of the building from these two accounts. Let's look at an example of a building with a net book value of $575,000:

Original cost	$1,250,000
Accumulated depreciation	($675,000)
Net book value	$575,000

Depreciation expense is an estimate of the amount of an asset written off in the current accounting period. Each class of fixed asset has an estimated useful life. Certain funding sources do not allow depreciation expense but they do allow an expense called a *use charge* (or other nomenclature that they specify) that might appear in a grant budget.

This estimated useful life for a nonprofit organization frequently follows IRS guidelines. Your auditor can also assist you in interpreting what generally accepted accounting principles (GAAP) require, which can vary from the IRS guidelines. (The Internal Revenue Code changes from time to time; current details are available at the IRS website [www.irs.gov].) Again we have a cautionary note: the books of an organization always need to be correct in reality as well as in theory. Furniture in a group home for adolescent clients is normally a fixed asset called *furniture*, but it is conceivable the wear and tear in a group home for adolescents will essentially use up the asset more quickly than the IRS's estimated useful life. When this situation arises, you correct the estimate and record the depreciation over the actual shorter useful life. Some funding sources might ask you to call the item *furniture expense*, since they know the furniture will need replacement in a year or less.

Specific regulations or rules attached to grants or certain monies received might require a distinct format. For example, federal guidelines exist in the form of Circular No. A-122 (Cost Principles for Non-Profit Organizations), which is issued and periodically revised by the U.S. OMB. (Please note that many states, counties, and cities use A-122 in the federal format or revise it for their purposes; excerpts from A-122 are included in Resource G of this book.) Therefore, you need to know the rules your particular organization is subject to when creating your chart of accounts.

Some grants specify that the cost of a fixed asset be completely expensed in the grant period it was acquired; at the same time, GAAP requires the fixed asset to be recorded in a fixed asset account (capitalized) and depreciated over the estimated useful life. These competing requirements can be handled by recording the fixed asset according to GAAP and creating documentation which provides a permanent record about the alternate accounting treatment. (Chapter Ten describes the creation and maintenance of a fixed asset record.)

Long-Term Investments and Other Assets

Another category of non-current assets is made up of items not likely to be converted into cash or consumed in the next year. The most common example of another asset is a security, which is a long-term investment.

Liability Accounts

The liability section of our chart of accounts generally contains the following sub-sections:

- Current liabilities
- Deferred revenue
- Refundable advances
- Mortgage and notes payable
- Other non-current liabilities

Within each section, there are accounts for each individual liability of the organization. The liabilities section of the modified UCOA is presented in Exhibit 3.2.

EXHIBIT 3.2	Modified Unified Chart of Accounts—Liabilities

2   Liabilities

2000   Payables:
   2010   Accounts Payable

2100   Accrued Liabilities:
   2110   Accrued Payroll
   2120   Accrued Paid Leave
   2130   Taxes Withheld
   2131   Federal Withholding Payable
   2132   FICA Payable
   2133   Medicare Payable
   2134   State Withholding Payable
   2135   State Disability Payable
   2137   Other Deductions Payable
   2140   Sales Tax Payable
   2150   Accrued Expenses

2300   Unearned/Deferred Revenue:
   2310   Deferred Contract Revenue
   2311   Unearned Grant Income
   2350   Unearned/Deferred Revenue—Other
   2351   Deferred Rental Income

   2410   Refundable Advances
   2420   Security Deposits Payable

2500   Short-Term Notes and Loans Payable:
   2550   Line of Credit
   2560   Current Portion—Long-Term Loan
   2570   Short-Term Liabilities—Other

2700   Long-Term Notes and Loans Payable:
   2710   Bonds Payable
   2730   Mortgages Payable
   2750   Capital Leases
   2770   Long-Term Liabilities—Other

        Total Liabilities

Current Liabilities

The current liabilities of an organization include the following types of accounts:

- Accounts payable

- Accrued expenses

- Taxes payable

- Other current liabilities

We previously described how we use accounts payable as a single-control account. The total of accounts payable always matches the total of all of the individual vendor account balances in our subsidiary accounts payable records. We can add and delete vendor accounts as needed without constantly changing the organization's chart of accounts.

Taxes payable and accrued expenses are accounts we use as we apply the matching principal. In the normal course of operation, certain activities obligate the organization to pay an amount in a future period. For example, if our organization collects sales tax in one accounting period, we will remit the tax collected to the tax authority in a subsequent period. The amount due is recorded as a *sales tax payable.*

Accrued expenses hold the amounts the organization owes to (but has yet to be billed by) vendors. For example, the electric company might bill for the thirty days ending on the 15th of each month. Our accrued expenses would include our liability for electricity consumed from the 16th until the end of the month. As we described earlier in this book, we use an accrual journal entry to set up this liability; we reverse the entry in the subsequent period, when the electric company bills us for our usage. The concept of materiality, discussed in Chapter Two, limits the accrual and reversal process to those amounts above the materiality threshold—that is, those amounts that are significant when viewed in the context of the organization's financial statement and that are considered to be important enough to be corrected if inaccurate.

Long-Term Liabilities

Long-term liabilities are not scheduled to be paid in full within one year (the normal business cycle). Examples might include bank loans longer than one year in duration and mortgages payable. The typical mortgage has a term of many years; while a small amount is due to be paid within the next year, payments due in later years are classified as a long-term liability. For convenience, an accounting system normally holds an entire mortgage balance in a long-term liability account. When preparing a balance sheet (also called the Statement of Financial Position, or the snapshot financial statement), the current portion (twelve months) of the mortgage payable is broken out and reported as a current liability.

Net Assets

Net assets are the equivalent of capital and retained earnings in a for-profit organization. Net assets contain the cumulative surpluses and deficits of the nonprofit organization's activities. Some nonprofit organizations have more than one class of net assets. The three classes of net assets are *unrestricted, temporarily restricted,* and *permanently restricted.* The underlying transactions determine the net asset class that is affected. Chapters Four and Ten examine the need for and classification of these net asset classes. The net assets section of the modified UCOA is presented in Exhibit 3.3.

EXHIBIT 3.3	Modified Unified Chart of Accounts—Net Assets

3   Net Assets

3000   Unrestricted Net Assets:
   3010   Unrestricted Net Assets
   3020   Board-Designated Net Assets
   3030   Board Designated Quasi-Endowment
   3040   Fixed Operating Net Assets

3100   Temporarily Restricted Net Assets:
   3110   Use Restricted Net Assets
   3120   Time Restricted Net Assets

3200   Permanently Restricted Net Assets:
   3210   Endowment Net Assets

      Total Net Assets

Support and Revenues

Support and *revenues* are generated from activities that constitute the organization's on-going major or central operation. The chart of accounts must be detailed enough to properly record the various types and sources of support and revenue; the UCOA structure has categories to cover the operations of most nonprofit organizations. As we discussed, your chart of accounts would normally be a subset of the UCOA. Your organization will need to add any accounts not listed in the UCOA.

Chapter Four will explore support and revenue categories in more detail. The support and revenue section of the modified UCOA chart of accounts is presented in Exhibit 3.4.

EXHIBIT 3.4	Modified Unified Chart of Accounts—Contributions, Support (Revenue)

4   Contributions, Support

4000   Revenue from Direct Contributions:
4010-***   Individual/Small Business Contributions
4015-***   Contribution Income—Temp. Restricted
4020-***   Corporate Contributions
4070-***   Legacies and Bequests
4075-***   Uncollectible Pledges—Estimated
4085-***   Long-Term Pledges Discount

4100   Donated Goods and Services Revenue:
4130-***   Donated Use of Facilities
4140-***   Gifts in Kind—Goods

4200   Revenue from Non-Government Grants:
4210-***   Corporate/Business Grants
4230-***   Foundation/Trust Grants
4250-***   Nonprofit Organization Grants
4255-***   Discounts—Long-Term Grants

4400   Revenue from Indirect Contributions:
4410-***   United Way or CFC Contributions
4420-***   Affiliated Organizations Revenue
4430-***   Fundraising Agencies Revenue

EXHIBIT 3.4   Modified Unified Chart of Accounts— Contributions, Support (Revenue) *(continued)*

4500	Revenue from Government Grants:
4510-***	Agency (Government) Grants
4520-***	Federal Grants
4530-***	State Grants
4540-***	Local Government Grants

5   **Earned Revenues**

5000	Revenue from Government Agencies:
5010-***	Agency (Government) Contracts/Fees
5020-***	Federal Contracts/Fees
5030-***	State Contracts/Fees
5040-***	Local Government Contracts/Fees
5080-***	Medicare/Medicaid Payments
5100	Revenue from Program-Related Sales and Fees:
5180-***	Program Service Fees
5185-***	Bad Debts, est.—Program Fees
5200	Revenue from Dues:
5210-***	Membership Dues—Individuals
5220-***	Assessments and Dues—Organizations
5300	Revenue from Investments:
5310-***	Interest Income
5320-***	Dividends and Interest—Securities
5330-***	Real Estate Rent—Debt-Financed
5335-***	Real Estate Rental Cost—Debt-Financed
5340-***	Real Estate Rent—Not Debt-Financed
5345-***	Real Estate Rental Cost—Not Debt-Financed
5360-***	Other Investment Income
5370-***	Securities Sales—Gross
5375-***	Securities Sales Cost
5400	Revenue from Other Sources:
5410-***	Non-Inventory Sales—Gross
5415-***	Non-Inventory Sales Cost
5440-***	Gross Sales—Inventory
5441-***	Freight Out
5445-***	Cost of Goods Sold
5446-***	Purchase Discount
5450-***	Advertising Revenue
5470-***	Royalty Income
5800	Special Events:
5810-***	Special Events—Non-Gift Revenue
5820-***	Special Events—Gift Revenue

6   **Other Revenue**

6710	Gain on the Sale of Fixed Assets
6800	Unrealized Gain (Loss):
6810-***	Unrealized Gain (Loss)—Investments
6820-***	Unrealized Gain (Loss)—Other Assets
6900	Net Assets Released from Restriction
6901-***	Temp. Restricted Net Asset Released from Restriction
6902-***	Unrestricted Net Asset Released from Restriction

Total Revenue, Gains, and Other Support

Expenses

Expenses are amounts consumed by activities that constitute the organization's ongoing major or central operation. The expense section of the chart of accounts should be detailed; it is easier to combine expense code totals than it is to separate postings into more detail after the fact. The UCOA structure provides a good guideline for most nonprofit organizations. As you design your chart of accounts, don't hesitate to delineate more finely some expense categories if it seems appropriate. Of course, you should follow the UCOA's lead on the placement of new expense codes. The expense section of the modified UCOA is presented in Exhibit 3.5.

EXHIBIT 3.5	Modified Unified Chart of Accounts—Expenses

7	**Expenses—Personnel-Related**
7000	Grants, Contracts, and Direct Assistance
7010-***	Contracts—Program-Related
7020-***	Grants to Other Organizations
7040-***	Awards and Grants—Individuals
7050-***	Specific Assistance—Individuals
7060-***	Benefits Paid to or for Members
7200	Salaries and Related Expenses:
7210-***	Officers and Directors Salaries
7220-***	Wage Expense
7230-***	Pension Plan Contributions
7240-***	Employee Benefits—Not Pension
7241-***	Health Insurance Expense
7250-***	Payroll Taxes, etc.
7251-***	FICA Expense
7252-***	Medicare Expense
7253-***	State Disability Expense
7500	Contract Service Expenses
7510-***	Fundraising Fees
7520-***	Accounting Fees
7530-***	Legal Fees
7540-***	Professional Fees—Other
7550-***	Temporary Help—Contract
7580-***	Donated Professional Services—GAAP
7590-***	Donated Other Services—Non-GAAP
8	**Non-Personnel-Related Expenses**
8100	Non-Personnel Expenses:
8110-***	Office Supplies
8120-***	Donated Materials and Supplies
8130-***	Telephone and Telecommunications
8140-***	Postage and Shipping
8150-***	Mailing Services

EXHIBIT 3.5	Modified Unified Chart of Accounts—Expenses (continued)

8170-***	Printing and Copying
8180-***	Books, Subscriptions, References
8190-***	In-house Publications
8200	Facility and Equipment Expenses:
8210-***	Rent, Parking, Other Occupancy
8220-***	Utilities
8230-***	Real Estate Tax Expense
8240-***	Personal Property Taxes
8250-***	Mortgage Interest
8260-***	Repairs and Maintenance
8265-***	Vehicle Repairs
8270-***	Deprec. and Amort.—Allowable
8280-***	Deprec. and Amort.—Not Allowable
8290-***	Donated Facilities
8300	Travel and Meetings Expenses:
8310-***	Travel
8320-***	Conferences, Conventions, Meetings
8500	Other Expenses:
8510-***	Interest—General
8520-***	Insurance Expense
8530-***	Membership Dues—Organization
8540-***	Staff Development
8550-***	List Rental
8560-***	Outside Computer Services
8570-***	Advertising Expenses
8580-***	Contingency Provisions
8590-***	Other Expenses
8595-***	Merchant Account Expense
8600	Business Expenses:
8610-***	Bad Debt Expense
8620-***	Sales Taxes
8630-***	UBI Taxes
8650-***	Taxes—Other
8660-***	Fines, Penalties, Judgments
8670-***	Organizational (Corp.) Expenses
	Total Expenses

Donated Services

GAAP dictates specific attributes of donations they consider recordable. FASB Statement 116 (Accounting for Contributions Received and Contributions Made) states that "Contributions of services shall be recognized if the services received (a) create or enhance nonfinancial assets or (b) require specialized skills, are provided by individuals possessing those skills, and would typically need to be purchased if not provided by donation" (para. 9, p. 6).

The UCOA, in accounts 7580 and 7590, provides the option of recording non-GAAP-eligible items (for example, donated services that aid the organization yet do not meet GAAP definitions). Discuss this matter with your accountant or auditor.

Account Numbering

There are a few things to note about the UCOA account numbering system. First, many of the individual account numbers end in zero. This effectively leaves a position available for at least nine accounts in between each standard account number. For example, if our organization has two checking accounts, we are free to add an account number (1011) for the second account that places it in its proper order in the chart of accounts.

Second, the actual account numbers have a meaning. All assets begin with the numeral 1; all accumulated depreciation accounts begin with 17 (the 1 tells us it is an asset account; the 7 tells us it is one of the accumulated depreciation accounts). By consistently using this type of numbering system, it is easier for the bookkeeper and the entire accounting staff to understand and remember the account numbers.

For organizations that must track activity by program or cost center, the revenue and expense account numbers all have room (represented by the *** suffix) to record a cost center, department, or program reference for the individual transaction. Recall that we are interested in posting each transaction one time while still being able to extract everything we need for analysis and reporting purposes. We will post a vendor's invoice for supplies to account 8110; this tells us what we purchased but not where the supplies were used. If we post the vendor invoice to 8110–123, we now know that we purchased supplies for program number 123—we not only know what we purchased, we also know where it was used. It is also a simple matter to total up all supplies purchased by ignoring the account suffix. Alternatively, we can develop a financial report for program 123 by accumulating all postings for that suffix, no matter which account number is used. This flexible numbering scheme is easily implemented in off-the-shelf software, particularly if the software comes with a job cost feature. Whenever you see *Job #*, think program or department. Support of a flexible account numbering system is a primary consideration in the selection of an accounting software package. A frequent use of this account numbering system is to provide detailed financial statements on a program, department, or location basis. Software specifically designed for nonprofit organizations has the capability to record specific program, location, and funding source information. Many organizations will also need the ability to view the financial results for a single suffix or for a combination of suffix categories.

Support, revenue, and expenses are segregated among the organization's activities, programs, and functions. At a minimum, a cost center code should be created for management, fundraising, and for every program in the organization. Careful planning will enable you to utilize the triple-asterisk suffix for every function, including special events and support service functions.

Summary

Designing a chart of accounts is an important first step in the bookkeeping process for a nonprofit organization. By using the UCOA as a starting point, you know you will have a structure that is useful for many required tasks, including the reporting of your organization's financial results on IRS Form 990. Placing new accounts into the UCOA to match the needs of your organization is easy, once you understand the concepts of the typical accounting structure and the meaning behind the UCOA account numbers.

PART TWO

Recording Transactions Correctly the First Time

The next eight chapters explore the day-to-day transactions that might occur in any nonprofit organization. Special emphasis is placed on topics unique to nonprofit organizations.

Each chapter addresses the internal control issues for the transactions being discussed. Suggested operating procedures and practical tips are presented for each accounting function. Depending on the size of your organization, you might not have the resources to implement some of these procedures in the manner suggested here. For example, many smaller nonprofit organizations will not have a separate purchasing department that issues formal purchase orders. Why take the time to read about a procedure that your organization is unlikely to follow? It is time well spent, because the description of the process helps to illustrate the concept and to highlight the suggested methodology. Understanding the process is important; with that understanding, you can design procedures that fit your organization and fulfill the goals we've established for your accounting system. In Part One, you learned about which transactions are recorded and why they are recorded. Part Two focuses on how the transactions are recorded.

This book doesn't focus on any particular accounting software package. Software constantly changes, and your organization's choice of accounting software is determined by many factors, including budget constraints, previous experiences, and local availability of technical support resources. In Resource C we present a list of features to look for in an accounting software package.

In the following chapters, we present balanced entries to show you how typical transactions are recorded for each topic. How do these entries relate to the task of posting transactions using accounting software? As we discussed in Chapter Two, every entry in an accounting system is really a balanced double entry. Accounting software is designed to facilitate the recording of transactions, and it simplifies posting tasks by automatically constructing and completing entries based on the information it has about your chart of accounts and based on an understanding of the transaction itself.

The configuration of the typical accounting software package includes several important tasks:

- Entry of the chart of accounts

- Classifying each account by type

- Specifying the accounts to use for specific purposes

The account code, account name, and account type are entered into the software for every account in the chart of accounts. The account type, such as asset, liability, net asset, revenue, and expense, indicates how the accounts will be handled on reports and during the fiscal year close. The software also needs to know which accounts are to be used for specific purposes: cash, accounts receivable, and accounts payable. The software will use these specific identifications to construct and complete the balanced entries just mentioned.

To give an example: every accounting software package has a cash receipts entry module. Using this entry screen, you record the details about a cash receipt, including the date, the person or company you received the money from, the amount received, and the reason for receipt of the money. At this point, the software takes over and constructs a balanced entry. It "knows" several things about cash receipts without prompting you for the information:

- The debit for the entry is posted to cash.

- The amount of the receipt is posted as a credit, even though you entered a positive number.

- If the receipt was in payment of an open A/R invoice, the credit for this entry is posted to A/R.

- If the receipt was for some event not previously billed, you are prompted for the account to receive the credit posting.

Exhibit II.1 illustrates how the software creates a balanced entry from a cash receipts entry screen.

This built-in knowledge about transactions is one of the primary reasons that accounting software is so useful. Here are several other examples of this ability to construct and complete a balanced entry:

Example Entry Created by Cash Receipts Software

Account	Description	Debit	Credit
1010	Cash in bank - Operating	4500.00	
4010-123	Individual/small business contrib		4500.00
	Totals	4500.00	4500.00

- The billing module knows that customer invoice amounts are credited to a revenue account and that the offsetting debit is posted to A/R.

- The purchases module knows that the offsetting credit for every purchase is posted to A/P.

- The check-writing module knows that the payment of open A/P items creates an entry that debits A/P and credits cash.

Every accounting software package has this construct-and-complete feature. If you understand the underlying entry being created, you have the ability (regardless of the software package you have selected) to create and maintain the accounting records in accordance with the goal we have established. The following chapters present each transaction in the form of the balanced, underlying entry that the software will create.

Properly tracking, recording, and documenting the sources and amounts of income of a nonprofit organization is one of the most important tasks in bookkeeping. Your organization needs an adequate system to document the receipt of funds and provide accurate information about each transaction. If your system fails, income can go uncollected, cash flow will suffer, and the organization's survival could be in jeopardy. In this chapter we will examine the methods and techniques to be used for a wide range of income sources.

The formal accounting literature and the Internal Revenue Service use special nomenclature to differentiate among different types of income received by nonprofit organizations. Normally, *support* is the title for contribution and grant income, and *revenue* is the title for most other income. In this chapter, we are going to keep it simple and use the term *income* for all types. Your auditor will be able to advise you as to the correct technical classification of the different types of income when your audited financial statements, tax returns, and other regulatory filings are prepared.

The typical nonprofit organization receives many types of income, including the following:

- Program service income

- Income from the sale of inventory

- Income from contributions

- Income from grants

- Interest, dividend, and royalty income

- Income from membership dues

- Income from special events

- Real estate and rental income

- Income from the sale of assets

Each type of income has its own distinctive set of characteristics, rules, and requirements. We'll discuss the accounting theory behind the transaction, how to post the transaction, the internal control implications, and the management of the collection process.

One recordkeeping task that is required for the accurate preparation of the IRS Forms 990 and 990-EZ is the tracking of any contribution from a disqualified person. The instructions for the forms are available on the IRS web site (http://www.irs.gov).

The Basic Entry

In its basic form, the entry required to record income performs two functions:

1. It debits an account to reflect the value received by the organization (that is, how the snapshot of assets and liabilities has changed due to the income event).

2. It credits an income account (creating a historical entry necessary to trace how the organization arrived at its current financial state).

The account to debit in a transaction that records an income event depends upon the facts surrounding the event. The most common accounts are cash and accounts receivable (or, in the case of contributions, some software has a separate *pledges receivable* control account and subsidiary records to distinguish this type of receivable). The conditions for the respective categories are as follows:

- *Cash* is debited if the organization receives a payment for some event that was not previously recorded in the accounting system.

- *A/R* is debited if payment has not been received; that is, if someone now owes the organization money (such as a pledge) as a result of the income event.

If cash is received in payment of a previously recorded event that is currently a part of the organization's A/R balance, the cash receipt is not income at all. (This transaction is discussed in Chapter Five.)

In less common transactions, the debit is posted to another account that reflects the reality of the event. For example, if cash was received in a prior period, but the income was not recognized at that time (that is, the organization received the funds prior to actually earning them), the original transaction would have debited cash and credited deferred income (a liability account, as the organization owes the money to the donor or funding source until the funds are earned). One example is a special-event sponsorship. The funds are not earned when the money is received; the funds are earned when the special event takes place. The entry recognizing the income in the current period would contain a debit to deferred income and a credit to income.

Receivable Tracking

Once you have established that someone owes you money, you have a receivable. A *receivable* is created when your organization earns income but has not yet collected the money it has earned. The recording and tracking of the asset called a receivable is of critical importance to the financial health of your organization.

When accounting records were manually kept in hand-written journals and ledgers, it was common to maintain the accounts receivable schedule on a *balance forward* method. Using this method, the A/R details for all preceding periods were summarized as a single amount rather than maintained separately for each unpaid item. The balance forward method sacrificed details but made the task more manageable in the manually maintained set of books. Depending on the software you are using, you might be offered the opportunity to choose between an *open item* system (where all details are tracked) and a balance forward system. We recommend you always select the open item system.

Program Service Income (Fees for Service)

For many nonprofits, charging fees for services is the largest source of income. Universities, health care agencies, mental health clinics, and hospitals all are common examples of nonprofits that derive a majority of their revenues from program service income. Smaller nonprofits often have substantial program service income as well: day-care facilities, private schools, and so on. Our focus will be on the smaller organization.

Proper documentation of the services billed is mandatory. For example, Medicare and Medicaid billing rules and guidelines must be adhered to in every aspect; improper billing and improperly documented billing under these programs can lead to serious financial (and possibly criminal) consequences.

Much like a for-profit enterprise, the challenges for the nonprofit organization offering services to the public include the following:

- Knowing who to bill

- Knowing when to bill

- Knowing how much to bill

- Knowing how to classify the income

- Knowing what to collect

- Knowing when to follow up on unpaid receivables

Let's look at each of these challenges in turn.

Knowing Who to Bill

Obtaining proper and complete client information is a critical part of the process. Often third-party reimbursement is involved; make sure you obtain accurate, updated information about coverage and about the third party's billing requirements at the time the service is rendered. Pre-registration, if possible, is highly recommended. Wrong or missing payer information will result in late payment or nonpayment of bills. Failure to obtain required authorization will also result in late payment or nonpayment from the third party coverage.

Knowing When to Bill

The organization must have a system in place to trigger the creation of a bill. To determine what the appropriate trigger is, you need to examine carefully the service rendered by your organization and the process by which the service is rendered. For example, in a medical clinic a bill would be triggered by each visit. In a day-care facility, enrollment and daily attendance records would trigger a periodic bill. Failure to issue bills promptly increases the possibility of nonpayment; in any event, late billing has a negative impact on the organization's cash flow.

Knowing How Much to Bill

Most nonprofit organizations use a sliding scale of standard rates for services the organization offers. Billing rates, if not currently used, should be developed and adhered to. Billing that varies from the standard should be recorded as a two-line entry: the standard rate as the first line; then the amount below or in excess of the standard rate as the second line. This multi-part entry eliminates any inadvertent billing rate errors (it makes the changing of the standard rate an affirmative process), and it provides management with more useful information about the billing for services rendered (the analysis of revenue can look beyond totals and averages and examine individual rate premiums or discounts by client or by individual bill).

Knowing How to Classify the Income

The chart of accounts used by the organization is designed to capture the transactions in a meaningful way. Usually there is a separate account for each of the services offered. It is important to understand both the range of services offered and the accounting system's goals for the recording and analysis of the transactions that result when services are rendered. Often a single point of contact will result in a multitude of transactions, each going to a separate account in the chart of accounts. Recording the transactions accurately and completely, as we have stressed, is a top priority.

Knowing What to Collect

This is divided into two separate processes. In many situations, particularly with third-party reimbursements, there is a co-payment due at the time the service is rendered; the balance of the bill becomes a receivable. The collection of the co-payment must be integrated into the delivery of service process, so there is no danger it will be overlooked. Since client privacy issues sometimes limit the organization's ability to mail out statements or reminders, proper staff training is essential to ensure the co-payment collection is a priority. The collection of the receivable involves knowledge of the third-party reimbursement contract details, if applicable, and the delineation of amounts due from the client versus amounts due from the third-party payer.

Knowing When to Follow Up on Unpaid Receivables

A high rate of uncollected bills often leads to high bad-debt expense. When possible, encourage payment in full at the time service is rendered. Regular late payment reminders should be mailed out, and requests for additional information from third-party payers should be answered quickly and accurately. The collection process is a mixture of persistence, politeness, and willingness and ability to document the amount due. As a last resort, you can consider engaging the services of a professional collection agency.

Some nonprofit organizations that offer confidential services have a policy of never mailing bills or statements or never calling or contacting clients. In those circumstances you need to develop an effective method of informing the front desk staff about billing and collection policies and utilizing them, as they manage appointments, to collect monies when due.

Let's look at a sample fee-for-service transaction. A client has two services provided during an office visit. Our organization charges $30 for service A and $55 for service B. We require a $10 co-payment at the time services are rendered, and we expect payment in full after thirty days. In our accounting system, the net result of that office visit is shown in Exhibit 4.1.

EXHIBIT 4.1   Posting to Record Co-Payment and Bill Client for Services

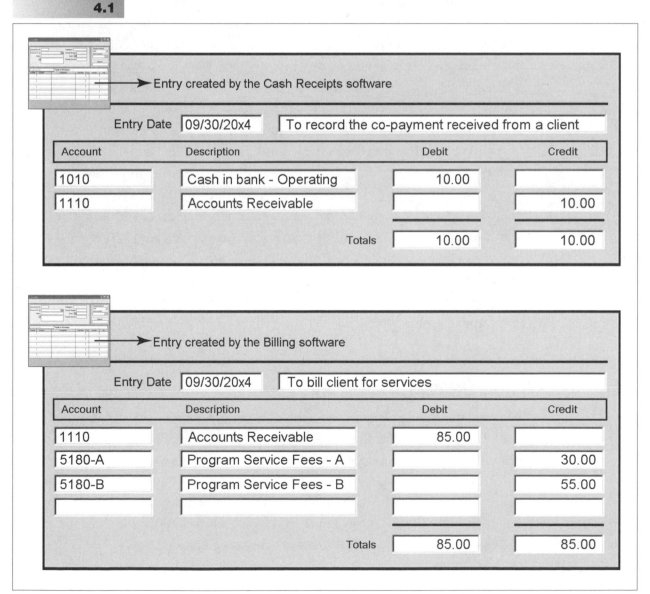

Entry created by the Cash Receipts software

Entry Date 09/30/20x4   To record the co-payment received from a client

Account	Description	Debit	Credit
1010	Cash in bank - Operating	10.00	
1110	Accounts Receivable		10.00
	Totals	10.00	10.00

Entry created by the Billing software

Entry Date 09/30/20x4   To bill client for services

Account	Description	Debit	Credit
1110	Accounts Receivable	85.00	
5180-A	Program Service Fees - A		30.00
5180-B	Program Service Fees - B		55.00
	Totals	85.00	85.00

The components of the transaction are as follows:

- We gather all necessary client information and set the client up in our accounting system.

- We collect $10 from the client and record it as a cash receipt, creating a credit amount in the client's A/R total (this debits *cash* and credits *accounts receivable* for the $10 received).

- We create a two-line bill for services rendered (each line debits *accounts receivable* and credits the appropriate *revenue* account):

  Service A for $30
  Service B for $55

The three entries into A/R (the two debits from the billing process and the credit from the cash receipt) combine to leave an unpaid balance of $75. The details are posted separately and are available to provide a trail from start to finish.

Since the fee-for-service model of generating revenue is so similar to the typical revenue model of a for-profit enterprise, most accounting software will work "as is." The nonprofit's client is equivalent to the customer of the for-profit company. Depending on the organization's structure and other issues discussed in Chapter Three, it is possible to use the account coding combined with job costing features of the accounting software to classify the transactions. Most accounting software will also allow you to categorize the customer list; this gives you the opportunity to use the A/R and billing components of the software for multiple kinds of revenue. If it is helpful in your organization, you should distinguish the fee-for-service clients from other customers, such as members billed for their annual dues.

If your organization does a large volume of billing, it makes sense to evaluate software written specifically for the type of fee for service you do. Third-party reimbursement billing, including electronic billing, is often incorporated into the software. You are able to record the results of any special function software into your accounting system by posting the summary results with a periodic journal entry or through an electronic import function.

Income from the Sale of Inventory

Many nonprofits supplement their cash flow through the sale of products. Gift shops, mail-order catalog operations, and the sale of promotional items with the organization's logo are sometimes a part of a typical nonprofit's revenue-raising strategy.

The sale of inventory items to the general public is a typical for-profit enterprise. Your organization will face the same challenges discussed in the section on program service income (fees for service), such as knowing when to bill, knowing whom to bill, and so on. A typical transaction to record the sale of a product from inventory in a gift shop is shown in Exhibit 4.2.

EXHIBIT 4.2   **Posting to Record Cash Sale of an Inventory Item**

Entry created by the Cash Receipts software

Entry Date	09/30/20x4	To record cash sale of inventory item	

Account	Description	Debit	Credit
1010	Cash in bank - Operating	15.00	
5440	Gross Sales - Inventory		15.00
	Totals	15.00	15.00

In addition to the challenges just outlined, when you sell a product from inventory there are other challenges:

- Knowing the proper level of inventory to maintain
- Knowing when to collect sales tax and how much sales tax to collect
- Knowing the impact of the Unrelated Business Income Tax (UBIT).

Knowing the Proper Level of Inventory to Maintain

The management of inventory is a complex topic. For most small organizations, there are essential points to consider:

- The need to employ effective purchasing strategies and to obtain favorable prices, delivery, and payment terms
- The need to use reliable suppliers to ensure quality products and responsive service
- The need to maintain a low total inventory to minimize the resources invested and to minimize potential loss from deterioration of products in stock
- The need to use drop-ship (fulfillment) arrangements when possible, in which the supplier maintains the inventory and arranges for shipment to your customer on a per-order basis
- The need to optimize your ordering versus holding costs by determining the *economic order quantity,* a calculation designed to minimize the costs associated with maintaining an inventory
- Establish controls to reduce *shrinkage,* or theft of products from the inventory

As you sell products from inventory, the cost of the goods sold (COGS) is recorded, and the inventory (the asset) is reduced by the same amount, as shown in Exhibit 4.3.

Posting to Record the Cost of a Sale of an Inventory Item

General Journal Entry

Journal Entry Date	09/30/20x4	To record the cost of a sale of inventory item	

Account	Description	Debit	Credit
5445	Cost of Goods Sold	6.75	
1410	Inventory		6.75
	Totals	6.75	6.75

Cost of goods sold is an expense account associated with inventory sales. Depending on the size of your inventory sales operation and on the accounting software you use, this COGS transaction can be calculated and recorded in several ways:

- At the time of the sale, the cost of the item sold can be debited to COGS and credited to inventory (if your software automates the process).

- At the end of the period, the cost of all items sold can be debited to COGS and credited to inventory (depending on the capabilities of your software, this information might be available for items removed from stock).

- At the end of the period, a physical count of inventory items can be taken, and the cost of that physical count can be calculated. By subtracting this ending inventory valuation from the sum of the beginning inventory valuation plus the cost of all purchases in the period, you will arrive at the cost of all goods sold in the period.

Inventory valuation is another complex topic that you must discuss with your auditor. What you should take away from this discussion is the awareness that recording the sale is one step in recording the entire transaction; the transfer of the inventory sold from asset to expense (cost of goods sold) is a necessary second step.

Knowing When to Collect Sales Tax

The laws of each state (and occasionally the laws of the county or municipality) determine the amount of sales tax to be collected. While every state's laws are different, here is a list of common factors that affect the taxation of your products.

The Product Itself. Certain jurisdictions collect a sales tax on clothing, for example, while clothing is tax exempt in other jurisdictions. Tax laws vary greatly; some jurisdictions exempt certain amounts of clothing sales from sales tax and only charge the tax on the amount over the threshold. In addition, depending upon your organization's exempt purpose, it is possible an item sold by you is tax exempt, while it would be taxable if it were sold by a for-profit business or by another exempt organization with a different charitable purpose. Also, items sold at certain special events might be exempt from sales tax. We recommend that you ask your CPA or attorney to do research in this complex area based on your organization's activities.

The Purchaser. Certain jurisdictions recognize the tax-exempt status of the organization buying the product and therefore exempt any sale to that organization from sales tax.

The Use of the Product. Certain jurisdictions recognize *exempt uses,* such as capital improvements, that will exempt the purchase of a product from sales tax.

The Geographic Location of the Purchaser. Your organization will be required to collect sales tax on behalf of states and other jurisdictions where you have a physical presence. (*Physical presence* is a complicated concept; states constantly seek to expand the definition in order to subject more organizations to the collection requirement. Check with your CPA or attorney for guidance.) Shipments of product to states other than those states where you are required to collect sales tax are exempt from sales tax.

The Organization's Exempt Purpose. In some states (the rules vary by jurisdiction), a nonprofit organization with a mission of promoting religious activities can sell religious books without collecting sales tax.

The Venue of the Sale. A one-time only sale to a member of the organization during a special event might be treated differently than a similar sale from a gift shop.

When determining the specifics of the sales tax law for your location, take a look at the treatment of shipping costs. Some jurisdictions include freight, postage, shipping, and handling in the taxable sale; other jurisdictions do not.

Sales tax laws are complex. With careful research and a discussion with your attorney and accountant, the organization can develop and implement the proper procedures.

Let's look at a sample sale with a sales tax transaction. A customer purchases an item for $10 plus sales tax, shipping, and handling. The net result of the sales transaction is shown in Exhibit 4.4.

The transaction posted when the purchaser remits payment for the sale is shown in Exhibit 4.5.

EXHIBIT 4.4 **Posting to Record a Sales Transaction**

Entry created by the Billing software

Entry Date 09/30/20x4   To record a sales transaction

Account	Description	Debit	Credit
1110	Accounts Receivable	14.10	
5440	Gross Sales - Inventory		10.00
2140	Sales Tax Payable		.60
5441	Freight Out		3.50
	Totals	14.10	14.10

EXHIBIT 4.5 **Posting to Record Payment by Customer**

Entry created by the Cash Receipts software

Entry Date 10/31/20x4   To record payment by customer

Account	Description	Debit	Credit
1010	Cash in bank - Operating	14.10	
1110	Accounts Receivable		14.10
	Totals	14.10	14.10

The Unrelated Business Income Tax (UBIT)

Nonprofits that derive income from activities that are not related to their tax-exempt purposes may be subject to UBIT on those earnings. Organizations that earn too much unrelated business income (UBI) might jeopardize their tax-exempt status.

Income earned from business activities substantially related to a nonprofit's tax-exempt purpose are not subject to UBIT. Business activities that are considered to be unrelated will generate UBI if all of the following are true:

1. The income is from a trade or business regularly carried on by the organization.

2. The activity itself is not substantially related to carrying out the organization's exempt purpose (regardless of what is eventually done with the income).

3. The activity or its income is not excluded from taxation, primarily under Internal Revenue Code sections 512, 513, and 514.

The IRS has listed forty exclusion categories that help define what is and is not subject to UBIT. In addition, there are steps that many organizations can take to avoid taxation legally and ethically; with proper planning, nonprofit organizations can ensure specific business activities fall into an exclusion category. For example, staffing a retail store with volunteers may avoid the UBIT. Tax planning to minimize the impact of UBIT is very important.

If the proceeds from the sale of inventory will be subject to UBIT, it is important that your organization budget for this. Pricing (knowing how much to charge) needs to be adjusted to account for the impact of UBIT. This area of taxation is confusing and subject to different interpretations; we suggest you consult your CPA or attorney regarding this topic.

Income Support from Contributions

Many nonprofit organizations depend almost entirely on contributions for support. Contributions are generated from a variety of methods, including special fundraising campaigns, direct-mail solicitations, and telemarketing activities.

The bookkeeper has to analyze transactions to categorize accurately those items that are contributions. Receipts of accounts receivable will often include an extra amount meant to be a contribution to the organization. The recording of the transaction must reflect this fact. In fundraising campaigns, the contributor might receive a gift for making a donation. When such gifts are under a certain dollar threshold (which increases periodically based on inflation), a contribution exists for the donor and is recorded by the organization. The organization should provide a written acknowledgment of all contributions. As the IRS states in Publication 1771 (Charitable Contributions—Substantiation and Disclosure Requirements), a donor is responsible for obtaining a written acknowledgment from a charity for any single contribution of $250 or more before the donor can claim a charitable contribution on his or her federal income tax return. A charitable organization is also required to provide a written disclosure to a donor who receives goods or services in exchange for a single payment in excess of $75. The written acknowledgment should include the donor's name and address, the amount of cash contributed (or a description of any other property contributed), and a statement on whether or not the donor received anything from the organization in exchange for the contribution.

If the organization sponsors a special event with a ticket price of $150, and attendees receive a meal worth $50, the actual contribution is $100. The actual contribution amount should be indicated on the solicitation for the event or on the ticket. (See the IRS publication for complete details.)

In a fundraising campaign, the organization solicits donations and receives pledges from potential contributors. In order to know when and how to record contributions in the accounting records, each promise should be analyzed:

- If the promise is unconditional, it must be recognized as income.

- If the promise is legally enforceable and without any conditions, it must be recognized as income.

Specialized software is available to track contributors and pledges. Summary information from the donor-tracking system should be posted as appropriate (but always at month end) in a journal entry to record the contribution activity.

As with any source of revenue, the receipt of funds due to a contribution is applied against any existing receivable, or if no receivable was previously recorded, the contribution is posted directly to the revenue account called *contribution income* (in Exhibit 4.6).

Promises to give can be unrestricted, temporarily restricted, or permanently restricted. The character of the underlying promise dictates the net asset classification of the transaction in the accounting records:

- *Unrestricted* contributions are given without any conditions from the donor.

- *Temporarily restricted* contributions are given by the donor for a specific purpose, for a specific time period, or for both a specific purpose and time period. For example, a donor specifies that the contribution is for a community hotline program for the year 20x5. Funds designated by the donor in this manner must be spent for the purpose and time period indicated.

EXHIBIT 4.6 **Posting to Record Receipt of Contribution**

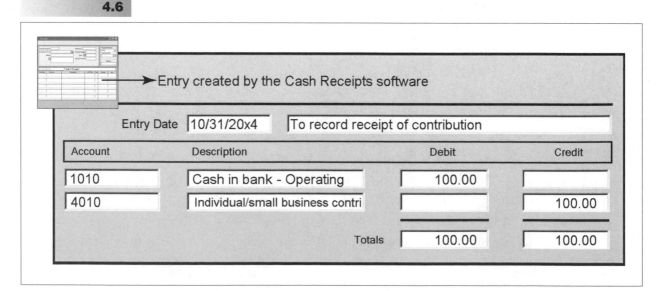

Entry created by the Cash Receipts software

Entry Date 10/31/20x4		To record receipt of contribution		

Account	Description	Debit	Credit
1010	Cash in bank - Operating	100.00	
4010	Individual/small business contri		100.00
	Totals	100.00	100.00

- *Permanently restricted* contributions are more common in large nonprofit organizations, such as colleges, universities, and hospitals. They might include endowment contributions designed to support a specific purpose, such as a Professor of Accounting chair at a University. Normally the organization can only use the income from the contribution to support the activity; the contributed amount is invested and cannot be spent. State laws governing endowments vary.

If no temporary or permanent restrictions apply, the contribution is unrestricted. *In-kind contributions* (non-cash contributions of goods or services) are recorded as a credit to income, with the offsetting debit recording the nature of the non-cash gift (inventory, assets, goods, or services received). Contributed services are recognized at fair value if the services require specialized skills, if the providers of the services possess the specialized skills, and if the organization would purchase the service if it were not donated.

Donated services that are not recognized under GAAP should still be recorded if the organization has a matching grant that requires these services. Under a *matching grant*, the funding source agrees to match resources acquired by the organization from other donors. Care must be taken to follow the requirements of the entity requesting the matching funds; often, there are many different types of special requirements for matches. Non-GAAP-donated services must be posted to a separate, clearly labeled account; this makes it easy to eliminate the effect of the transaction when financial statements according to GAAP are needed. The identification of donated services is also required to properly prepare IRS Form 990.

Income from Grants

Nonprofit organizations often receive grants for a substantial percentage of their funding. Organizations that manage to follow all of the rules and regulations related to their grants are rewarded with a very stable income stream. When you are awarded a grant, the money is committed; if your organization fulfills the requirements of the grantor, the funds will be received.

Grant income requires the organization to account properly for all transactions related to the grant; there must be systems in place to ensure compliance with the terms specified by the funding source. Failure to comply with any one requirement could possibly cause the revocation of the grant and a loss of grant income. See Chapter Eleven and Resources F and G for descriptions about allowable and non-allowable costs related to federally funded grants.

There are many types of grants, including the following:

- *Private sector unrestricted grants*—essentially the same as a contribution

- *Private sector targeted grants*—given with a designated purpose for the use of the funds

- *Private sector restricted grants*—stipulate that the funds be used for a specific purpose and/or a specific period of time, often specifying a specific goal and expected results

- *Government grants*—often require specific services

The recognition of income from a grant must be evaluated based on the requirements and restrictions of the grant contract. Private sector unrestricted grants are recognized as income in the period that the grant is made. For example, an organization is awarded an unrestricted grant for the year 20x4 in the amount of $50,000, payable four times per year at the end of each calendar quarter. The income is recorded and a receivable is established at the start of the year (Exhibit 4.7).

As each payment is received, the receivable is reduced (Exhibit 4.8).

EXHIBIT 4.7	Journal Entry to Record an Unrestricted Grant Award

General Journal Entry

Journal Entry Date 01/31/20x4   To record an unrestricted grant award

Account	Description	Debit	Credit
1240	Grants Receivable	50000.00	
4230	Foundation/trust grants		50000.00
	Totals	50000.00	50000.00

EXHIBIT 4.8	Posting to Record Receipt of Grant Payment

Entry created by the Cash Receipts software

Entry Date 03/31/20x4   To record receipt of grant payment

Account	Description	Debit	Credit
1010	Cash in bank - Operating	12500.00	
1240	Grants Receivable		12500.00
	Totals	12500.00	12500.00

Performance-based grants, cost reimbursement grants, and other types of restricted grants are recognized as income as the requirements of the grant award are met: that is, when you actually spend the money on grant-related activities or perform the services specified. Receipt of funds prior to the organization fulfilling the requirements of the grant establishes a liability, as shown in Exhibit 4.9.

EXHIBIT 4.9   **Posting to Record Receipt of Grant Payment When Requirement Not Met**

→ Entry created by the Cash Receipts software

Entry Date 05/31/20x4   receipt of grant payment - requirement not met

Account	Description	Debit	Credit
1010	Cash in bank - Operating	12500.00	
2311	Unearned Grant Income		12500.00
	Totals	12500.00	12500.00

Frequently, the grant period does not coincide with the organization's fiscal year. This can lead to classifying unearned grant funds as either a refundable advance (deferred revenue) or as a balance due to the funding source (liability). If the grant period is not yet over, grant funds received but not yet earned are called *refundable advances* (deferred revenue, which is a liability). At the fiscal year end, these refundable advances are distinguished from other liabilities since their classification is due to a timing difference: the likelihood exists that the grant requirements will be met before the grant period ends. Grant funds received that were never earned during the grant period are recorded as a liability due to the funding source. Once the grant period ends, the unearned grant monies must be returned to the funding source unless the funding source allows for a different disposition of monies.

Grants are a major source of funding for nonprofits of all sizes. Careful record keeping, in accordance with the goals we have established for our accounting system, help provide management with the tools it needs to satisfy the requirements of the grantor. A useful checklist for organizations receiving grants is located in Resource F of this book.

Interest, Dividend, and Royalty Income

Interest, dividends, and royalties are often supplementary sources of income for nonprofit organizations. Investments in certificates of deposit, bonds, and money market funds generate interest income. Stocks and mutual funds generate dividends. Royalty income is generated from the sales of publications and other types of media, including books, compact discs, audiotapes, and videotapes; royalties are also generated by *affinity credit cards*, which carry the organization's name and pay a percentage of each purchase to the organization.

All of these income items are reported to the organization on periodic statements of account. Depending on the financial arrangement, the income generated can be added to the original investment (reinvested) or the income can be disbursed directly to the organization. When the organization receives the check, or when the income is reported to the organization, the financial transaction is recorded (as in Exhibits 4.10 and 4.11).

At the end of a fiscal period, it is often necessary to accrue interest income earned but not yet credited to the organization by the bank. Since interest income is often

EXHIBIT 4.10   **Journal Entry to Record Savings Account Interest**

General Journal Entry

Journal Entry Date 05/31/20x4   To record savings account interest

Account	Description	Debit	Credit
1070	Cash - Savings Account	14.52	
5310	Interest Income		14.52
	Totals	14.52	14.52

EXHIBIT 4.11   **Posting to Record Receipt of Royalty Payment**

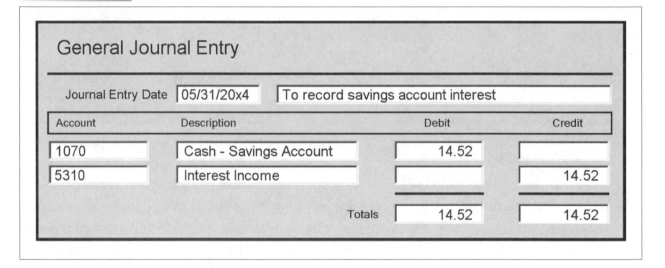

→ Entry created by the Cash Receipts software

Entry Date 07/31/20x4   To record receipt of royalty payment

Account	Description	Debit	Credit
1010	Cash in bank - Operating	253.25	
5470	Royalty Income		253.25
	Totals	253.25	253.25

earned at a fixed rate and is guaranteed to be paid, a material amount of interest can be recorded in a journal entry prior to actual receipt of the funds. Dividends and royalty payments are more uncertain and should not be accrued unless definitive information is available, and the payment amounts are material.

Income from Membership Dues

Membership dues are a major source of revenue for professional organizations, alumni associations, and fraternal organizations. Dues are distinguished from other revenue sources since they are paid by individuals on an ongoing basis and are paid without the expectation of receiving products or services from the organization. While donations from members and sale of services and products to members are other sources of revenue, dues are paid periodically in exchange for the right to be a member.

Membership dues that provide services to members, such as access to a health club facility, should be distinguished from the traditional concept of membership dues. If the purpose of joining the organization and paying the dues is to obtain an economic or other direct benefit, the dues should be treated as a fee for service transaction. These dues are recognized in the period when the benefit is provided.

Some organizations combine an offer of membership with a subscription to the organization's periodical; when accounting for the transaction, segregate the dues component from the periodical subscription component (subscription income).

Membership tracking software is available; depending on the size of the organization, it is also possible to utilize a general accounting package to track membership events. Since the renewal of membership dues is voluntary, the organization cannot recognize revenue until payment is received from the individual. If your organization uses a general accounting package to handle membership billing, it is important to segregate the membership from other customers and post the revenue and the receivable to memo accounts.

Memo accounts are additional accounts in the chart of accounts designed for a specific purpose. They are created in pairs and are clearly labeled with the word *memo* in the account name. These accounts occur in pairs to allow the posting of balanced entries; they are useful when you need to track activity but do not want to impact the general ledger.

To use memo accounts for tracking memberships, create two general ledger accounts: one for the receivable and one for the dues. The balance in these accounts will always be the mirror image of each other at the end of each accounting period. When billing the members for dues, set up the software to debit the *Memo: Receivable* account with the receivable and credit the *Memo: Dues* account with the revenue not yet earned. As cash is received from the members, the *Memo: Receivable* account is credited (cash is debited). At the end of the accounting period, the difference between the two memo account balances represents the dues revenue for the period. A simple journal entry reclassifies the amount from memo to revenue.

Normally, dues are paid for a time period and are not refundable. To record the payment of dues when you do not use your accounting software to track membership, post the receipts as shown in Exhibit 4.12.

EXHIBIT 4.12 **Posting to Record Receipt of Unbilled Membership Dues**

→ Entry created by the Cash Receipts software

| Entry Date | 05/31/20x4 | To record receipt of unbilled membership dues |

Account	Description	Debit	Credit
1010	Cash in bank - Operating	275.00	
5210	Membership dues - individua		275.00
	Totals	275.00	275.00

This same transaction format is used if your organization utilizes separate membership tracking software.

Income from Special Events

Many nonprofit organizations hold special events to supplement their existing sources of revenue. Special events provide the organization with a favorable publicity opportunity and a chance to broaden the reach of membership promotions, product sales, and other revenue sources. Income from a special event can come from a variety of sources:

- The organization can arrange for sponsorship of the event.
- Participants of the event pay a fee to attend.
- Additional contributions can be solicited at the event.

When accounting for a special event, it is important to segregate the revenue and expenses of the event from other activities of the organization. Management will always be interested in the profitability of the event, and so future event planning will be based on the performance of past events. Depending on your accounting software, it is usually possible to establish a new cost center (often labeled a *job*) for the event. Your auditor or accountant will need this information when preparing the organization's financial statements and tax returns, since specific disclosure of fundraising revenue and costs is required.

Recording the revenue transactions from a special event is similar to accounting for the sale of inventory and accounting for contributions. In fact, ticket sales for many special events are actually part sale and part contribution. Monies received in advance (for example, ticket sales prior to the event) are recorded as *deferred income* (a liability), since the income is earned when the event takes place. Sponsorship income is almost always unrestricted in nature and is recorded when the commitment is made by the sponsor.

Real Estate and Rental Income

Real estate property management is the main purpose of some nonprofit organizations operating in areas where such services are needed. Specialty software is available to track tenant information, leases, rent rolls, insurance, utilities, maintenance and repair issues, and tenant complaints.

The accounting issues in real estate management include the following:

- Security deposits
- Prepaid rent
- Rental income

A security deposit is received from the tenant at the beginning of the lease term. This amount is a liability of the organization; the amount is to be returned with interest, minus the cost of any damages to the premises at the termination of the lease. The security deposit should be segregated from the other funds of the organization in an interest-bearing bank account. Many banks offer special real estate security deposit account services that are excellent ways to fulfill the responsibilities associated with such monies. Many jurisdictions have specific rules governing security deposit accounts; check with your attorney for the rules in your area. The entry in Exhibit 4.13 records the receipt of the security deposit.

EXHIBIT 4.13   **Journal Entry to Record the Receipt of Rent Security Deposit**

General Journal Entry

Journal Entry Date 08/31/20x4   To record receipt of rent security deposit

Account	Description	Debit	Credit
1050	Cash - Security Deposits	650.00	
2420	Security Deposits Payable		650.00
	Totals	650.00	650.00

Prepaid rent is an amount received prior to the period covered by the rental payment. If a tenant pays two months' rent on June 1, the June rent is classified as rental income, but the July rent is a liability of the organization until July 1. The entry in Exhibit 4.14 illustrates how to record both the prepaid rent and the rental income.

On July 1, the deferred income is reclassified (Exhibit 4.15).

Rental income is earned and recognized by the organization during the period represented by the lease payment.

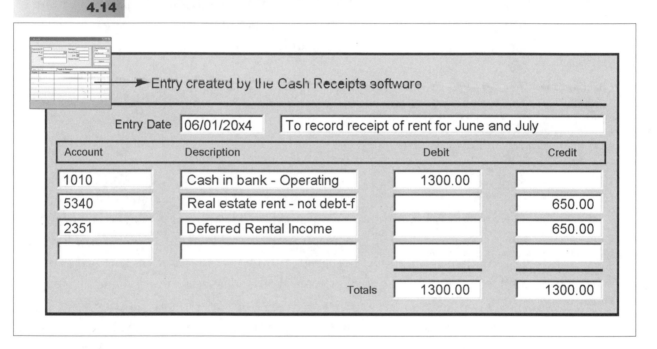

EXHIBIT 4.14   Posting to Record Receipt of Rent for Two Months

Entry created by the Cash Receipts software

Entry Date	06/01/20x4	To record receipt of rent for June and July		
Account	Description		Debit	Credit
1010	Cash in bank - Operating		1300.00	
5340	Real estate rent - not debt-f			650.00
2351	Deferred Rental Income			650.00
		Totals	1300.00	1300.00

EXHIBIT 4.15   Journal Entry to Reclassify Deferred Rent to Rental Income

General Journal Entry

Journal Entry Date	07/01/20x4	To reclassify a July payment received in June		
Account	Description		Debit	Credit
2351	Deferred Rental Income		650.00	
5340	Real estate rent - not debt-f			650.00
		Totals	650.00	650.00

Income from the Sale of Assets

The sale of assets can generate income for the nonprofit organization under several circumstances:

- The organization sells securities previously held for investment.

- A donor makes a non-cash contribution of securities for the nonprofit to sell.

- The nonprofit organization decides to sell property (such as a building) it previously acquired via purchase or donation.

Assets are recorded in the accounting records of the organization at the time of acquisition. Regardless of the type of asset being sold, the transaction must record two items: the removal of the asset (and any related accumulated depreciation) being sold from the balance sheet of the organization and the creation of a new asset (cash or receivable) that is received at the time of the sale. The transaction in Exhibit 4.16 illustrates how to record the sale by the organization of a small building and land for cash.

In the example, the cost of the land and building were recorded at the time of purchase. The building was partially depreciated over the years, which had the effect of reducing the net book value of the asset. At the time of sale, the gain equals the sales price minus the net book value of the asset.

EXHIBIT 4.16   **Posting to Record the Sale of a Building**

→ Entry created by the Cash Receipts software

Entry Date 10/31/20x4   To record the sale of a building

Account	Description	Debit	Credit
1010	Cash in bank - Operating	72000.00	
1610	Land - operating		10000.00
1620	Building - operating		21000.00
1725	Accum Deprec - building	6000.00	
6710	Gain on Sale of Fixed Assets		47000.00
	Totals	78000.00	78000.00

Debt-Financed Revenue

Keeping track of debt-financed versus non debt-financed revenue is important for the nonprofit organization. A surplus of revenue over expenses associated with debt-financed property might be considered unrelated business income, thereby making it subject to Unrelated Business Income Taxes (UBIT).

Internal Control Considerations

The Committee of Sponsoring Organizations of the Treadway Commission (COSO) issued this definition of internal controls:

> *Internal control* is broadly defined as a process, affected by an entity's board of directors, management, and other personnel, designed to provide reasonable assurance regarding the achievement of objectives in the following categories:
>
> • Effectiveness and efficiency of operations
>
> • Reliability of financial reporting
>
> • Compliance with applicable laws and regulations
>
> (COSO, 1985)

For example, in an accounting system, there are several rules that should generally apply:

• No single individual has complete control over financial transactions. For example, the physical receipt of funds is handled by someone other than the person recording the transaction.

• Bank reconciliations are prepared by someone other than the individuals responsible for the receipt and disbursement of funds.

• Periodically, bank reconciliations and other critical tasks are performed by someone other than the individual normally responsible for the task.

In the case of revenue and support, the internal control system must focus on these critical points:

• Proper billing for every billable event

• Accurate pricing on each bill

• Complete recording of each transaction

Many of the internal control issues specific to revenue and support are intertwined with the collection of funds; these issues are addressed in Chapter Five.

Summary

Understanding, tracking, and recording the income of an organization are vitally important. Proper recognition and classification of revenue and support are the most important and complicated aspects of maintaining good financial records in a nonprofit organization. In this chapter, we have explored some of the common sources of revenue and support, focusing on evaluating and recording each transaction in your accounting system.

Cash Receipts

The process of receiving, recording, and documenting funds is essential to the success of the organization. Cash is the most desirable type of asset, the most liquid asset, and the most readily transported asset of any entity; safeguarding the asset is the primary task of the cash receipt system. All nonprofit organizations depend on adequate cash flow to maintain operations; the efficient working of the cash receipt system maximizes cash flow. (In Chapter Fourteen we go into some detail on cash flow forecasting and reporting.)

In this chapter, we will examine both the process of recording cash receipts in the accounting system and the procedures that should be in place to safeguard cash and maximize cash flow.

Sources of Cash

As we noted in Chapter Four, the typical nonprofit has many potential sources of funds:

- Program service income (fee for service)
- Income from the sale of inventory
- Income from contributions
- Income from grants
- Interest, dividend, and royalty income
- Income from membership dues
- Income from special events
- Real estate and rental income
- Income from the sale of assets

Funds collected from each of these sources are processed by the cash receipt system. For some of the revenue sources, a bill was generated at the point of service or at the shipment of product. For these items, an accounts receivable open item exists in the accounting system (Exhibit 5.1).

Other revenue sources are recorded at the point that the funds are received; in this case, the cash receipt must also be properly classified and posted to the correct revenue account (Exhibit 5.2).

EXHIBIT 5.1   **Posting to Record the Receipt of an Open A/R Item**

→ Entry created by the Cash Receipts software

Entry Date	10/31/20x4	To record the collection of an open A/R item

Account	Description	Debit	Credit
1010	Cash in bank - Operating	52.50	
1110	Accounts Receivable		52.50
	Totals	52.50	52.50

EXHIBIT 5.2   **Journal Entry to Record Savings Account Interest**

General Journal Entry

Journal Entry Date	10/31/20x4	To record savings account interest

Account	Description	Debit	Credit
1070	Cash - Savings Account	100.00	
5310	Interest Income		100.00
	Totals	100.00	100.00

Aside from funds generated by revenue sources, every cash receipt system has to handle the occasional general ledger receipt (these are sometimes called *non-A/R receipts,* because the receipt is payment for an item or event that has not been billed and entered into the A/R system). Examples of a general ledger receipt include the following:

- Insurance claim proceeds
- Supplier refund
- Return of deposit
- Transfer of funds between bank accounts

Whenever possible, all contributions should be processed through the standard billing subsystem. The reasons for this include the following:

- All contributions of $250 or more must be acknowledged in writing.

- The billing sub-system captures information about the donor, which becomes a valuable resource in future fundraising efforts.

Every contributor should be thanked. Experienced fundraisers send the thank-you acknowledgment with a self-addressed envelope for use by the individual to facilitate future contributions.

The bookkeeper's task is to understand the nature of the general ledger receipt and to properly record the transaction. Let's look at two examples:

1. The insurance claim proceeds reimburse the organization for funds expended to repair a vehicle. Was the reimbursement anticipated in some prior transaction? If so, there might be a receivable (debit) sitting in a balance sheet account, representing the money due from the insurance company. If not, the insurance proceeds should be posted as a credit to the same account where the organization charged the vehicle repair.

2. The supplier refund is due to the return of a purchase; in this case, the refund should be credited to the account originally charged. If the supplier refund is the result of an outstanding credit from the supplier, the credit was already posted to the account originally charged, and the refund should offset the existing credit memo in accounts payable.

While the task of processing A/R cash receipts is fairly straightforward, recording general ledger receipts usually involves some careful analysis (illustrated in Exhibits 5.3, 5.4, 5.5, and 5.6).

EXHIBIT 5.3   **Posting to Record Receipt of Insurance Claim Proceeds**

Entry created by the Cash Receipts software

Entry Date 04/30/20x4   To record the receipt of an insurance claim proceeds

Account	Description	Debit	Credit
1010	Cash in bank - Operating	550.00	
8265	Vehicle Repairs		550.00
	Totals	550.00	550.00

EXHIBIT 5.4 **Posting to Record Supplier Refund for Existing Credit Memo**

→ Entry created by the Cash Receipts software

Entry Date 04/30/20x4 | To record supplier refund for existing credit memo

Account	Description	Debit	Credit
1010	Cash in bank - Operating	25.00	
2010	Accounts Payable		25.00
	Totals	25.00	25.00

EXHIBIT 5.5 **Posting to Record the Return of a Deposit**

→ Entry created by the Cash Receipts software

Entry Date 04/30/20x4 | To record the return of a deposit

Account	Description	Debit	Credit
1010	Cash in bank - Operating	100.00	
1330	Deposits Receivable		100.00
	Totals	100.00	100.00

Form of Receipts

Any organization can receive funds in various forms:

- Currency
- Checks
- Lockbox receipt advice
- Wire transfers
- Credit card receipts

EXHIBIT
5.6 **Posting to Record the Transfer of Funds**

➤ Entry created by the Cash Receipts software

Entry Date	04/30/20x4	To record the transfer of funds	

Account	Description	Debit	Credit
1010	Cash in bank - Operating	10000.00	
1070	Cash - Savings Account		10000.00
	Totals	10000.00	10000.00

Each form of receipt has its own variation in the handling and recording process, but for every receipt the following information must be recorded:

- Date of receipt
- Source
- Amount
- Payment reference
- Payment form

The *source* of the receipt is the person or organization that remitted the funds. Enough information is recorded to completely identify the source and to document the transaction so that it is completely traceable. In the case of an accounts receivable item, the source includes the client (customer) number and name.

The *payment reference* describes what is being paid. In the case of an accounts receivable item, the payment reference is the invoice number. In the case of a grant, the reference is the program contract information. For each non-A/R receipt, the reference includes a brief description of the reason for the payment and the account code where the credit will be posted.

The *payment form* specifies if the payment was currency, check (including check number), lockbox advice (reference number), wire (reference number), or credit card (credit card merchant account reference).

Currency

In situations where currency is collected on a regular basis, such as at a gift shop or the front desk of an organization that offers counseling services, it is advisable to use a cash register that produces two copies of a receipt. In other situations, pre-numbered receipts should be used. A copy of the receipt is always given to the client (customer), and a copy of the receipt becomes a permanent part of the accounting system's records. Be sure to maintain physical control over the cash register drawer and over the stock of pre-numbered receipts.

Checks

Checks should be photocopied or scanned after being stamped on the back with a restrictive endorsement (such as "For Deposit Only, Universal Nonprofit, account #12–3456"). If a remittance advice is included with the check, it should be filed with the daily deposit register as part of the complete documentation of the transaction.

Lockbox Arrangement

A lockbox arrangement is a valuable way to safeguard an asset, speed up the availability of the collected funds, and document the receipts. Rather than mailing payment to your organization, your client (customer) mails the check and remittance advice to a post office box number. The bank collects the mail, photocopies the checks, deposits the checks into your organization's bank account, and then sends you a summary of the day's receipts. The transaction summary is mailed, faxed, or emailed to your organization once per day. Funds are generally available more quickly since the bank deposits checks directly upon receipt, and the separation of duties is built into the arrangement. Bank fees for implementing a lockbox arrangement vary and might be too costly for some nonprofits. In addition, there are certain volume minimums below which it does not make sense to set up such a relationship.

Wire Transfers

Funding sources, third-party payers, and other payers often use electronic funds transfers (EFT) to make payments. The payer initiates the transaction, and your bank notifies you by credit memo when the funds have been received into your bank account. The funds are immediately available, and safeguarding the asset is not an issue; this type of payment is highly desirable. The credit memo document serves as the remittance advice.

Credit Card Receipts

Many nonprofit organizations accept payments by credit card for dues, membership fees, sales of merchandise, contributions, fees for services, and so on. By establishing a *merchant account*, your organization benefits from these advantages:

- Quicker payments (funds are typically transferred to your account within forty-eight hours)
- Simplified cash receipt processing
- Increased transactions (ease of payment usually increases the percentage of potential customers and donors who actually make the purchase and contribution)
- The ability to sell products and accept contributions over the telephone or via the internet

Fees for payments processed in a merchant account vary; normally there is a minimum fee for very small transactions and a 2 or 3 percent charge on larger transactions. The transaction amount minus the merchant account fee is transferred to your bank. A typical contribution transaction where the donor paid with a credit card is shown in Exhibit 5.7).

Merchant accounts have various rules and procedures about accepting credit cards when you (as the merchant) do not physically swipe the card. One safeguard that is now commonly used is to require the CVV2 or CVC2 security code, printed on the signature strip on the back of the credit card but not anywhere else. This security code requires the person using the card to have it in their possession or to have memorized the security code.

Controlling the Cash Receipt Process

No matter what the source of funds is or what part of the organization generates the revenue, there are some basic internal control principles that always apply. Depending on the size of your organization, some modifications might be necessary, but the theory behind the principles remains the same.

Opening the Mail

Someone other than the person responsible for recording and depositing the funds should open the mail. Any currency is counted and noted on a separate register, which will later be compared to the transactions posted by accounting. Checks are immedi-

| EXHIBIT 5.7 | Posting to Record the Receipt of an Unbilled Contribution by Credit Card |

→ Entry created by the Cash Receipts software

| Entry Date | 05/31/20x4 | To record receipt of an unbilled contribution by C.C. |

Account	Description	Debit	Credit
1010	Cash in bank - Operating	49.00	
8595	Merchant Account Expense	1.00	
4010	Individual/small business contri		50.00
	Totals	50.00	50.00

ately stamped on the back with a restrictive endorsement (for deposit only) with the organization's name and bank account number. Some organizations will not accept currency; payment can be made by check, money order, or credit card.

Checks should be photocopied or scanned to produce a permanent record of the payment received. This provides the organization with information not necessarily recorded in the typical accounting system.

Setting Up the Cashier

In locations where cash is regularly collected, each transaction is immediately recorded by a cash register receipt or by a pre-numbered receipt. A copy of the receipt is given to the client (customer). The cash drawer is counted at the beginning and at the end of the shift, and the remaining cash total is proved to the transaction summary for the shift. Your organization may also need to set up a cashier when you have a special fundraising event, such as a casino night. Some organizations have found it helpful to use a laptop computer at special events to track financial activity.

Accounting for Cash As It Is Received

In all cases the transaction is immediately recorded in some preliminary document. This hand-written document serves two purposes: (1) it is the primary document showing that currency or check was received and by whom, and (2) it documents and assists in the cash receipt recording process when a copy is given to accounting. The application of the payment to an open A/R item or to some other general ledger account can be completed at the appropriate later time.

Separating Cash Handling Duties

The collection, depositing, posting, and reconciling of cash receipts should each be the responsibility of different people, if possible (depending on the size of the organization). Many good internal control ideas can be implemented regardless of the size of the organization. Some ideas will require the assistance of volunteers and/or other staff to "help" the accounting staff bolster internal controls.

Safeguarding the Asset

Until deposited in a bank account, the funds should be held in a protected environment, such as a safe. Funds should not be held on the premises in any amount or for any length of time that is greater than necessary.

Promptly Depositing the Funds

At least once per day, all funds should be deposited in the organization's bank account. Only employees with proper authorization should deposit funds. The deposit slip is stamped by the bank and returned to the organization to be used as a part of the reconciliation process. The stamped deposit slip is also a basic control against deposits being lost or stolen. If the organization receives a substantial amount of currency on a regular basis, a professionally installed safe is essential to safeguard the funds between bank deposits.

Daily Reconciliation

Once each day, the cash receipt process should be reconciled. The registers, photocopies of checks, bank deposit slips, and accounting system postings are examined by someone not involved in the process to assure the completeness and accuracy of the transaction recording and to assure that all funds received have, in fact, been recorded and deposited.

Monthly Bank Reconciliation

An employee who is not involved in either the cash receipt or cash disbursement processes should complete a monthly reconciliation of each bank account. In smaller organizations, a board member or consultant can be assigned to perform the bank reconciliation. The reconciliation procedure should include a visual examination of the payee, amount, authorized signature, and endorsement on cancelled checks; an analysis of outstanding items (deposits in transit and outstanding checks); and an investigation of any discrepancy.

Monitoring the Process

Management should periodically spot-check the process and, at random times, select the recording and depositing of funds on a single day for a complete review. The unopened bank statement should be delivered to the executive director of the organization for an initial perusal of the checks and signatures. Then the bank statement should

---

CHECKLIST 5.1   **Internal Control Checklist for Cash Receipts**

☐ Does the person who opens the mail not have access to the accounting records?

☐ Are checks immediately stamped with a restrictive endorsement ("For Deposit Only")?

☐ Are all checks photocopied or scanned?

☐ Are all receipts recorded on a schedule of cash receipts that is then used in the daily reconciliation of cash receipts?

☐ Are deposits made at least once each day?

☐ Is it a requirement to post all cash receipts to the accounting system every day?

☐ Does someone other than the people responsible for opening the mail, taking the deposit to the bank, and posting the transactions reconcile the cash receipts process every day?

☐ Does management spot-check the cash receipts process on a regular basis?

be given to the person responsible for the reconciliation for immediate analysis. The executive director or a supervisory individual should review the completed reconciliation and indicate approval in writing. Any errors identified during the reconciliation process should be discussed; methodologies to prevent such errors in the future need to be discussed and implemented. It is important to give the bookkeeper in charge of cash accounts any entries needed to correct the organization's books.

Other Issues

As a part of the cash receipt process, the bookkeeper has to occasionally deal with bank debit memos resulting from returned checks and associated bank fees. *Returned checks* are checks presented to the bank for deposit into your account that eventually prove to be non-negotiable for one of these reasons:

- *NSF (not sufficient funds)*—the check was drawn on a valid account, but the account does not have sufficient funds available to cover the check.

- *Stop payment*—the check was drawn on a valid account, but the check issuer directed its bank to not honor the check when presented for payment.

- *Account closed*—the check was drawn on an account that is no longer active.

When a bank returns an NSF check, it is the usual practice to re-deposit the check; often the issuer of the check had funds in the account to cover the check, but they were not yet available. Every jurisdiction and every bank has a policy regarding the availability of funds. A common policy is for payroll checks to be immediately available upon deposit; out-of-state checks to be held for five days before becoming available; and all other checks to be held for two days. Often the amount of the check plays a role in determining when the funds will be available; larger checks might have a longer holding period. The holding period enables the bank to have time to present the check for payment and to report back any difficulties encountered. Because of the holding period, most bank accounts have a smaller amount of cash available than the actual account balance. In certain cases, making a phone call to the issuer of the check prior to re-depositing it is helpful to ensure they are aware that the bank did not honor the check.

If an issuer puts a *stop payment* on a check, it is usually because the check was issued in error, or the issuer of the check had reason to be concerned that the payment would not go to the intended party. Personal communication resolves these issues.

Checks written on a *closed bank account* often signal a serious problem. You should attempt to contact the check's issuer immediately.

Bank charges resulting from returned checks are normally assessed to the check's issuer. Your organization's policy should specify the amount to be charged in the event of a returned check, and it should list acceptable reasons, if any, when the returned check charge will be waived. Returned check charges are billed to the customer or client and become an additional receivable.

Collections

In addition to recording cash receipt transactions, the bookkeeper must regularly analyze the A/R open items. Working from an aged A/R report, which places all open items into columns such as *current, over thirty days, over sixty days,* and so on, the bookkeeper can make phone calls and generate reminders in an attempt to encourage payment of bills that are past due. The accounting software should generate statements of each customer's account once per period, and additional reminders can be sent as appropriate.

The collection process involves accurate note taking and persistence. If a client or customer makes a promise to pay, this promise should be noted both in the book-keeper's records and with a brief e-mail or other communication sent to the customer. A reminder system will facilitate your ability to follow up on any promises when it is necessary. A pleasant manner should always prevail in any conversation, but accurate facts and a persistent demeanor will often result in payment of the item.

Special Considerations for Nonprofits

Privacy concerns make collection procedures in nonprofit organizations more complicated. Privacy statutes or internally defined principles might govern certain services offered by your organization. Your organization's billing and collection policies need to be reviewed and understood by the board of directors and by all staff members before the bookkeeper can take collection action. A balance must be struck between the privacy rights of the clients of the organization and the economic reality the organization faces if receivables remain uncollected. This is a very sensitive and important issue that needs to be carefully reviewed and documented within your organization with clear policies and effective training.

Care must be taken in the decision to employ a collection agency to pursue bad debts; there are some professional and competent collection agencies that understand the nonprofit environment. Collection agencies are seldom used by smaller nonprofit organizations. Management should consult with other nonprofit organizations for recommendations in this area.

Write-Offs

After every attempt has been made to collect an open item, it is necessary to write off the receivable as a bad debt. One of our goals is to have the asset balances in our accounting system represent real-world amounts; when a bill is clearly never going to be collected, it has no place in our books as a receivable. The transaction to be recorded is similar to the transaction used to record the receipt of payment: instead of being posted to cash, the debit goes to an account for bad debts. Bad debt can be accounted for as an expense (bad debts) or as a reduction of assets in an account called *allowance for bad debts.* The organization's auditor will determine the best method for handling these transactions. The direct bad-debt write-off method is very simple, and it is the method of choice for many small nonprofits. A transaction recording a bad debt using the direct write-off method is shown in Exhibit 5.8.

EXHIBIT 5.8 **Posting to Write-Off a Bad Debt**

Entry created by the Cash Receipts software

Entry Date 08/31/20x4   To record write-off of a bad debt

Account	Description	Debit	Credit
1010	Cash in bank - Operating	0.00	
8610	Bad Debt Expense	75.50	
1110	Accounts Receivable		75.50

This is an example of offsetting entries on a form.
No cash received, but a multi-line posting results.

| | Totals | 75.50 | 75.50 |

The entry in Exhibit 5.8 is made using the cash receipt software, since the subsidiary records that contain the A/R open item details must be adjusted. A general journal entry is able to correctly record the bad debt expense, but it is the wrong choice for recording this transaction, since it cannot change the A/R subsidiary details. Always use the appropriate software module when you are posting to one of the control accounts (A/R or A/P).

Approvals for writing off a bad debt should be documented in your organization's accounting manual. Normally, the size of the write-off will determine the level of approval necessary. For example, the board of directors might be required to approve the write-off of a very large receivable, while the office manager might be able to approve the write-off of a small bill. This is an important issue, because one popular way to commit fraud is to steal the actual money collected, and then write off the A/R item being paid as a bad debt. Careful analysis of bad debt expense is an important part of managing the cash receipt process.

When we need to correct an error: cash receipt documents should only be voided with appropriate approvals; all voided documents should be retained as a part of the accounting records. The correction of an error should be noted and approved on a separate document.

Summary

The cash receipt function is closely connected to the revenue and support function, and both play a vital role in the financial health of the organization. A clear set of controls and procedures helps to safeguard the funds and make the process efficient.

S alaries, wages, and fringe benefits might be close to 80 percent of a nonprofit organization's budget; accounting for them properly is an important task. Payroll is the most highly regulated area of accounting. Many governmental departments at the federal, state, and local level promulgate rules and regulations affecting the employment process. Compliance with every rule, regulation, and reporting requirement can be a very complicated task.

The process of calculating an employee's gross pay, calculating the correct deductions, and producing a paycheck is fairly straightforward. The complications arise when payroll tax rates change, when electronic filing is required, when filing requirements are modified, and when fringe benefit plans are implemented. The decision to keep payroll functions in-house versus using a payroll service company is often made easier by a thorough appreciation of the entire payroll process. Many payroll and human resource (HR) tasks remain the responsibility of the accounting department whether or not a payroll service is used; any tasks that can be better accomplished by a specialist should be delegated. A payroll service company helps to ease the compliance burden.

Confidentiality

All accounting records are confidential. Accounting information belongs to the organization and is disseminated to stakeholders through the publication of financial statements.

Payroll information is confidential for two reasons: (1) payroll records are accounting records; (2) the employee has a right to privacy regarding his or her payroll information. This right to privacy covers not only salary or wage information; it also covers marital status, health history, family information, and a wide range of information collected by the employer.

The annual IRS Form 990, which is available to the public, discloses the salaries of highly compensated personnel. Many nonprofit organizations also produce and disclose detailed program budgets, which contain the salary information of some or all staff members. Employees of nonprofit organizations might have more access to payroll information than do the employees of a for-profit organization. The accounting manual must identify how the organization will balance the need for confidentiality with the competing need for disclosure.

The standard operating procedure for the payroll process should include safeguards to ensure the payroll information is treated in a confidential manner.

Payroll Bank Account

When it is feasible, the organization should set up a separate checking account to be used only for payroll checks. The separation of payroll from other cash transactions often makes sense for a few reasons:

- Payroll checks often have different signature requirements than general cash disbursements checks have.

- The confidential nature of payroll checks necessitates that only authorized staff can examine the cancelled checks, as is often done as a part of the bank reconciliation process.

- Bank fee structures are often different for payroll checking accounts. Adding a high volume of payroll checks to the regular checking account might result in higher bank fees.

Payroll checks should be pre-numbered. Unused payroll checks must be kept in a secure location.

The payroll checking account is normally set up with an opening balance; it is then maintained as an imprest account. *Imprest* accounts have a fixed balance; the transactions for each period equal each other, leaving the balance unchanged. For example, to set up the payroll checking account, we transfer $1,000 from the regular checking account (Exhibit 6.1).

Normally, the payroll checking account book balance does not change. Every check written on the account is matched by an amount transferred from the regular checking account. In order to illustrate this procedure, we will first show the transfer as a separate transaction producing two entries: transfer and disbursement. Once the mechanics of these transactions are understood, we will combine them into a single transaction. This single transaction is the usual method of recording the reimbursement of an imprest account—the reason for the reimbursement is recorded, but the account receiving the reimbursement is never mentioned.

As each payroll is processed, we transfer the total amount of the payroll checks written from the regular checking account to the payroll checking account (Exhibit 6.2).

The payroll summary entry in Exhibit 6.3 (simplified for the purposes of this illustration) completes our posting of the transaction.

EXHIBIT 6.1   Posting to Establish a Payroll Checking Account

Entry created by the Cash Disbursements software

Entry Date 01/31/20x4   To establish a payroll checking account

Account	Description	Debit	Credit
1020	Cash - Payroll Account	1000.00	
1010	Cash in bank - Operating		1000.00
	Totals	1000.00	1000.00

EXHIBIT 6.2   Posting to Transfer Net Pay to Payroll Account

Entry created by the Cash Disbursements software

Entry Date 03/31/20x4   To transfer net pay

Account	Description	Debit	Credit
1020	Cash - Payroll Account	5150.00	
1010	Cash in bank - Operating		5150.00
	Totals	5150.00	5150.00

As you can see, we have debited the payroll checking account when we recorded the transfer and credited the payroll checking account as a part of the weekly payroll summary posting. These amounts will always offset each other exactly; the net effect of the two postings on the payroll checking account is zero.

In practice, we combine the two postings into a single posting. When we record the transfer, we record all of the details from the payroll summary. The payroll checking account debit and credit entries are unnecessary, since they will always offset one another (Exhibit 6.4).

EXHIBIT 6.3   Journal Entry to Record the Weekly Payroll (Simplified)

General Journal Entry

Journal Entry Date [03/31/20x4]   [To record the weekly payroll (simplified)]

Account	Description	Debit	Credit
7220	Wage Expense	7000.00	
2130	Taxes Withheld		1100.00
2137	Other Deductions Payable		750.00
1020	Cash - Payroll Account		5150.00
	Totals	7000.00	7000.00

EXHIBIT 6.4   Posting to Record the Weekly Payroll (Simplified)

→ Entry created by the Cash Disbursements software

Entry Date [03/31/20x4]   [To record the weekly payroll (simplified)]

Account	Description	Debit	Credit
7220	Wage Expense	7000.00	
2130	Taxes Withheld		1100.00
2137	Other Deductions Payable		750.00
1020	Cash - Payroll (not posted)		5150.00
1020	Cash - Payroll (not posted)	5150.00	
1010	Cash in bank - Operating		5150.00
	Totals	12150.00	12150.00

Some organizations also use the payroll cash account for the disbursement of payroll taxes; this is very common when a payroll service company handles the filing of payroll tax forms and remits the taxes due directly to the taxing authority on behalf of the organization. A sample entry to record the transfer of funds to cover payroll tax disbursements from the payroll cash account is shown in Exhibit 6.5.

Similar to the entry recording the weekly payroll, this entry does not affect the imprest balance of the payroll cash account.

Direct Deposit

One of the options available to your employees when your organization uses a payroll service is to have the net pay from each paycheck electronically transferred to the employee's personal bank account. This method, called *Direct Deposit*, has many benefits:

- The employee is saved from making a trip to the bank
- Lost paychecks are no longer a problem.
- The bank reconciliation for the payroll checking account is simplified.

When funds are electronically deposited, the employee receives a non-negotiable facsimile of the paycheck with the usual pay stub information.

Human Resources

Human Resources is the name given to the task of managing the employment, fringe benefit, and employee relationship functions in an organization; it was formerly

EXHIBIT 6.5   Posting to Record the Payroll Tax Payment

Entry created by the Cash Disbursements software

Entry Date 03/31/20x4   To record the payroll tax payment

Account	Description	Debit	Credit
2130	Taxes Withheld	1100.00	
1010	Cash in bank - Operating		1100.00
	Totals	1100.00	1100.00

called the *Personnel Department.* In smaller organizations without an HR department, these vital functions are still carried out by department managers and the finance department.

Employment Process

When a position opens up in the organization, management will seek to fill the position from a variety of sources:

- Referrals from current employees
- Applications from current employees looking to advance their careers
- Newspaper classified advertisements
- Open jobs listing on the organization's web site
- Internet job hunting websites
- Employment agencies

The job posting or classified advertising should seek to qualify any potential applicant; the requirements of the position should be clearly explained.

Applicants will usually fill out a job application that details personal information, work experience, and references. The organization should get detailed legal advice regarding the development and use of a job application form; issues of privacy and discrimination have shaped the types of information that can be acquired, as well as the manner in which the information is solicited. All information on the job application is confidential, whether or not the applicant is eventually hired.

New Hires

After an offer of employment has been extended and accepted, the new employee will:

- Complete documents required by the employer and required by law
- Participate in the creation of the employee ID, if applicable
- Receive the employee manual
- Participate in a new hire orientation program

At some organizations, these steps are done informally, but the information received from the employee and by the employee remains basically the same. Using a standard operating procedure when hiring a new employee and providing some type of orientation to new hires is recommended.

I-9

One of the documents required by law comes from the Immigration and Naturalization Service (INS), a part of the U.S. Department of Justice. The *Employment Eligibility Verification* Form I-9 is filled out by the employee and employer and kept on file by the employer as a part of the employee's personnel file. Form I-9 is the record that verifies the following:

- The employee has adequate documents that establish both identity and employment eligibility.
- The employer has examined the documents supplied by the employee.

The employer is allowed to photocopy any documents supplied with the I-9; the photocopies should be filed in the employee's personnel folder. Under current law, the employer must keep a copy of the I-9 for three years after the date of hire or one year after employment ends, whichever is later. It is a good idea to make the completed I-9 and any supporting documents a permanent part of the employee's personnel folder.

W-4

At the start of employment, the employee fills out the *Employee's Withholding Allowance Certificate* Federal Form W-4 (and the corresponding state form). This form, from the IRS, includes a worksheet the employee can use to calculate the number of withholding allowances and marital status to claim for withholding purposes. The employee should be encouraged to review this information once each year and submit a new W-4, since withholding tax amounts are only estimates of taxes owed. A current calculation using the W-4 worksheet will help the employee accurately estimate the amount of tax to be withheld.

The W-4 information is used in the calculation of the employee's withholding taxes. Changes submitted by the employee are recorded in the payroll data, and the completed W-4 is then filed in the employee's personnel folder. In certain circumstances, a copy of the W-4 is required to be sent to the IRS. IRS publishes a new version of Circular E (Employer's Tax Guide) every year; the bookkeeper should use this publication as a valuable reference on payroll requirements.

Earned Income Credit

The *Earned Income Credit* (EIC) is a refundable tax credit for certain workers. The organization is required to inform any employee from whom no income tax was withheld of the EIC. Employees can claim the EIC on their tax returns, but certain employees are eligible to receive a portion of the EIC with their pay throughout the year. To begin receiving the Advance EIC payments, the employee must complete form W-5 and submit it to the organization. The Earned Income Credit is designed to help lower-income wage earners; the advance EIC payments provide eligible workers with additional cash flow to help meet living expenses.

Employee File

Each employee should have a permanent folder containing documents from the hiring process and from the period of employment, including (but not limited to) the following:

- Employment application
- Correspondence from the hiring process
- Employment contract (if applicable)
- Employment covenants (if applicable)
- Employment forms (W-4, I-9)
- Periodic performance reviews
- Pay rate history
- Fringe benefit documents
- Voluntary deduction documentation
- History of paid time off (vacations, personal days, leave)
- Paid time off hours available
- Documents about any employment-related illness or injury
- Documents about union-related benefits

A common practice is to maintain a master folder containing permanent documents that span the years of employment, plus a series of yearly folders containing documents specific to a single year. Maintaining accurate and exhaustive employment records on every employee will help you to comply with the many regulations and requirements of the employment process.

Employee ID

Employee identification badges or cards are common at larger organizations. Security concerns associated with terrorism have sharply increased their use and importance. Advances in technology have brought the ability to create Employee IDs to organizations of any size. ID cards or badges can be used to control access to facilities, to provide information when dealing with individuals outside of the organization, and for other purposes. A disadvantage of issuing IDs is that the organization must retrieve the card or badge from individuals upon the termination of their employment. If your organization decides to issue Employee ID badges or cards, be sure to add a "valid through" date to mitigate the consequences of lost or stolen IDs.

Employee Manual

A detailed description of employee benefits and responsibilities should be published and distributed to all employees. Topics covered should include the following:

- Timesheet recording
- Appropriate attire
- Rules concerning discipline and conflict resolution
- Performance review procedures

- Paid time-off calculations: vacation, holiday, sick, personal, bereavement, voting time, and so on

- Health insurance and other benefits

- Special licensing requirements (for health care workers, teachers, school bus drivers, and so on)

Using technology to publish and maintain the benefits manual can dramatically reduce costs. The manual can be made available over the local area network (LAN) as a series of web pages. (For more information on this concept, see Resource C plus many resources on the topic of running an intranet that are available online.) Please consult with your legal counsel on this topic since some state laws might consider the manual to be a part of an employment agreement, which can lead to various legal issues. Properly written, an employee manual is a valuable tool.

The Payroll Process

The actual payroll process begins with the accumulation of time cards or timesheets by the department managers. The entries made by the employees are reviewed by the manager, checking for accuracy and comparing time reported with any employee schedule that might have been prepared. The manager calculates the time to be paid and marks the entry with her or his approval. The information is forwarded to the accounting department.

In accounting, the time cards or timesheets are once again reviewed; the calculation of hours is checked for accuracy; and any discrepancies are resolved by contacting the appropriate manager. Overtime worked by the employee must be separately approved by management; the calculation of the overtime pay rate is determined by the organization's policy, formulated in conjunction with the current wage and hour laws of the federal and state departments of labor.

Any pay rate changes scheduled to go into effect are made to the employee's existing rate. This action is also noted by a permanent entry in the employee's personnel folder.

Pay requested for vacation, holiday, sick, personal, or bereavement time is analyzed to determine if the paid time off was approved and if the employee has unused time available for that category. In some payroll systems, the employees earn a specific number of paid time off hours per pay period; in other systems, the hours are awarded at the beginning of the year or on the employee's anniversary date. In any case, payment for hours not worked should be documented by category, providing the details necessary to determine any hours still available to the employee.

Certain employees are paid on an hourly basis, while other employees are paid a salary. In some instances, an hourly employee might have a minimum gross pay (otherwise known as a *Guarantee*). The payroll system normally makes these calculations, but a review of the gross pay calculation should be a part of the payroll process. The U.S. Department of Labor (www.dol.gov) issues and implements regulations governing the applicability of overtime payment rules; check the website for the tests to use in determining if an employee is exempt from overtime protection. State and local overtime rules vary from federal rules; organizations must follow the rules providing the greatest benefit for the employee.

As a by-product of entering and computing the gross pay for an employee, it is desirable to allocate the gross pay, taxes, and fringe benefits to the appropriate departments and programs. This allocation is done in a variety of ways depending on the rules your funding sources have attached to the income stream. If no government funds are utilized by your organization, you can normally use the actual timesheet entries or a computation based on an agreed-upon percentage for the employee. If you receive any government money, you need to read and understand Circular A-122 promulgated by the U.S. OMB or, in other circumstances, the rules issued by your state's OMB. While it is possible to process the payroll and then allocate the gross pay after the fact, making the allocation as a part of the payroll process is very efficient and hopefully more accurate. Most accounting software allows the gross pay of an individual to be distributed to a number of cost centers and expense codes. Payroll service bureaus also offer the ability to record and track these gross pay distributions for a small additional fee.

Payroll checks are printed, as are payroll journals and summary reports, and these documents are compared to the underlying time cards or timesheets. Control totals, such as *total overtime hours* and *total sick pay hours,* are helpful when attempting to "prove out" the payroll prior to the distribution of paychecks. The payroll checks are then signed; if the organization uses a payroll service, it is likely the paychecks are machine-signed and sealed in envelopes. With direct deposit, no signature is needed, as there is no physical paycheck.

Internal Control Issues in Payroll Where Direct Deposit Is Used

It is important when using direct deposit in a payroll system that your payroll procedures are strictly adhered to. Since management does not sign the payroll checks, the payroll details must be reviewed carefully to prevent incorrect payments or payments made to former or non-existent employees. The payroll journal, which lists the details of every paycheck, should be reviewed and approved by management in writing to ensure that all payroll disbursements are accurate and are being made to current employees. Payroll service companies are able to provide a report that identifies people coming on or off the payroll and those individuals receiving salary or hourly increases. This *exception report* allows management to quickly spot any changes in the payroll roster or pay scales.

Manually Written Checks

On occasion, you will need to calculate and write a paycheck during the period between paydays. There are several reasons for creating manually written paychecks:

- Error correction

- Additional check for vacation pay

- Final paycheck when employment is terminated

Manual checks should be subjected to the same calculations, verifications, and approvals as computer-generated paychecks. When creating the manual paycheck, all of the information is recorded in the usual manner; however, the timing of the posting to the general ledger is different. Unless the manual check is written in one calendar quarter, and the next regular payroll cycle falls into a subsequent quarter, the usual practice is to include the manual check in the next regular payroll's totals. If the check date comes at the end of a quarter, separate payroll totals for the manual check are computed and posted in the current quarter. The end of each payroll quarter is significant due to payroll tax reporting to the IRS and state taxation departments; paychecks should be reported in the quarter in which they are written.

When the calendar quarter is not an issue, it is acceptable to post any manually written paychecks with the next scheduled payroll totals. One caveat: since the payroll checking account is not reimbursed for checks written until the regular payroll totals are posted, you have to make sure the manually written paychecks do not exceed the imprest balance of the account. In the previous example, we funded the payroll checking account by transferring $1,000 from the regular checking account. The amount with which you fund the payroll checking account should be based on two things:

1. The bank's fee structure and minimum balance rules

2. The typical amount of manual check totals written between pay periods

Expense Reimbursement

Payroll checks are frequently a convenient way of providing employees with expense reimbursement. Keep in mind that these items are subject to the same authorization and approval requirements as if they were disbursed on an accounts payable check or through the petty cash fund. Expenses are paid to the employee after taxes; that is, any expense amount added to a paycheck is not included in gross pay, but rather is added to net pay after all taxes and other deductions are subtracted. The miscellaneous addition to the net paycheck is posted in the same way it would have been posted if disbursed in some other way, as shown in the simplified example in Exhibit 6.6.

In this example, the employee's net paycheck equals the gross pay amount ($500) minus the payroll tax amounts ($125) plus the travel expense reimbursement ($25), for a total of $400.

Statutory Deductions

Gross pay is the amount of money the organization pays an employee for work performed; this gross pay amount is the wage or salary expense recorded in the accounting system. The employee's *take home pay* (or *net pay*) equals the gross pay minus all payroll deductions. Some deductions are *elective*; that is, the employee agrees to have an amount taken from each paycheck for a particular purpose. Some deductions are *statutory*; that is, they are required by law.

| EXHIBIT 6.6 | Posting to Record the Payroll with Travel Reimbursement (Simplified) |

➤ Entry created by the Cash Disbursements software

Entry Date [03/31/20x4]   [Record payroll with travel reimbursement (simplified)]

Account	Description	Debit	Credit
7220	Wage Expense	500.00	
2130	Taxes Withheld		125.00
8310	Travel	25.00	
1010	Cash in bank - Operating		400.00
	Totals	525.00	525.00

Withholding Taxes

One category of statutory deductions is *withholding tax.* This amount is based on the wages in the pay period and exemptions claimed. It is an estimated tax payment, not a calculation of the final tax amount. The actual amount of income tax due at the local, state, and federal level is usually calculated from total income at the end of each calendar year on an individual tax return. The withholding tax is simply an estimate of the tax due on the wages paid. Withholding taxes are collected by the employer and remitted to the government on behalf of the employee. The employee is responsible for correctly computing the number of exemptions claimed; at the federal level, the IRS provides the W-4 Worksheet to help in this effort.

During the payroll process, withholding tax amounts are subtracted from the employee's pay and become a liability of the organization. Depositary rules vary, based on factors such as the amount of the deposit and the taxing authority. Taxes withheld from gross pay are considered *trust funds;* failure to make timely deposits will result in penalties and interest assessments and, in extreme cases, serious criminal charges. The rules have no flexibility to allow for human error. Board members, executive staff, and bookkeepers have been held liable for failure to make a timely deposit of trust funds; make sure all payroll taxes are paid in accordance with the depositary rules. A payroll service can be engaged to remit payroll taxes and prepare the required payroll tax returns.

Payroll Taxes

Another category of statutory deductions is the *payroll tax.* These taxes are computed based on gross pay and represent the exact amount due. Examples include FICA (Federal Insurance Contributions Act—commonly known as Social Security), Medicare,

State Unemployment, and State Disability. In many cases, these taxes are based on a maximum annual gross pay; once the employee reaches the maximum taxable wage, the deduction is stopped. Normally, tax-exempt organizations under Section 501(c)(3) of the law are exempt from federal unemployment taxes (FUTA). Check the determination letter received from the IRS to verify the organization's status, and then notify the payroll service company or payroll department of the exemption.

Payroll taxes deducted become a liability of the organization. The amount of payroll taxes deducted from the employee is often matched by the employer's share of the tax. The combined tax (employee and employer share) is recorded as a liability and remitted to the taxing authority in the same manner as the withholding taxes.

Elective Deductions

In addition to the statutory deductions, there can be a wide variety of elective deductions from an employee's gross pay:

- Deferred pay, such as 403(b) plans
- Cafeteria plans (in which employees select benefits from a menu of choices)
- Health insurance premiums
- After-tax savings plans

As with any deduction from the employee's pay, the amounts are potential liabilities of the organization. In some cases, the money is due to the organization—for example, the health insurance premium deduction is a reimbursement to the organization for a health insurance premium paid.

Certain elective deductions have an effect on the statutory deductions. For example, a deferred pay elective deduction, if structured properly to comply with the applicable laws, might be subject to certain payroll taxes but not subject to withholding taxes. The laws in this area change frequently; your tax advisor and your payroll service company can provide you with the current law.

Payroll deductions also might include court-ordered child support or other various wage garnishments. Care must be taken to withhold the proper amount, to remit the amount withheld promptly to the authority that issued the order, and to stop the withholding once the total garnishment has been satisfied.

Recording the Payroll Transaction

Exhibit 6.7 illustrates a sample transaction, taken from a summary of the weekly payroll for an organization.

In the example in Exhibit 6.7, the organization transfers the net pay amount from the regular checking account to the payroll checking account. The transfer is recorded without reference to the payroll checking account, which is treated as an imprest fund. Total gross pay of $5,000 was debited to various department payroll expense accounts,

EXHIBIT 6.7   Posting to Record the Payroll (Detailed)

Entry created by the Cash Disbursements software

Entry Date   05/31/20x4   To record payroll

Account	Description	Debit	Credit
7220-A	Wage Expense - Dept A	2,500.00	
7220-B	Wage Expense - Dept B	1,000.00	
7220-C	Wage Expense - Dept C	1,500.00	
2131	Federal Withholding Payable		1,400.00
2132	FICA Payable		310.00
2133	Medicare Payable		72.50
2134	State Withholding Payable		150.00
2135	State Disability Payable		25.00
7241-A	Health Insurance Expense - Dept A		325.00
7251-A	FICA Expense - Dept A	155.00	
7251-B	FICA Expense - Dept B	62.00	
7251-C	FICA Expense - Dept C	93.00	
7252-A	Medicare Expense - Dept A	36.25	
7252-B	Medicare Expense - Dept B	14.50	
7252-C	Medicare Expense - Dept C	21.75	
7253-A	State Disability Expense - Dept A	56.25	
7253-B	State Disability Expense - Dept B	22.50	
7253-C	State Disability Expense - Dept C	33.75	
2132	FICA Payable		310.00
2133	Medicare Payable		72.50
2135	State Disability Payable		112.50
1010	Cash - Operating Account		2,717.50
	Totals	5,495.00	5,495.00

and the statutory deductions are credited to liability accounts. These taxes will be paid at a later time by the A/P system or by the payroll service (if requested by the organization). The health insurance deduction is a reimbursement to the organization for that portion of the premium paid by the employee.

The second half of the transaction records the employer's share of the payroll taxes. Under current law, the FICA and Medicare taxes are assessed equally to the employee and employer, so the example shows a matching amount for each tax recorded as the employer's share of the liability. Other payroll taxes, such as the disability amount in the example, have various rate structures for employees and employers.

This entry reflects the true cost of the payroll to the organization. Gross wages equaled $5,000, yet the total expense posted in the transaction is $5,495. The employer's share of payroll tax expense makes up the difference.

Those nonprofit organizations having staff members in a union might have special deductions and employer costs in addition to the payroll described here. Union staff might receive special pay for specific holidays; union dues might be deducted from the employee's pay. The bookkeeper should obtain a copy of the union contract to make sure the payroll processing conforms to the union contract in all aspects.

Payroll Tax Reporting

As we mentioned earlier, the depositary rules for payroll taxes vary based on circumstances. Some of the rules for reporting wages and payroll taxes also vary, but the federal reporting process includes the forms and periods covered shown in Exhibit 6.8.

Using a payroll service greatly simplifies the compliance with reporting wage and payroll tax information to local, state, and federal agencies.

Payroll Accrual

At the end of each accounting period (typically at the end of each month), you need to make adjusting entries to match revenues with expenses. A common entry is to make a *payroll accrual,* to record any wages earned by the employees but not yet included on a paycheck. With the payroll accrual entry, you charge (debit) payroll wage expense and credit a current liability, typically called accrued payroll. As with any accrual journal entry, you are shifting a monetary transaction from the period in which it is posted into the period where it belongs.

For example, the hotline service of a Community Mental Health Center is open 24 hours per day, 7 days per week. The pay period ends on Saturday and the paychecks are dated the following Wednesday.

In this example (see Exhibit 6.9), the last paychecks posted in October are dated October 26th (the last Wednesday in the month). Those paychecks represented wages earned by employees up through October 22nd (the preceding Saturday). Wages earned from October 23rd through October 31st will be paid on paychecks dated after October. The pay period ending October 29th is paid on November 2nd, and the wages earned on October 30th and 31st are included in the week ending November 5th, paid

EXHIBIT 6.8	Federal Payroll Tax Forms		
FORM	PERIOD COVERED	AGENCY	INFORMATION REPORTED
941	Calendar Quarter	IRS	Organization Totals
W-2	Calendar Year	Social Security Administration	Individual Totals

on November 9th. Therefore, the payroll accrual will be the total wages earned during the last nine days of October, from the 23rd to the 31st.

The entry to post the payroll accrual is shown in Exhibit 6.10.

Payroll Reversal

Whenever you make an entry accruing a transaction, you must remember to reverse your accrual in the subsequent period. In the example, the payroll accrual entry moved $2,600 of wage expense into October; the actual wages were paid in November. When the November payroll is posted, total wages will include all of the paychecks written

EXHIBIT 6.9   **Calendar Used to Calculate a Payroll Accrual**

SUNDAY	MONDAY	TUESDAY	WEDNESDAY	THURSDAY	FRIDAY	SATURDAY
October 23	24	25	26	27	28	29
30	31	November 1	2	3	4	5

EXHIBIT 6.10   **Journal Entry to Record the Payroll Accrual**

General Journal Entry

Journal Entry Date 10/31/20x4   To record the payroll accrual

Account	Description	Debit	Credit
7220-A	Wage Expense - Dept A	1500.00	
7220-B	Wage Expense - Dept B	800.00	
7220-C	Wage Expense - Dept C	300.00	
2110	Accrued Payroll		2600.00
	Totals	2600.00	2600.00

in November, including the amount already posted in October by way of the payroll accrual entry. By reversing the payroll accrual in November, the duplicate expense is eliminated. If you fail to reverse the accrual, the wages you accrued will be posted in both October and November.

The entry to reverse the payroll accrual is shown in Exhibit 6.11.

Highly Compensated Employees

Bookkeepers have busy and challenging roles in the nonprofit environment. One challenge is to be aware of IRS requirements that affect the organization. The executive staff, controller, and auditor all have a responsibility to monitor many aspects of tax compliance at the federal, state, and local level; the bookkeeper must also stay involved.

One current issue relates to salary levels within the nonprofit organization. Due to some abuses, which the IRS and Congress wanted to control more effectively, legislation containing intermediate sanctions was enacted. Before this legislation, the IRS had only one major tool to control a tax-exempt entity they thought was acting improperly. That tool was to revoke the organization's tax exemption. Revocation is tantamount to closing the organization's operations. The new rules are designed to fine and otherwise punish individuals and organizations that were violating various rules against using the entity for personal gain, labeled *excess benefit transactions.* The rules are complex and largely untested in the courts.

The rules pertaining to salaries of staff of organizations exempt under section 501(c)(3) or 501(c)(4) specify the following. Salaries up to $90,000 per employee con-

EXHIBIT 6.11	Journal Entry to Reverse the Payroll Accrual

General Journal Entry

Journal Entry Date 11/30/20x4   To reverse the payroll accrual

Account	Description	Debit	Credit
7220-A	Wage Expense - Dept A		1500.00
7220-B	Wage Expense - Dept B		800.00
7220-C	Wage Expense - Dept C		300.00
2110	Accrued Payroll	2600.00	
	Totals	2600.00	2600.00

stitute a safe harbor and require no special documentation. Salaries over $90,000 (this is the threshold as of 2004; increases have been periodically approved based on inflation) must be documented by the maintenance of adequate records. The board of directors must maintain records that board approval of such salaries took place in advance of payment, that the board used appropriate comparable data, and that proper minutes documenting their actions were maintained. The board must also prove that their approval did not relate to any conflict of interest with the person being paid. Organizations with less than $1 million in average revenue over a three-year period have easier rules to follow. The actual IRS regulations are lengthy and complicated. Recent adverse publicity regarding salaries paid by nonprofit organizations and IRS initiatives in this area make it desirable for nonprofits to closely monitor salary levels. Discuss this issue with your auditor and use the IRS web site for research and updated information.

Qualified Transportation Fringe Benefit

Employers are able to provide employees with a transportation fringe benefit that is not subject to withholding or payroll taxes. The cost of the benefits might be paid directly by the employer or reimbursed to the employee, and they are excluded from the employee's gross income (subject to dollar limitations) when they provide one or more of these benefits:

- Transit passes
- Tokens
- Fare cards
- Van-pool transportation in a commuter vehicle to and from work
- Qualified parking at or near the place of work

If the employer reimburses the employee, a procedure must be in place to ensure that the employee has incurred the expense covered by the reimbursement. Consult with your auditor, accountant, or tax attorney for specific dollar limits and the complete regulations for this fringe benefit.

Summary

Payroll is a highly regulated area of accounting, and for most organizations it is the single biggest expense and use of funds. Using a payroll service helps to ease the compliance burden. Whether your payroll is processed in house or by a service, your organization needs sound procedures and well-organized documentation to meet the goals of the accounting system.

The bookkeeper's understanding of the organization, its programs, departments, activities, and operations, is the key to effectively recording purchases. No other area of the accounting system touches the entire spectrum of the chart of accounts on a regular basis. In no other bookkeeping function is the bookkeeper's ability to analyze the transaction more important to the goal of accurately and completely recording a financial entry.

Purchases *(vendor invoices)* are recorded in the accounts payable system; they become the open items that are the liability called *accounts payable.* The *cash disbursements* function, discussed in the next chapter, completes the process by selecting the open items and creating checks to pay those items. Not every non-payroll cash disbursement begins with the recording of a purchase, but most significant expenditures follow the procedures discussed in this chapter.

Funding sources have rules about the timing of payments of expenses to be reimbursed. For example, if a payment is not made within the period mandated by the grant guidelines (frequently within ninety days of the grant's ending date), that amount may be disallowed as an expense of that grant. Expenses incurred before the grant period but paid during the grant period are normally not allowable. Failure to comply with funding source rules could lead to a loss of reimbursement. A purchase order system helps the organization comply with these rules. The management of the organization should require that the documentation for all purchases and miscellaneous disbursements, whether or not subject to the creation of a formal purchase order, is forwarded to the accounting department on a regular basis (but always by the end of the month).

Vendors

The entry and maintenance of a vendor record is the starting point for all A/P software modules. In addition to the usual name and address information, the following data is frequently maintained for each vendor:

- Payment remittance address
- Credit terms
- Default expense code

The default expense code is the account in the chart of accounts that is most often used in the posting of invoices from the vendor. Having a G/L account associated with a vendor can speed up the invoice posting process, but it places the responsibility on the bookkeeper to verify that the default expense code is the appropriate account for a particular invoice.

For example, Central Power and Light's vendor record has *utility expense* as its default expense code. For most CP&L invoices, the default expense code is the appropriate account to debit. If a CP&L invoice comes in for the replacement of the main electric panel of the building, the bookkeeper should override the default expense code and post the invoice to a more appropriate G/L account (either a repair expense account or a building improvement fixed asset account, depending on the reason for the purchase and on the amount of the invoice).

Accounting software is designed to facilitate entries; care must be exercised to ensure that the accuracy of each posting is not compromised by software features that accept entries without requiring the bookkeeper to think.

Purchase Order System

Implementing a purchase order system is important to the financial health of the organization, and it is an extremely useful part of the effort to make sure all transactions are fully documented and traceable. A formal purchase order process places better controls on spending, provides a framework for measuring purchases against budgets, and provides the accounting department with a wealth of information about the transaction, from quantities and pricing to the cost allocations to be used. Smaller organizations without the resources to implement fully a purchase order system can still benefit from an understanding of the principles and procedures involved.

Not every purchase must be made using a formal purchase order. The organization should establish procedures that dictate when a purchase order is required and which approvals are required for different types of purchases.

The purchase order process begins with a purchase requisition, which specifies the person, department, or program requesting the purchase, the reason for the purchase, the budget authority allowing the purchase, and other pertinent details. In some circumstances where a large or unusual purchase is contemplated, a *request for proposal* (RFP) is prepared; interested vendors are encouraged to submit proposals. In other cases, competitive prices are obtained from several appropriate vendors. Often a funding source will have requirements that dictate rules to be adhered to during the purchase process. Organizations receiving governmental funds should be familiar with OMB Circular A-110, *Uniform Administrative Requirements for Grants and Agreements with Institutions of Higher Education, Hospitals, and Other Non-Profit Organizations*, which discusses a number of rules governing administration and recordkeeping.

The decision to purchase from a particular vendor is driven by many factors:

- Price

- Delivery date

- Product quality

- Product features

- Payment terms

When the particulars of a purchase have been finalized and when authorization for the purchase has been received from management, the purchase order is forwarded to the accounting department. Nonprofit organizations must make sure the proposed purchase fits under the budget (including budget flexibility guidelines where appropriate); it is the bookkeeper's responsibility (together with the program manager) to analyze the proposed expenditure and determine if there is room in the budget under the appropriate cost category. For example, in a cost reimbursement grant, the funding source might not pay for expenses that exceed the budget unless a formal budget modification form is submitted to and approved by the funding source. The management, program staff, and bookkeeper should all monitor expenses on an ongoing basis. The bookkeeper, with information from the program budget and current accounting data, should have final budget approval of the proposed purchase.

After the bookkeeper determines that money is available in the budget, a purchase order (PO) is issued to the vendor. *Purchase orders* are pre-numbered, multi-part documents that serve to document the proposed transaction and notify the vendor and interested parties within the organization of the decision to buy. In this example, the original plus five copies of the PO are distributed as follows:

- To the vendor (original)

- To accounting

- To the receiving department

- To the author of the requisition

The remaining two copies are filed within the purchase order system to be used for expediting delivery, verifying price and delivery, providing a permanent record as a part of the overall traceability and documentation of the transaction.

Unprocessed Vendor Invoice File

In the accounting department, the PO is filed in the *unprocessed vendor invoice* file. As other documents arrive, they are filed with the PO until the entire set of documents can be matched, analyzed, and posted into the accounting system. At a minimum, most purchases have the following documentation:

- Purchase order

- Receiving report

- Packing slip

- Vendor invoice

Prior to posting the vendor invoice, the bookkeeper analyzes the documents. The quantity listed on the vendor invoice should match the packing slip and receiving report and, depending on policy, the quantity should match or be within an acceptable range of the PO quantity. The price on the vendor invoice should match the price on the PO. The terms extended by the vendor should match the terms specified on the PO. The vendor invoice is checked for proper totals, including the extension of each line (quantity multiplied by price). Freight charges are verified, and the applicability of any sales tax charged by the vendor is analyzed. In many jurisdictions, nonprofit organizations are exempt from paying sales tax on their purchases. Vendors normally require their tax exempt customers to complete a *sales tax exemption form* before the purchase is made to allow the vendor to not charge sales. In most states there is a process where the nonprofit organization can submit proof that the Internal Revenue Service has approved the organization's tax-exempt status to the sales tax bureau. The result of this process is approval of the organization's exemption from paying state sales tax. This is a complex topic. The best strategy is to check with your accountant concerning the laws in your area applicable to your type of tax-exempt organization.

A similar topic of less impact but still worth noting is the federal excise tax. Certain exempt organizations meeting a specific classification as an educational organization may be exempt from certain fuel and other excise taxes. (Visit www.irs.gov for more information.)

Using the information on the requisition and on the PO, the bookkeeper prepares the chart of accounts coding of the purchase, including the program and department allocations. The combination of cost centers and account classifications should be documented on the invoice packet prior to the paperwork being submitted for approval. Management is approving not only the purchase and eventual cash disbursement; it is also approving the allocation of the expense. The staff person most knowledgeable about the budget and operations of the organization should approve the cost center and account classifications and understand how the actual dollar allocations were prepared. The approval might be made at the executive director level or delegated to a person closer to the actual program operation, such as the program director. The key is having the approval done by the people with the most information to make the allocation as accurate as possible.

Invoice Posting

The completed invoice packet is posted to the A/P system after written approval is indicated by the responsible parties. The paperwork is then filed in the *processed vendor invoice* file, where it remains until payment is issued to the vendor.

Posting a vendor invoice creates an open item in the A/P system, as illustrated by Exhibit 7.1.

EXHIBIT
7.1

Posting to Record a Vendor Invoice

➤ Entry created by the Purchase software

Entry Date	02/28/20x4	Posting a vendor invoice

Account	Description	Debit	Credit
8110-B	Office Supplies - Program B	52.75	
8110-C	Office Supplies - Program C	14.25	
8110-2	Office Supplies - Dept 2	19.95	
2010	Accounts Payable		86.95
	Totals	86.95	86.95

No Invoice Number

Some vendors do not issue invoices with invoice numbers. The proper procedure in this case is to create a unique invoice number for the invoice, write the number on the vendor invoice, and refer to this number as if it had been originally printed on the invoice. Unique invoice numbers are important to avoid the possibility of duplicating the entry (and possible double-payment) of an invoice. Most accounting software warns you if you attempt to enter the same invoice number twice for a single vendor; often this warning can be by-passed. A simple suggestion is to create a unique invoice number, where none exists, by combining the invoice date with time you are posting the invoice. Adding the posting time is a commonly used device, particularly in the data processing field, for creating a unique value. For example, a vendor invoice is dated 09/16/04, and it has no invoice number. If you are posting the invoice at 2:00 P.M., the unique invoice number is 091604–0200. This simple technique allows for the possibility that a single vendor will have more than one invoice with the same date.

Vendor Credits

Goods returned to the vendor and price adjustments are two of the many reasons a vendor will issue a credit memo to a customer. Credits should be matched to the original invoice packet and posted in the same manner as an invoice. The credit amount is a negative number, so the resulting entry takes the form shown in Exhibit 7.2.

EXHIBIT 7.2 **Posting to Record a Vendor Credit Memo**

Entry created by the Purchase software

Entry Date	03/28/20x4	Posting a vendor credit memo		
Account	Description		Debit	Credit
8110-B	Office Supplies - Program B			52.75
8110-C	Office Supplies - Program C			14.25
8110-2	Office Supplies - Dept 2			19.95
2010	Accounts Payable		86.95	
		Totals	86.95	86.95

Accounting software varies in the treatment of credits posted to a vendor account. Some software allows you to apply the credit against the original invoice, if it is still an open item. To facilitate future traceability, it is better to create a separate open item with a negative open amount. The original invoice and credit memo offset one another and can be selected for payment together during the next payment cycle.

Vendor Statements

Some vendors mail periodic statements of account to their customers. Certain vendors do not invoice their customers for every transaction; they issue statements to the customers that act as invoices. The bookkeeper must be aware of the different types of invoices and statements issued by vendors and treat each type in the proper way.

Vendors that invoice for every transaction will often send out periodic statements of account as a collection tool. If a vendor invoices for every transaction, the bookkeeper must be careful to compare the vendor's information with the A/P open items report, but then dispose of the vendor statement. Too often, the vendor statement has been mistakenly processed as an invoice. Once the comparison is completed, the vendor statement serves no useful purpose in the accounting system and should be destroyed.

Vendors that do not invoice for every transaction, such as credit card companies and utility companies, send out statements that are in effect invoices. Statements of this type are treated in the same manner as a vendor invoice. Credit card statements must be matched up with the individual receipts from the unprocessed vendor invoice file.

Other Issues

Most nonprofit organizations are too small to have separate purchasing and receiving departments. For internal control purposes, the separation of these functions from accounting and from each other is desirable. If complete separation is not feasible, the organization's procedures should implement additional management approval requirements.

The organization should have a rule prohibiting the purchase of goods for the personal use of an employee or board member. One danger is the possibility the expenditure will incorrectly be charged to a program or department expense. Another danger is the possibility the organization will never be reimbursed for the expenditure. Even when the individual properly reimburses the organization, there are other concerns. In some circumstances, major problems with sales tax authorities have occurred due to the practice of allowing employees or board members to use the tax identification number of the exempt entity to purchase items for personal use.

There should be a strict prohibition of the receipt of gifts of any amount by employees or board members from vendors or potential vendors. The possibility of a conflict of interest, or even the appearance of a conflict of interest, exists when vendors bestow gifts on individuals in a position to purchase goods or services. Employees and board members have a responsibility to the organization. Accepting a gift might imply that there is an inappropriate responsibility to the vendor.

An organization-wide coordination of the purchase of supplies helps to reduce costs in several ways. Economic order quantities can be calculated, carrying costs reduced, and favorable prices negotiated for items used by many departments and programs within the organization. Some organizations engage experts to help control costs, such as a nutritionist to help them purchase food economically.

Each month, health insurance premiums should be compared to the payroll system's list of active employees and health insurance payroll deduction amounts. Employee enrollment and coverage information from the payroll system must match the invoice prior to it being posted to accounts payable.

IRS Form 1099

The Internal Revenue Service requires the organization to issue a Form 1099 for the total of payments made throughout the calendar year to any individual, partnership, or estate for rent, services, and other various fees. Payments made to employees must be made through the payroll system. They are reported on a W-2, not on a 1099. Payments made to a corporation are generally not reportable. Payments for merchandise, telephone, and freight are not subject to 1099 reporting. Rent or service payment totals of less than $600 are not subject to 1099 reporting. Other types of payments have different dollar thresholds. The rules are available at http://www.irs.gov, as is IRS Form W-9

(Request for Taxpayer Identification Number and Certification). Nonprofit organizations may issue 1099s for the following types of payments: rent, legal fees, auditing fees, and consulting fees.

Summary

Purchasing is the area of accounting with perhaps the biggest learning curve for the bookkeeper. To properly post transactions, the bookkeeper must have the following:

- Knowledge about the programs and departments in the organization
- Knowledge about the budgets and funding sources for the various programs and departments
- Knowledge about the chart of account structure
- Knowledge about how purchasing, receiving, and cash disbursements all fit together
- Effective communications with all areas of the organization

The purchasing process creates open items in the A/P system.

Cash Disbursements

As we discussed in Chapter Seven, most of the vendor invoices and other transactions requiring the disbursement of funds are recorded in the accounting system prior to the cash disbursement process. Accurate and well-documented cash disbursements records are vital to the financial health of the organization as well. Proper procedures designed to safeguard cash and to complete the process of fully documenting expenditures are key to disbursing funds efficiently and effectively.

Smaller nonprofits might be tempted to eliminate the purchases process and record all vendor invoices at the time of payment. The end result is the same, since the transactions are eventually posted to the same general ledger accounts. Without the purchase process, however, it is not possible to meet one of the goals of the bookkeeping system: up-to-date information. By eliminating the purchase process, the nonprofit would limit access to information that is vital to the efficient operation, cash flow planning, and financial health of the organization. (Without the purchases process, only paid invoices have been recorded; your financial reports might be missing expenses you have incurred.) Unless staffing is so limited as to make a purchasing process impossible, it is better to take full advantage of the information it provides.

The Basic Entry

A cash disbursement event does one of two things. It either pays a previously recorded liability or it pays an amount for an event or activity that was not previously recorded in the books.

The purchase function (described in Chapter Seven) records transactions and simultaneously establishes a liability in the A/P account. The posting of this purchase transaction debits an appropriate account and credits A/P. A cash disbursement that pays an open A/P item is recorded by debiting A/P and crediting cash. This type of disbursement is sometimes referred to as the *check writing function*.

A cash disbursement for any item not already in accounts payable is recorded by debiting the appropriate account and crediting cash; this type of disbursement usually occurs when payment must be made on a date other than the date of the normally scheduled printing of checks.

Accounts Payable

In Resource B, two sets of files are created for unpaid vendor invoices. In the one set of files, *unprocessed vendor invoices* and related paperwork are accumulated until the information packet is completed, that is, until all documentation, from requisition to purchase order to receiving documents to vendor invoice, is available. The second set of files contains the *processed vendor invoices;* these invoices have been matched to all the documentation and have been posted to the A/P system. Unpaid processed vendor invoices make up the A/P open items.

Payment of A/P open items is a matter of selecting the items for payment and printing the checks. The selection process includes the following:

- Determining the proper payment date, based on any agreements with the vendor, the vendor's terms, the invoice's due date, and the organization's payment policies

- Examining the invoice packet for payment approvals and for the completeness of the underlying documentation

- The current cash flow situation

Decisions about taking a discount offered under a vendor's terms can only be made in conjunction with management's analysis of the organization's current cash balance and anticipated cash flow requirements. Purchase discounts are not commonly offered to nonprofit organizations. Discounts for early payment are offered by distributors of merchandise and in other for-profit industries. Nonprofit organizations that purchase large quantities of merchandise for resale might be able to take advantage of this type of payment terms.

Establish a schedule for the payment of vendor invoices and train staff members and vendors to follow this schedule. If checks are printed every Thursday, for example, vendors will often modify their billing procedures to conform to this schedule, which in turn improves their own cash flow. Staff members will prepare and submit paperwork in a timely manner if they are aware of the disbursement schedule's requirements. This will help to avoid the need for manually written checks.

Most accounting software provides a flexible method of selecting invoices for payment, based on a wide variety of criteria:

- Invoice date

- Discount date

- Due date

- Individual vendors

- Individual invoices

- Invoice amounts

Purchase discounts are available from certain vendors if the invoice is paid prior to a specific discount date. This practice is more common in the for-profit world, although a nonprofit organization might be offered payment terms that include a discount from an inventory supplier or similar type of vendor. The decision about whether to take the discount depends on the organization's cash flow situation.

Typical accounting software prints a single three-part check per page. (The actual layout and intended uses of forms vary widely among software packages; check the software's documentation for the specifics of your forms.) One section of the page contains the remittance advice to be sent to the vendor, listing all invoices paid on the check. Another section of the page contains the actual check. The third section of the page contains the remittance advice details plus the vendor name, check date, and the amount of the check; this portion is attached to the invoice packet and retained by the organization to complete the documentation for the transaction. Each invoice in the packet should be marked "paid" to avoid confusion if the invoice packet becomes separated.

All checks must be pre-numbered. The supply of unused checks must be kept in a secure location. Void checks are retained, with the word *void* written across the face and with the signature area of the check ripped off, for filing with the monthly bank reconciliation.

The organization should have a firm policy against writing checks made payable to *Cash* or *Bearer.* Signing a blank check should be prohibited. The board of directors authorizes which employees and board members can be signatories; a copy of the board approval is kept on file with the signature card at the bank. Many organizations require two signatures on all checks or on any checks over a particular dollar amount. The bank is notified of this policy by the board. When possible, the signatories should not record cash receipts or cash disbursements or have other responsibilities in accounting for cash.

The unsigned check, together with the invoice packet including all documentation, is given to the check signatory for final review and signature. The check signatory should carefully review the check and all attached documentation. The invoice packet, now topped with one-third of the check page, is returned to A/P for filing in the paid invoice file. The signed check and remittance advice are sent to another staff member for mailing to the vendor.

The transaction summary resulting from the selection and payment of A/P open items is in Exhibit 8.1.

Manually Written Checks

Manually written checks should be avoided. Despite this rule, not every disbursement begins with a requisition and purchase order, and often payment of an invoice or other disbursement must be made before the next scheduled vendor check printing. A manually written check is created to fill this need. While manually written checks are drawn on the same bank account as the computer generated checks, it is advisable to main-

EXHIBIT 8.1 Posting to Record the Printing of A/P Checks in Payment of Open Items

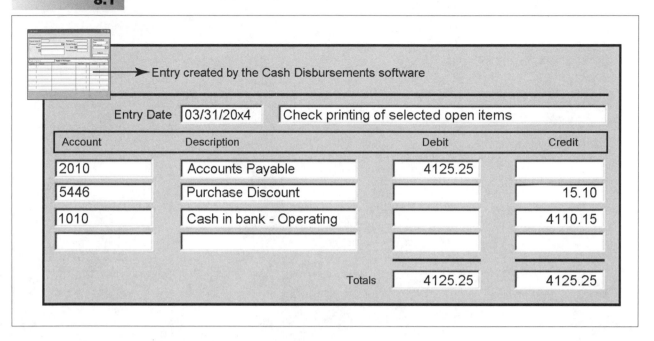

Entry created by the Cash Disbursements software

Entry Date	03/31/20x4	Check printing of selected open items		
Account	Description		Debit	Credit
2010	Accounts Payable		4125.25	
5446	Purchase Discount			15.10
1010	Cash in bank - Operating			4110.15
		Totals	4125.25	4125.25

tain a separate checkbook for the hand-written checks. This checkbook has a series of check numbers selected to distinguish the two types of checks on the monthly bank statement, and it has a payment stub attached to each check for further documenting the transaction. Manually written checks require the same levels of documentation, authorization, and approval as other checks; the accounting manual might specify additional procedures to follow.

If it is necessary to write a check manually to pay a processed vendor invoice, the posting of the transaction is the same as a posting made by the process of selecting and paying invoices by computer-generated check. Since the invoice was previously posted, the expense coding and allocation information has already been recorded; the payment transaction affects A/P, cash, and purchase discount (if any). Payment of any item not previously posted involves the capture of expense coding and allocation information in addition to recording the actual disbursement.

Manually written checks might be needed for cash transfers, payment of taxes, and to pay any vendors with payment terms too rigid to conform to the organization's normal cash disbursement cycle.

For example, a freight company invoice for the delivery of an overnight letter must be paid within seven days; the organization makes the payment with a manual check. The transaction is illustrated in Exhibit 8.2.

If the invoice had been posted through the normal purchases procedure, the entry would have been a debit to the expense and a credit to A/P (lines 1 and 2 of the entry). When the open item was paid, the entry would have been a debit to A/P and a credit to cash (lines 3 and 4). By writing a manual check, the two postings are combined in a single transaction; the debit and the credit to A/P offset each other and are not posted.

| EXHIBIT 8.2 | Posting to Record a Manual Check in Payment of an Unrecorded Invoice |

→ Entry created by the Cash Disbursements software

Entry Date 03/31/20x4   Record manual check paying an unrecorded invoice

Account	Description	Debit	Credit
8140	Freight Expense	52.50	
2010	Accounts Payable (not posted)		52.50
2010	Accounts Payable (not posted)	52.50	
1010	Cash in bank - Operating		52.50
	Totals	105.00	105.00

Void Checks

A check that has been recorded in the accounting system and is later voided must be recorded as a void check, preferably in the same accounting module used to record the check originally. Depending on the accounting software, the act of voiding the check can have one of two effects: (1) the cash is added back, and the invoice is re-established as an open item in the A/P system; or (2) the cash is added back, and the expense accounts originally charged when the invoices were posted are credited.

The first effect reverses the check-writing process, but it does not have any impact on the purchases process. The second effect essentially removes the vendor invoices and associated payment from the accounting system, as if the invoices had never been posted in the first place. Some accounting software offers you the choice; select the appropriate effect for the situation at hand. Most software automatically re-establishes the open item.

Daily Check Register

Part of the process of documenting the transactions in the accounting system is the production of summary reports for each function. A daily check register showing date, check number, vendor, and check amount should be printed; a copy of this report should be filed, and a copy should be made available to management. It is a good practice to print the daily check register even on days without any disbursements; the filed copy of the report with zero totals eliminates the possibility of a missing check register report containing actual disbursements.

CHECKLIST 8.1   **Internal Control Checklist for Cash Disbursements**

- ☐ Are all disbursements (other than petty cash) made by prenumbered checks?
- ☐ Is the signature section torn off of all voided checks and are they marked as "Void" and retained for use in the bank reconciliation process?
- ☐ Is it prohibited to make a check payable to "Cash" or to "Bearer"?
- ☐ Are all check-signatories authorized by the board?
- ☐ Are authorized signatories people without responsibility for recording cash receipts or disbursements?
- ☐ Is there a written prohibition against signing blank checks?
- ☐ Are vouchers or other explanatory documents presented with each check submitted for signature?
- ☐ Are check-signers required to examine back-up documentation before signing a check?
- ☐ Are signed checks mailed by someone not responsible for preparing them?

Bank Reconciliation

The monthly reconciliation of the bank statement to the general ledger book balance for each cash account should be assigned to an individual with no responsibility for the cash receipts or cash disbursements processes. A monthly check register, listing every check written in the period in check number order, is supplied for the purposes of performing the bank reconciliation. This monthly check register also provides additional documentation for the activity posted to the general ledger by the A/P system. (For more information on the bank reconciliation process, see Chapter Ten.)

Petty Cash

Every organization occasionally makes a disbursement where a check is not necessary or appropriate; perhaps the payment is very small, or the supplier does not accept checks. The petty cash fund is set up for those times. Maintained as an imprest fund, petty cash is originally created by cashing an organization check for the amount of the fund (Exhibit 8.3).

Petty cash is kept in a locked box or drawer; only one employee (the custodian) has access to the fund and is responsible for safeguarding the funds and for properly accounting for the funds and all related documentation.

The amount of the petty cash fund should be large enough for the daily needs of the organization, but small enough to require reimbursement on a regular basis. The concept behind petty cash is to eliminate needless check preparation while still maintaining control and timely, accurate accounting over the disbursement.

EXHIBIT 8.3   **Posting to Establish a Petty Cash Fund**

Entry created by the Cash Disbursements software

Entry Date 01/01/20x4   To establish a petty cash fund

Account	Description	Debit	Credit
1040	Cash - Petty Cash	300.00	
1010	Cash in bank - Operating		300.00
	Totals	300.00	300.00

Once the fund is established, no other entries are made to the account called petty cash unless the imprest amount of the fund is being increased or decreased. Since it is an imprest account, petty cash reimbursement entries are posted directly to the expense codes for each petty cash receipt. For example, at the end of the month, the petty cash box has $135.50 remaining in currency; the balance of the $300.00 ($164.50) is represented by the petty cash vouchers in the box. To reimburse the fund, a check is written and recorded as illustrated in Exhibit 8.4.

The fund custodian fills out a petty cash voucher whenever money is disbursed. The voucher lists the date, amount of the transaction, person receiving the funds, the reason for the disbursement, and the proper coding of the transaction. Any documentation supporting the transaction is attached to the voucher. The person receiving the funds signs the voucher, and the voucher is kept with the petty cash fund until it is used as documentation during the petty cash reimbursement process. The organization should have a specific dollar limit on the size of any petty cash disbursement to prevent the use of petty cash to by-pass the normal purchasing policies and procedures.

When the remaining cash in the fund drops to a previously determined amount, the custodian of the fund requests a check to be used to reimburse the fund. At any point in time, the cash in the fund plus the petty cash vouchers should equal the imprest fund balance. The custodian analyzes the vouchers, verifying the petty cash fund is in balance and creating a summary transaction to support the check request. Management reviews the request for reimbursement with all supporting documentation. The reimbursement check is made payable to the custodian, who cashes the check at the bank and returns the funds to the petty cash box.

The custodian is the only person with access to the petty cash box; this lessens the possibility funds will be removed without the proper documentation. Since the

EXHIBIT 8.4 Posting to Record the Petty Cash Fund Reimbursement

➤ Entry created by the Cash Disbursements software

Entry Date	01/31/20x4	Petty Cash fund reimbursement		
Account	Description		Debit	Credit
8310-A	Travel - Program A		76.05	
8310-B	Travel - Program B		12.00	
8110-B	Office Supplies - Program B		21.50	
8110-3	Office Supplies - Dept 3		9.95	
8260-B	Repairs & Maint - Program B		45.00	
1010	Cash in bank - Operating			164.50
		Totals	164.50	164.50

custodian is responsible for safeguarding the asset and maintaining accurate and complete documentation, eliminating the errors and potential misdeeds of others is both necessary and fair. On occasion, management should assign someone other than the custodian to, on a surprise basis, reconcile the fund balance and vouchers in the presence of the custodian.

Giving an IOU to the petty cash fund and the cashing of personal checks from the fund should be prohibited. As a practical matter, employees are occasionally advanced a small amount of money when they are assigned to purchase some supplies. These advances are recorded on a voucher in the same manner as any other transaction; special care should be taken by the custodian to obtain the actual purchase receipt and any balance of funds remaining from the advance in order to complete the transaction. Normally all petty cash transactions are completed in a single day. On the rare occasion when the petty cash fund must be reimbursed between the time an advance was disbursed and the time the advance transaction is completed, the custodian should not include the advance voucher in the request for reimbursement. The advance and the related documentation obtained when the transaction is completed are always submitted together; expenses are reimbursed, not advances.

Travel and other expenses are frequently paid from the petty cash fund. Proper documentation is required for all expenses; undocumented expense reimbursement can be construed as income to the employee. Consult with your accountant concerning the level and type of documentation required; most tax authorities and other agencies have a *de minimus* rule in effect where very small items require less documentation.

Summary

Cash disbursements is an important function in the pursuit of the goal we set for our bookkeeping system. While much of the actual account coding and expense allocation is accomplished prior to the disbursement of funds, the final documentation packet supporting each check is critical to the goal of a fully documented, completely traceable transaction. In addition, the timing of disbursements has a direct impact on the cash flow and overall financial health of the organization.

General Journal Entries

All transactions are recorded in the accounting system in the form of entries. Depending on the software used, many of the transactions are entered on forms designed to capture all of the details for a single transaction and create the appropriate entry. For example, the recording of an office product supplier's invoice in the purchases screen of the typical accounting software captures all of the essential data, including the vendor identification, invoice number, purchase amount, and the allocation of the purchase to various departments, programs, and expense codes. The software uses the data entered on the form to automatically create an entry; in this case, it debits the department, program, and expense code combinations and credits accounts payable.

General Journal

The *general journal* is the place to post any entry that is not normally handled by one of the accounting software's specialty modules, such as billing, cash receipts, cash disbursements, purchasing, and payroll. Each entry has a posting reference and is made up of numerous debits and credits to any combination of department, program, and expense codes from the chart of accounts. As with all transactions, the debits must equal the credits. When do you use a general journal entry (GJE)? Here are some examples:

- To allocate expenses between departments and programs
- To record an accrual of income or expense
- To reverse a previous accrual
- To record the depreciation of assets
- To record the expense portion of a prepaid expense as it is used up
- To record in-kind contributions
- To correct an error

When Not to Use a General Journal Entry

While any entry can, in theory, be posted as a general journal entry (GJE), transactions that affect accounts receivable or accounts payable open items should not be posted through the general journal. Part of the goal of our bookkeeping system is to record the transaction fully; a GJE records the transaction in the general ledger, but it has no impact on the subsidiary records maintained by the system. Posting a purchase through a GJE debits the expense and credits the liability properly, but the accounts payable system has no record of the vendor invoice. Accounting software has specific modules to handle the tasks that affect A/R (billing and cash receipts) and A/P (purchases and cash disbursements). The correction of errors in A/R or A/P should be accomplished in those modules as well. Always use the appropriate module for these tasks; a GJE is the wrong tool.

Which Accounts to Avoid in a General Journal Entry

Certain accounts (often called *control accounts*) are maintained by specific software modules, and they have associated with them details that, when added together, equal the account balance. As we just discussed, the A/R and A/P accounts work this way. At any point in time, the general ledger balance in the account called accounts payable should equal the open item report from the A/P module. This will remain true if you never make a GJE to the general ledger account called accounts payable. Whenever a subsidiary set of records exists for an account in the chart of accounts, avoid posting a GJE to that account. If a correction is required, use the appropriate module; a GJE is the wrong tool.

When the chart of accounts is designed, each of these control accounts (with subsidiary records) should have a matching non-control account. For example:

- 1110 Accounts receivable (control)

- 1120 Accounts receivable—other (non-control)

There are times when an entry is necessary that affects an account with subsidiary records. For example, it might be necessary to record the billing of a client in December, when the actual bill was created by the A/R module and posted in January. In this case, the technique is to post the entry to the non-control account in December (shown in Exhibit 9.1).

The general ledger has two accounts that make up the total of accounts receivable (including the $10,000 GJE), yet the A/R control account still matches the open item report from the A/R module. In January, when the actual billing is posted by the A/R module, this accrual entry will be reversed (see Exhibit 9.2).

This method of using alternate (non-control) accounts has the advantage of highlighting any balances that need to be analyzed. For example, the balance of *accounts receivable—other* would normally be zero. A debit balance indicates a prior entry might still require adjustment.

Recurring Entries

The typical interim accounting period is the month, and most accounting systems are designed to produce some reports on an interim basis. Nonprofit organizations must

EXHIBIT 9.1   Journal Entry to Accrue Revenue

General Journal Entry

Journal Entry Date 12/31/20x4   Revenue Accrual

Account	Description	Debit	Credit
1120	Accounts Receivable Other	10000.00	
5180	Program Service Fee		10000.00
	Totals	10000.00	10000.00

EXHIBIT 9.2   Journal Entry to Reverse the Revenue Accrual

General Journal Entry

Journal Entry Date 01/31/20x5   Reverse a prior Revenue Accrual

Account	Description	Debit	Credit
1120	Accounts Receivable Other		10000.00
5180	Program Service Fee	10000.00	
	Totals	10000.00	10000.00

also produce reports based on the period covered by a grant. Resource C describes the need to select accounting software with the capability to handle a wide range of reporting periods.

In order to make the interim financial reports as accurate as possible, certain adjusting journal entries are necessary. In an attempt to match revenue and expenses, large expenditures are allocated to each interim period throughout the year. Without the need for interim reports, a large expenditure could be expensed in a single month. (See the discussion of prepaid expenses in Chapter Ten.)

This allocation process produces a series of journal entries (one per month), which are either identical or nearly identical. These *recurring entries* are posted as part of the analysis performed by the accounting staff at the end of each period. Examples of recurring entries include the following:

- Depreciation

- Prepaid insurance adjustment to record expense

The structure of the journal entry remains the same from period to period; the debit and credit amounts are often the same as well. Most accounting software has the ability to structure a recurring entry; this is often called *memorizing an entry*. To post the recurring entry with the software, select the memorized entry from the list, verify or modify the amounts, and save the changes (thereby posting the entry).

Accruals and Reversals

Recording a transaction correctly is more than simply a matter of getting the debits and credits right. Another important component to any transaction is the timing of the entry. While this is particularly true between fiscal years, the timing of entries also has an effect on the accounting data for interim periods. Ideally, each transaction is recorded in the proper period as a part of the natural course of workflow.

There are times when the transaction belongs in one period, but it is naturally recorded in another period. Recall our example from Chapter Six:

A community mental health center Hotline is open twenty-four hours per day, seven days per week. The pay period ends on Saturday, and the paychecks are dated the following Wednesday.

In this example (see Exhibit 9.3), the last paychecks posted in October are dated October 26th (the last Wednesday in the month). Those paychecks represented wages earned by employees up through October 22nd (the preceding Saturday). Wages earned from October 23rd through October 31st will be paid on paychecks dated after October. The pay period ending October 29th is paid on November 2nd, and the wages earned on October 30th and 31st are included in the week ending November 5th, paid on November 9th. Therefore, the payroll accrual will be the total wages earned for the last nine days of October, from the 23rd to the 31st.

The entry to post the payroll accrual is shown in Exhibit 9.4.

Whenever you make an entry accruing a transaction, you must remember to reverse your accrual in the subsequent period. In the example, the payroll accrual entry moved $2,600 of wage expense into October; the actual wages were paid in November. When the November payroll is posted, total wages will include all of the paychecks written in November, including the amount already posted in October by way of the payroll accrual entry. By reversing the payroll accrual in November, the duplicate expense is eliminated. If you fail to reverse the accrual, the wages you accrued will be posted in both October and November.

The entry to reverse the payroll accrual is shown in Exhibit 9.5.

**EXHIBIT
9.3**   **Calendar to Calculate a Payroll Accrual**

SUNDAY	MONDAY	TUESDAY	WEDNESDAY	THURSDAY	FRIDAY	SATURDAY
October						
23	24	25	26	27	28	29
		November				
30	31	1	2	3	4	5

**EXHIBIT
9.4**   **Journal Entry to Record the Payroll Accrual**

General Journal Entry

Journal Entry Date 10/31/20x4   To record the payroll accrual

Account	Description	Debit	Credit
7220-A	Wage Expense - Dept A	1500.00	
7220-B	Wage Expense - Dept B	800.00	
7220-C	Wage Expense - Dept C	300.00	
2110	Accrued Payroll		2600.00
	Totals	2600.00	2600.00

The accrual and reversal process is the technique used to shift transactions from the period they are posted in to the period in which they belong. Every accrual should be followed, in a subsequent period, by a reversal of the accrual.

Materiality

Materiality is a threshold amount in accounting, which will vary based on the size of the nonprofit organization and based on the type of account (asset, liability, net asset, income, or expense) in question. An amount below the threshold is not important

EXHIBIT 9.5   Journal Entry to Reverse the Payroll Accrual

General Journal Entry

| Journal Entry Date | 11/30/20x4 | To reverse the payroll accrual | | |

Account	Description	Debit	Credit
7220-A	Wage Expense - Dept A		1500.00
7220-B	Wage Expense - Dept B		800.00
7220-C	Wage Expense - Dept C		300.00
2110	Accrued Payroll	2600.00	
	Totals	2600.00	2600.00

enough to warrant special analysis. Amounts above the threshold are important and must be corrected if inaccurate. Accrual journal entries are made after determining that the impact of the entry is material to the financial results of the organization.

Documentation

General journal entries are less automatically self-documenting than other types of transactions. What appears obvious at the time the entry is made can often be obscure upon later analysis. One of the goals of the bookkeeping system is to have each transaction be fully documented and traceable. With GJE, attaining this goal requires a special effort.

Work papers, photocopies, and other documentation should be attached to the GJE and permanently filed after posting. The explanation must be clear and complete, and it should cite and/or identify how any assumptions or calculations support the entry.

When correcting an error on a previous entry, always reverse the prior amount as originally posted and then post the correct amount. Posting an entry for the net difference hides the purpose of the entry and should always be avoided.

All general journal entries have a GJE reference number, a posting date, and a memo (description) field to provide a way to trace the general ledger posting back to its source. For the sake of clarity and brevity, the example entries throughout this book do not show these essential components.

The reference number is often pre-assigned by the accounting software; if it is not, a common numbering scheme is to use the date combined with a sequential value (for example, Feb2004–1, Feb2004–2, and so on).

The memo field is a brief summary of the purpose of the GJE. Don't rely on the memo to be the sole documentation for the entry; always attach the appropriate documentation to the printed copy of the GJE before filing.

Approvals

Journal entries should be reviewed by the accounting manager and approved in writing prior to posting. This process provides a way of checking the logic of the entry and the completeness of the documentation.

Summary

A general journal entry is an important and powerful tool to help keep your books accurate. In many cases, it is the only tool available to record certain transactions. The experienced bookkeeper also recognizes that the general journal entry should not be used when working on the control accounts for subsidiary records; cash balance adjustments should be made through the cash receipt and cash disbursement subsystems.

The Month-End Close and Account Analysis

W e normally maintain accounting records in monthly increments. While many funding sources and governmental agencies require quarterly and annual reports, internal reporting is more useful to management if it is produced more frequently. The end of each month is a good time to summarize results with printed reports, to finalize the postings for the month, and to analyze the records. The month-end close and account analysis procedures are an essential part of the accounting process.

One of the views produced by our accounting system is the snapshot of things our organization owns and amounts our organization owes. We established asset, liability, and net asset accounts in our chart of accounts (often called *balance sheet accounts*) to represent each of these real-world items. GAAP uses the term *statement of financial position* to describe what we are referring to as the balance sheet. *Asset accounts* represent tangible items, such as equipment or cash or contributions due to us. *Liability accounts* are real financial obligations, such as amounts due to vendors or bank loans. Each account balance is derived from all previously recorded transactions. In this chapter, we'll explore the techniques you will use to verify the correctness of these balances.

Interim Periods

As we've described, organizations have a natural business cycle, typically one year. It is common to divide the business cycle into month-long periods when posting transactions and recording financial events. Our economy revolves around the monthly cycle: utility companies bill once per month; vendors generate monthly statements of account; grants and other contracts have monthly payments; and so on. Your organization might have a valid business reason for using a business cycle other than one year, or your organization's interim periods might be more or less than one month long. In this chapter, we're going to assume a business cycle made up of twelve monthly periods.

Every organization takes in revenue and pays expenses. For all but the smallest organizations, this inflow and outflow of funds is managed with the following accounting subsystems:

- Accounts receivable—billing
- Accounts receivable—cash receipts
- Accounts payable—purchases
- Accounts payable—cash disbursements
- Payroll

The focus in this chapter is on how these subsystems interrelate and how the reports produced by these subsystems are used to track activity and account balances. At the end of each monthly period, each of these subsystems closes its activity by finalizing the postings for the month and then printing the usual set of month-end reports. The accounting department uses the reports to prepare adjusting journal entries prior to printing the final version of the standard general ledger reports:

- General journal
- Trial balance
- General ledger

Most software packages create these general ledger reports automatically as a result of the transactions being posted; they are available at any time, but are most commonly used during the month-end process.

The billing subsystem typically generates bills for services or products on the same day or, in some instances when the shipment of product is involved, on the next day. When the last bill for the month has been created and printed, the monthly billing summary reports are printed and the subsystem for that month is closed. *Closing* a subsystem means that no further postings to that system can be made; additional postings or adjustments must be posted instead to a subsequent month. One important reason for closing a subsystem is that other parts of the accounting system are using and relying on the totals of each subsystem. Without a formal subsystem close, totals in the accounting system become moving targets—yesterday's total is no longer accurate because another transaction was posted since the reports were printed. You should only use an accounting software product that provides a method to close a subsystem for each accounting period. Without the ability to close a subsystem, your books are vulnerable to errors and postings designed to hide fraudulent activity. If your accounting software lacks the ability to close subsystems, and the organization is unable to replace the software, you will need to devise procedures that limit the exposure. These procedures might include printing and permanently retaining various reports on a daily or weekly basis and assigning someone without access to the accounting system to analyze and be the custodian of those reports.

The *cash receipts* subsystem typically records payments received on the day of the receipt. The monthly cash receipt summary reports are printed after the final day's receipts have been recorded, and the subsystem is closed.

The *purchases* subsystem records invoices received from vendors as they arrive and are matched up with supporting documentation. Since the arrival of invoices depends on the action of the vendors (each vendor has a billing subsystem to generate bills) and on the performance of the Postal Service, the purchases subsystem must be kept open for several days beyond the end of the period. Most accounting software has this capability; the accounting staff should follow a set of procedures designed to avoid confusion during the transition from one month to the next. After the last vendor invoice has been posted, the monthly purchases summary reports are printed and the subsystem is closed. Any vendor invoices that arrive after closing are posted in the subsequent period, and are also candidates for an accrual general journal entry.

The *cash disbursements* subsystem records cash disbursements on the day the checks are written. The monthly check register report is printed at the end of the last day of each period, and the subsystem is closed.

The *payroll* subsystem is always recorded on a cash basis; checks are recorded on the check date, regardless of when the employee worked to earn the paycheck. Every pay date produces a set of reports, and the last pay date in each month produces a monthly payroll summary report. Since the payroll subsystem is run on pay date cycles, which can be weekly, bi-weekly, semi-monthly, or monthly, there is normally no need to close the subsystem. Any transactions posted between pay dates are automatically included in the reports of the next pay cycle. The cash-basis nature of payroll and the use of pay cycles make payroll the most common candidate for month-end accrual and reversing general journal entries.

General Ledger Posting

Most accounting software automatically posts the transaction totals from the subsystems to the general ledger. The month-end reports from each subsystem could be used to post the totals to the general ledger manually, but they also provide a method of cross-checking the accounting software's automatic entries and tracing a general ledger posting back to its source transaction in a subsystem.

Account Analysis

A critical part of maintaining accounting records is to verify the accuracy of those records. When the totals from all subsystems have been posted to the general ledger, the preliminary version of the *general ledger* and *trial balance* reports are printed. A careful analysis of each account balance is prepared, in order to produce any adjusting journal entries that might be required and to provide assurance about the accuracy of the transactions recorded in the month.

A general ledger has the following details for all accounts in the chart of accounts:

- Opening balance for the period

- Every transaction in the period posted as a debit or credit, with posting date, posting source, and reference (Some software summarizes control account transactions [A/R and A/P] into daily or batch totals, which makes the general ledger more compact and offers transaction details on subsystem reports.)

- Ending balance for the period

The trial balance report lists every account in the chart of accounts with the ending debit or credit balance for each account.

Account analysis methods depend on the type of account; this chapter will describe common analysis techniques for various account types. All account analysis has one thing in common: it proves that the general ledger account balance is correct as of the period ending date.

Most accounting software provides comparative balances (for example, this year versus last year) that facilitate the analysis of many accounts (particularly support, revenue, and expense accounts) in the general ledger. Comparative information helps to highlight trends. Multi-year balance information is also very helpful in developing accurate budgets. (This is discussed in more detail in Chapter Thirteen.) The one area where comparative financial information is less helpful is in the analysis of certain grants. As the grant activity evolves from year to year, the budget can change dramatically. Since each grant stands on its own, comparing a grant in year two to the same grant in year one is often useless from an analytical stand point.

Bank Reconciliation

For cash accounts, account analysis takes the form of a reconciliation between the general ledger (book) balance and the bank statement balance. For savings accounts with little activity, the reconciliation often shows the need to record the monthly interest income credited by the bank as the only reconciling item. The reconciliation of the regular and payroll checking accounts is more complicated.

Cash checking accounts frequently have daily deposits and a large number of checks written in the month. As noted earlier, your organization closes the cash receipts and cash disbursements subsystems on the last day of each month. Banks also close the books on accounts once per month. If it is possible, the organization should request the bank make the closing date for the account the same as the date used by the organization—the end of the month. Some banks charge additional fees for this service; other banks will not be able to accommodate the request. Regardless of the bank closing date, the process of reconciling the account remains the same. Closing dates that coincide will produce fewer reconciling items.

For control purposes, the bank statement should be given unopened to the executive director (ED) or to another manager selected to examine the statement and cancelled checks prior to the reconciliation being done. This examination includes a look at the payee on each check, the amount of each check, the signatures on each check, and the endorsement on the back of each check. For more information about the safeguarding of cash and about controlling the receipt and disbursement processes, see Chapters Five and Eight.

When reconciling a payroll checking account, carefully examine the endorsement on the back of each check. Multiple endorsements or unusual endorsements might indicate a problem and in many cases will warrant an investigation. In all but the smallest organizations, the payroll department will not have personal contact with every employee; payroll fraud is a real and potentially costly possibility. Multiple endorsements where the second endorser is a supervisor also might indicate an illegal kickback agreement between the employee and the supervisor.

The bank reconciliation is designed to reconcile the bank balance with the book balance. The differences are almost always due to the timing of events: checks written on the books that have not yet cleared the bank, or deposits recorded on the books that were posted by the bank in the subsequent period. Other differences, such as bank fees, will require entering the fees in the disbursement records. Do not make these adjustments through general journal entries. All adjustments to cash receipt items should be made through the cash receipt subsystem. All adjustments to cash disbursement items should be made through the cash disbursement subsystem.

The monthly cash receipts summary report shows every deposit made by the organization and recorded in the accounting records. An item-by-item comparison with the deposits credited to the account by the bank will reveal whether the bank still needs to record any deposits. These missing amounts are called *deposits-in-transit*. Care must be taken to ensure that the deposits are not listed on the bank statement because the date of the bank statement came prior to the deposit date, and not because the deposit never made it to the bank. The individual deposit slips, filed with the daily cash receipts documentation, are stamped with the date the bank received and posted the deposit.

Amounts credited to the bank account but not listed in the accounting records might indicate a major problem with the accounting system's procedures. This type of accounting error, where the bank records a deposit that your books do not contain, is very serious and is a reconciling item that should never occur; when it does occur, it is a symptom of a structural flaw in the bookkeeping system. Quickly investigate and determine the cause of such errors and create a series of checks and balances that ensures that every deposit is entered in the records before being sent to the bank.

Amounts credited to the bank that do not exactly match the deposit recorded in the accounting records indicate an error; a careful analysis of the cash receipts documentation for the deposit will reveal if the error was made by the bank or by the organization.

The monthly check register report lists every check written in the period in check number order. An item-by-item comparison with the checks that cleared the bank will reveal the checks that remain *outstanding* at the end of the period. Some of the checks listed on the bank statement will have been written and recorded by the organization in prior periods; they will be on the outstanding checklist from the previous month's bank reconciliation. Care must be taken to analyze the outstanding checklist for checks that were written more than one month ago; these older outstanding checks are in danger of becoming stale, meaning that the bank will no longer honor the check because it was written too far in the past. Old outstanding checks also indicate a possible problem in the accounts payable system. One possibility is that the payment was never sent to the vendor, and the check was never voided in the system. Another possibility is that the payment was lost; if the vendor never received payment, the organization's credit history and relationship with the vendor could suffer.

Checks that clear the bank but were never recorded in the accounting records indicate a major problem with the accounting system's procedures. This should never happen; when it does, it indicates a complete lack of control by management.

The bank statement might contain miscellaneous debits and credits. The most common reasons for this type of activity are the fees charged by the bank and interest earned from the bank. Every miscellaneous debit and credit must be analyzed and recorded as an adjustment. The entire bank reconciliation and all of the adjustments relating to transactions incorrectly recorded or transactions missing from the records must be approved by management in writing before posting to the appropriate subsystem.

To complete the bank reconciliation, the reconciling items are combined with the book balance, and the total is compared to the bank balance (see Exhibit 10.1 for an example).

Outstanding checks and deposits-in-transit are items in the accounting records that the bank knows nothing about. To match the bank balance, add outstanding checks back to the book balance and subtract deposits-in-transit from the book balance; notice that items not on the bank statement must be removed from the book balance. This adjusted book balance should equal the bank statement balance. Bank service charges must be entered as a disbursement to reflect the reduction in the cash balance.

On bank statements with a large number of transactions, the first attempt at the bank reconciliation might not be successful. Check the following to see where the error is:

- Have all miscellaneous debits and credits been accounted for?

- Is the outstanding check total correct? To prove it is, add last month's outstanding check total to the total of checks written in the current month. This is the pool of checks that could have cleared the bank. Now subtract the total of the checks that did clear the bank (from the bank statement). The result should equal the current outstanding checklist total; if it does not, the outstanding checklist is incorrect. One possibility to watch for is a manually written check that was never posted.

- Was there a deposit-in-transit on last month's reconciliation? Did it clear the bank in the current month?

EXHIBIT 10.1	Sample Bank Reconciliation

Cash Account #12345
National State Bank

Bank Reconciliation
as of 10/31/20x4

			Total
Book Balance			5,250.97
Minus Bank Service Charge			(10.00)
Plus Outstanding Checks	#107	15.25	
	#110	124.50	
	#111	175.00	
	#113	7.95	
	#120	100.00	
	#121	150.00	
	#122	5.00	
	Total O/S Checks		577.70
Minus Deposits-In-Transit	Deposit dated 10/31/20x4 (recorded by bank on 11/1/20x4)	650.00	
	Total D-I-T		(650.00)
Bank Statement Balance	10/31/20x4		5,178.67
Prepared by:	John Smith Bookkeeper	11/12/20x4	
Approved by:	Mary Jones Executive Director	11/14/20x4	

- The bank prints the amount charged to your account on each cleared check in the lower right hand corner (right after the account number). Does this amount match the face amount of the check? Does this amount match the cash disbursement records? Banks can make errors; if this amount is incorrect, notify the bank immediately. Sometimes the bank makes mistakes for a few cents and sometimes for thousands of dollars.

Each cash account is reconciled separately. The book balance in the general ledger must be reconciled exactly to the bank statement balance every month. A $1.00 difference could be an error in a deposit of $1,000.00 and an error in a disbursement of $999.00; the person doing the bank reconciliation should be a person who enjoys details and reconciles accounts to the penny.

Accounting software often provides a bank reconciliation module. The process might be different from the method presented here, but the concept is the same.

| CHECKLIST 10.1 | Internal Control Checklist for Bank Accounts |

☐ Are unused bank accounts closed and is the bank notified in writing not to process any future transactions?

☐ Are all unused checks for closed accounts destroyed?

☐ Are all check-signers clearly designated by the Board in the minutes of their meetings?

☐ Is the bank notified in writing when an individual is no longer authorized to sign checks?

☐ Are monthly bank statements and cancelled checks directly received and reviewed by someone other than a person involved in the cash receipts and cash disbursement functions?

☐ Are bank statements reconciled to the general ledger as soon as possible every month?

☐ Are bank reconciliations done in writing?

☐ Is the sequence of check numbers accounted for as a part of the reconciliation?

☐ Are cancelled checks examined for date, name, authorized signatures, cancellation, and endorsement?

☐ Is the reconciliation reviewed and approved in writing by management?

Control Accounts

The accounts receivable and accounts payable subsystems are each represented in the general ledger by *control accounts*. The A/R control account is debited by the billing subsystem when a bill is generated, and it is credited by the cash receipts subsystem when payment is received for a bill. The A/R open item report is a list of every unpaid bill; the total of each bill's unpaid balance equals the balance of the accounts receivable account in the general ledger.

In a similar manner, the A/P control account is credited by the purchases subsystem when each vendor invoice is posted, and it is debited by the cash disbursements subsystem when each vendor invoice is paid. The A/P open item report is a list of every unpaid vendor invoice; the total of these invoices equals the balance of the accounts payable account in the general ledger.

It is important not to make a general journal entry to one of these control accounts. (For more information on this topic, turn to Chapter Nine.) The control accounts are designed to be maintained by the subsystems; adjustments and error corrections to these accounts should be made through the appropriate controlling subsystem. If the general ledger balance does not equal the open item report total, it is likely that a general ledger journal entry is the reason.

Comparing the general ledger balance to the open item report balance is the first step in the account analysis process. The bookkeeper must also analyze the details of the open item report. Most systems provide the ability to print an aged version of the open items, classifying each open item into columns based on a comparison of the report date to the transaction date. Open items in the oldest columns should be scrutinized. In the

A/R system, very old open items indicate a collection problem and possible bad debt. In the A/P system, very old open items indicate a problem with the invoice posting and a possible duplication of an expense. They also might indicate a cash flow problem that needs to be addressed.

Prepaid Expenses

Prepaid expenses are amounts recorded in the accounting system prior to the period when the expense should be recognized.

Matching is the concept of recording expenses incurred in generating revenue in the same period that we record the revenue. We try to match revenue with expenses. Invoices from vendors arrive according to the vendor's schedule. Often the time frame of the expense covered by the vendor invoice is for more than a single month. A typical example is an insurance premium—the premium is due at the inception of the policy, but the term of the coverage is one full year. Applying the matching principle, the insurance premium is recorded as a prepaid expense, and then a general journal entry records one-twelfth of the premium as the expense each month. If the total premium is $3,900.00 for the entire year, the monthly write-off or expense is $325.00 each month ($3,900.00 divided by 12 months), as illustrated in Exhibit 10.2.

Various expenses are candidates for being treated in this manner, including prepaid real estate taxes, prepaid insurance, and prepaid interest expense. The bookkeeper should prepare a schedule for each prepaid asset account, showing the initial amount of the vendor payment and all subsequent entries. The purpose of the schedule is twofold: to tie out the current general ledger account balance, and to provide further documentation of the logic of handling the vendor payment in this manner. It is very important to understand and analyze invoices as they are received. For example, with-

EXHIBIT 10.2   **Journal Entry to Write-Off One Month's Insurance Premium**

General Journal Entry

Journal Entry Date 04/30/20x4   To write-off one month's insurance premium

Account	Description	Debit	Credit
8520	Insurance Expense	325.00	
1450	Prepaid Expenses		325.00
	Totals	325.00	325.00

out careful analysis an insurance bill that covers a three-year period might be written off in one year. Real estate tax bills can be extremely confusing depending on the local taxing authority's rules and procedures. All financial transactions should be reviewed by a knowledgeable person to ensure accuracy.

Fixed Assets (Land, Buildings, and Equipment)

Purchases classified as land, buildings, and equipment have useful lives that exceed a single accounting period. A portion of the cost is expensed every month by making a depreciation entry. Various governmental funding sources mandate different methods to compute depreciation. Depreciation might be given a different name such as *usage charges* or other names by a funding source and be capped according to a formula they require. Where depreciation is allowed, most funding sources require it to be shown as an item in the budget submitted for approval. If not in the budget, such costs might be disallowed and therefore not chargeable to the funding source. Unfortunately this area of accounting is further confused by the fact that the IRS might require a different method than the funding source for calculating depreciation expense. Discuss the rules applicable to your organization with your funding source representative and with your auditor to keep your tax reporting and funding source reporting correct. (A more complete discussion of this topic can be found in Chapter Three.)

Funds received from government grants (and from certain private grants) for the purchase of a fixed asset might create a *reversionary interest* in that fixed asset. This means that the organization cannot dispose of the fixed asset without the permission of the funding source. When the organization no longer uses the fixed asset, the fixed asset must (technically) be returned or transferred to the funding source. This reversionary interest should be disclosed in financial statements; the bookkeeper must be able to identify which fixed assets are subject to this type of restriction.

Account analysis of fixed assets requires the creation and maintenance of an asset record for each acquisition. A perpetual record of equipment is often required by grant guidelines; whether or not it is specified by a funding source, a fixed asset record for each acquisition is essential. An asset record includes the complete details about the asset:

- Cost
- Acquisition date
- Description
- Vendor
- Funding source
- Grant name
- Grant period
- Reversionary interest
- Serial number (or other identifying characteristics)

The asset record also includes information on the depreciation of the asset:

- Estimated useful life

- Depreciation method

- Depreciation expense for each year

- Accumulated depreciation balances for each year

This asset record is the place to document differences between expensing for grant purposes and capitalizing and depreciating for GAAP. Individual asset records also support any insurance claims filed for losses due to theft, fire, or other hazards.

The asset record fully describes the acquisition and life of an asset. Added together, all of the asset records make up the general ledger balances for the fixed assets and for the associated accumulated depreciation accounts.

Marketable Securities

The summary of FASB Statement No. 124 (Accounting for Certain Investments Held by Not-for-Profit Organizations) states:

> This Statement establishes standards for accounting for certain investments held by not-for-profit organizations. It requires that investments in equity securities with readily determinable fair values and all investments in debt securities be reported at fair value with gains and losses included in a statement of activities. This Statement requires certain disclosures about investments held by not-for-profit organizations and the return on those investments. This Statement also establishes standards for reporting losses on investments held because of a donor's stipulation to invest a gift in perpetuity or for a specified term.

In general, marketable securities are carried on the books at their fair market value. If the market value of the security is higher than the existing book value, an adjustment is made and the gain is reported on the statement of activities as an increase in unrestricted net assets (unless the use of the security is temporarily or permanently restricted by donor restrictions or by law). If the market value is lower than the existing book value, the value of the asset is adjusted to the market value, and the resultant loss is reported on the statement of activities. Discuss any proposed adjustments with your auditor. The treatment of investments related to permanently restricted net assets can be affected by state law; discuss this area with the organization's attorney and auditor.

Accrued Expenses

If your organization receives government grant money, study the rules governing your grant carefully. Many jurisdictions have different rules that govern the time period in which an invoice must be paid to include it in the expenses attributable to a specific grant. One common rule is that expenses must be paid within ninety days of the end of the grant period; payments made after that date might be disallowed by the funding source.

Materiality for Nonprofit Organizations

Materiality is a threshold amount in accounting. An amount below the threshold is not important enough to warrant special analysis. Amounts above the threshold are important and must be corrected if inaccurate. The decision to accrue an expense is made by considering if the amount of the accrual is material to the financial results of the organization. The concept of materiality for grant funds is further complicated by the need to consider the threshold amount at the grant level, as opposed to the material amount for the organization as a whole.

In the earlier description of prepaid expenses, vendor invoices were posted to the prepaid asset account in an attempt to match expenses to revenues. For prepaid expenses, the vendor invoice is posted ahead of time and needs to be written off over a series of months. *Accrued expenses* are the mirror image of a prepaid expense; the activity incurring the cost has taken place, but the expense has not been posted. This happens for several reasons. Payroll expenses follow a cash basis, pay date cycle—the pay period seldom, if ever, coincides with the payroll check date. Or purchases of goods and services are used in one period, and the invoices often arrive in subsequent periods.

Various expenses are candidates for accrual, including payroll, audit and professional fees, real estate taxes, payroll taxes, and interest expense. An audit fee, for example, is agreed upon prior to the beginning of the engagement, but it is often invoiced at a later date. Some controversy exists over the accrual of audit fees; some organizations accrue the year-end fee in the year just ended, others do not. Discuss this matter with the funding source and with the auditor.

Notice that certain expenses are candidates to be both prepaid and accrued expenses. Real estate taxes, as illustrated in the following paragraphs, are a good example of this.

Depending on where your organization is located, it might be possible to have an attorney petition the local government to waive real estate taxes. In some jurisdictions local authorities might negotiate and accept a PILOT (Payment In Lieu Of Taxes) agreement that sometimes is relatively close to the original amount of taxes and sometimes is lower. Since state budgetary pressures affect many local tax jurisdictions, some localities have stopped exempting nonprofit organizations from property taxes or greatly narrowed the type of exempt organization that might qualify for tax abatement. Your organization should consult with a local attorney regarding these issues.

In some jurisdictions, real estate taxes are paid for a calendar quarter at the beginning of the second month of the quarter. In the first month of the quarter (October), the organization must accrue one month's real estate tax expense. In Exhibit 10.3, the quarterly tax bill equals $6,300; the one-month expense is $2,100, which is $6,300 divided by three months.

In the second month of the quarter (November), the quarterly taxes are paid; the amount is charged to a Prepaid expense account, and entries are made to reverse the October accrual and to record the October and November expense, as illustrated in Exhibit 10.4.

The net effect of these entries in November is to zero out the accrued expense (the actual expense has been recorded), to charge the month with the correct amount of expense, and to establish an amount representing December's real estate tax as a prepaid expense.

As Exhibit 10.5 shows, in the third month of the quarter (December) the prepaid amount remaining is written off, leaving a zero balance in the prepaid asset account.

In this example, the timing of the real estate tax payment caused it to be accrued in one month and prepaid in another month.

Account analysis of accrued expense accounts entails the preparation of detailed schedules that show the reason for the accrual and the calculation of the accrued amount. The bookkeeper must reverse accruals in the appropriate month; the timing of the reversal is dictated by the payment of the expense through the Payroll or A/P systems.

Notes Payable

The payment of debt service includes interest expense and (usually) the payment of principal. Whether the lending institution invoices the organization, or the loan payment is made according to a loan amortization schedule, the bookkeeper must separate

---

EXHIBIT 10.3   Journal Entry to Accrue One Month's Real Estate Tax

General Journal Entry

Journal Entry Date 10/31/20x4   To accrue October's real estate tax

Account	Description	Debit	Credit
8230	Real Estate Tax Expense	2100.00	
2150	Accrued Expenses		2100.00
	Totals	2100.00	2100.00

EXHIBIT 10.4 Entries to Record the Payment of the Quarterly Real Estate Tax Bill, Reversing an Accrual and Writing-Off the Prepaid Portion

Your software's Cash Disbursements entry screen completes the balanced entry by automatically crediting the Cash account.

Entry Date 11/30/20x4   To record the payment of quarterly real estate taxes

Account	Description	Debit	Credit
1450	Prepaid Expenses	6300.00	
1010	Cash in bank - operating		6300.00
	Totals	6300.00	6300.00

General Journal Entry

Journal Entry Date 11/30/20x4   To reverse October's real estate tax accrual

Account	Description	Debit	Credit
2150	Accrued Expenses	2100.00	
8230	Real Estate Tax Expense		2100.00

Journal Entry Date 11/30/20x4   To write-off Oct's portion of the Prepaid Expense

Account	Description	Debit	Credit
8230	Real Estate Tax Expense	2100.00	
1450	Prepaid Expenses		2100.00

Journal Entry Date 11/30/20x4   To write-off Nov's portion of the Prepaid Expense

Account	Description	Debit	Credit
8230	Real Estate Tax Expense	2100.00	
1450	Prepaid Expenses		2100.00
	Totals	6300.00	6300.00

EXHIBIT 10.5 **Journal Entry to Write-Off One Month's Prepaid Real Estate Tax**

General Journal Entry

Journal Entry Date 12/31/20x4   To write-off December's real estate tax

Account	Description	Debit	Credit
8230	Real Estate Tax Expense	2100.00	
1450	Prepaid Expenses		2100.00
	Totals	2100.00	2100.00

the interest component from the payment of loan principal. Account analysis for accounts that represent notes or loans payable by the organization should always include a schedule comparing the book balance to any available loan statement balance prepared by the lender, plus a detailed analysis of the related interest expense. Interest expense is an example of an expense not chargeable to most private or governmental grants. Non-grant funds must be used to pay for interest in most situations.

Net Assets

There are several kinds of net assets. Net asset types take their character from the underlying transaction that created them. If no temporary or permanent restrictions apply to the support received by the organization, the resulting amount is an unrestricted net asset.

The Financial Accounting Standards Board (FASB) has created three classifications for net assets applicable to nonprofit organizations:

• *Unrestricted net assets* are defined in FASB Statement of Financial Standards No. 116 as "neither permanently restricted nor temporarily restricted by donor-imposed stipulation" (para. 209, glossary, p. 59). They come from support sources that place no conditions or stipulations on the funds.

• *Temporarily restricted net assets* are assets for which use is limited to specific purposes or time periods, as specified in contracts, grant agreements, or other written or oral statements. They arise from support sources that place conditions regarding the use of the funds for a specific purpose, for a specific time period, or for both a specific purpose and time period. For example, a donor specifies that a contribution is for a community hotline program for the year 20x5. Funds designated by the donor in this manner must be spent for the purpose and in the time period indicated. If the conditions placed on temporarily restricted net assets are met in the current accounting period, the net assets are recorded as unrestricted (or, if previously recorded as temporarily restricted, those net assets are reclassified as unrestricted using a journal entry).

• *Permanently restricted net assets* arise from conditions placed on support by the donor that permanently restrict the use of the funds. The funds are held in perpetuity for a specific purpose. Permanently restricted net assets are more common in large nonprofit organizations, such as colleges, universities, and hospitals. For example, endowment contributions are designed to support a specific purpose, such as a Professor of Accounting chair at a university. Normally the organization can only use the income from the contribution to support the activity; the contributed amount is invested and cannot be spent. Restrictions on the use of net assets might be conveyed either orally or in writing and might be made by the donor at the time the funds are given *(donor restriction)* or as a result of specific statements or commitments made when the organization originally solicited the contribution. State laws governing endowments vary. Misuse of these types of funds have led to criminal charges being filed against the organization's CEO, CFO, legal counsel, and board members; it is important to understand and adhere to the requirements of any restrictions.

In some cases, the nonprofit organization can classify income generated from the principal amount as temporarily restricted or unrestricted, depending on donor stipulations. Some donors want the income from their endowment contribution to be used for the general operations of the organization; in this case, the endowment creates a permanently restricted net asset that produces unrestricted income from the investment. Donor restrictions can only be changed by the donor; similarly, restrictions placed on contributions by the organization at the time of solicitation may only be changed with the consent of the donor.

Contributions that are not specifically designated as temporarily or permanently restricted will be considered unrestricted. Funds received as a result of fundraising campaigns or special events are unrestricted unless the organization stated that the contribution would be used for a specific purpose when it was solicited.

Funds received from government agencies often have specific performance requirements attached to them; despite the many rules specified by the funding source, these funds are considered unrestricted net assets by the FASB.

Unrestricted Net Asset–Designated Funds

The board of directors of the organization has the ability to designate funds for a specific purpose, such as the building of a new facility. The board passes a formal resolution, included in the board minutes, to authorize the organization to create this sub-classification of unrestricted net assets. At any time, the board can pass a new resolution removing the designation. The designations of funds by the board of directors are internal classifications of net assets.

Posting to Net Assets

Net asset accounts are usually maintained by the accounting software. The accounting equation discussed in Chapter Two shows how the net asset balance is calculated:

assets – liabilities = (previous net assets balance + revenues – expenses)

This calculation is performed whenever financial reports are created from the accounting records; monthly (interim) financial reports contain accurate balances for the net asset accounts. Despite the need to make this calculation often, no formal entry is made to record the net asset change until the books are closed at the end of the fiscal year. During the year-end close, the accounting software creates a journal entry that debits every revenue (and expense) account with a credit balance, credits every expense (and revenue) account with a debit balance, and balances the entry by posting an amount to net assets.

This year-end closing journal entry does two things: (1) it posts an amount to the net asset accounts that reflects the financial results from the fiscal year just ended; and (2) it zeroes out every revenue and expense account in preparation for the new fiscal year.

A closing journal entry is not made during the month-end close; the books are maintained for each fiscal year. Interim reporting and analysis is performed for management and other purposes, but fiscal year totals must be maintained. A formal month-end closing journal entry would reset the revenue and expense account balances to zero each month; we would lose the history view for the entire business cycle of the organization.

Accounting software that recognizes the distinction between the various classes of net assets will create a year-end closing entry that maintains the character of the account classifications. For example, temporarily restricted revenue and expense activity will be closed to the temporarily restricted net asset account. Software without this built-in intelligence can still be used, but it requires the bookkeeper to maintain the distribution of net asset account balances manually.

In general, you should not post an entry to the net asset accounts used by the computer software when posting the year-end closing entry. It is good practice to post all transactions affecting net assets to the appropriate revenue or expense account, leaving a posting-free or clean net asset account. If the accounting software does not recognize and maintain the classes of net assets required, you should create additional net asset accounts to allow you to post transfers among the net asset classifications without touching the net asset account used by the software. For example, if the software uses account number 3000 (called *net assets*) for its closing entry, you could create four additional accounts to use when transferring balances:

1. 3001—net asset transfer

2. 3010—unrestricted net assets

3. 3110—temporarily restricted net assets

4. 3210—permanently restricted net assets

To transfer a credit balance from the account (3000) used by the accounting software to the appropriate net asset categories, you debit account 3001 for the total to be transferred and credit accounts 3010, 3110, and 3210 as required to properly classify the net asset total. The primary account (3000) remains free of journal entries, and the balances in 3000 and 3001 offset each other.

Why maintain the primary net asset account free from journal entries? Most accounting transactions should be part of the history view; they belong in the revenue and expense accounts created for that purpose. In addition, it is easier to check on the integrity of the data maintained by the accounting software if the primary net asset account balance is maintained by the system.

Temporarily Restricted Net Asset Transactions

As shown in Exhibit 10.6, on December 15, 20x4, the organization receives a contribution from a donor who specified that the funds were to be used only for the expenses of a community health hotline during the calendar year 20x5.

At the end of 20x4, the $10,000 is a temporarily restricted net asset, reflected by the $10,000 of temporarily restricted income for the year ended 12/31/20x4. As Exhibit 10.7 shows, during the year 20x5, the organization sets up the hotline, incurring $10,000 in costs attributable to the project.

The donor's conditions having been met, the organization reclassifies the temporarily restricted net asset to an unrestricted net asset in 20x5. The income was recorded in December 20x4 as temporarily restricted; the reclassification entry transfers the amount by using two offsetting income accounts designed for this purpose. The net effect on total income of the entry in Exhibit 10.8 is zero; this reflects the fact that no new income was earned in 20x5 as a result of the donor's conditions being

EXHIBIT 10.6	Posting to Record a Temporarily Restricted Contribution

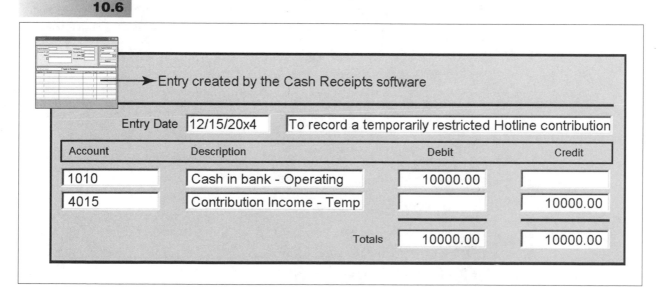

Entry created by the Cash Receipts software

Entry Date 12/15/20x4   To record a temporarily restricted Hotline contribution

Account	Description	Debit	Credit
1010	Cash in bank - Operating	10000.00	
4015	Contribution Income - Temp		10000.00
	Totals	10000.00	10000.00

EXHIBIT 10.7 Posting to Record Various Hotline-Related Expenses

Entry created by the Cash Disbursements software

Entry Date 12/31/20x5   Various Hotline related expenses are recorded

Account	Description	Debit	Credit
(various)	Hotline expenses	10000.00	
1010	Cash in bank - Operating		10000.00
	Totals	10000.00	10000.00

EXHIBIT 10.8 Journal Entry to Reclassify a Temporarily Restricted Net Asset

General Journal Entry

Journal Entry Date 12/31/20x5   To reclassify a temp. restricted net asset as unrestric

Account	Description	Debit	Credit
6901	Temp. Restricted Net Asset	10000.00	
6902	Unrestricted Net Asset relea		10000.00
	Totals	10000.00	10000.00

met. The purpose of this entry is to transfer the previously recorded income from a temporarily restricted net asset to an unrestricted net asset.

Recall the accounting equation:

assets – liabilities = (previous net assets balance + revenues – expenses)

The income recorded in 20x4 was temporarily restricted; using the accounting equation, it became a part of the temporarily restricted net assets of the organization in that year. When the accounting equation is applied to the entry in Exhibit 10.8, the temporarily restricted net assets are reduced, and the unrestricted net assets are increased, transferring the net assets to reflect the fact that the donor's conditions have been met. No additional income is recorded because no new income was earned; only the character of the income was changed by events.

The underlying character of the hotline contribution was originally recorded with the temporary restrictions. When the conditions specified by the donor were satisfied, the restricted nature of the funds changed, and the new underlying character is reflected by the reclassification of the net asset.

Summary

The month-end close and account analysis functions are an important part of the accounting system. Tracking assets, liabilities and net assets involves taking a second look at transactions. The first look occurs as the transaction is recorded; the second look happens through the detailed account analysis of the balance sheet accounts. Every account balance represents something real; the numbers on the trial balance are not simply totals. Each account balance can be independently verified by the bookkeeper through the account analysis process. Account analysis takes on different forms, depending on the account being analyzed. Using the traceability of the accounting system, the bookkeeper can substantiate that the accounting system information is accurate and reliable.

CHAPTER 11 Allocating Costs

M ost nonprofits run more than a single program or offer more than one service to their clients. While costs associated with a single program or service are easy to identify and record, how do you record a cost that represents money spent on several programs or activities, or money spent by the organization that is not associated with any program at all?

This is a key area you need to discuss and plan with your organization's program staff and auditor. In performing the audit, your auditor must review allocation methods to determine their correctness in accordance with accounting principles and regulations defined in your grant agreements or contracts with funding sources. It is also important to consider the funding realities: a grant can fund multiple programs, and multiple grants can fund a single program.

Allocation Challenges

Costs incurred for several programs *(direct costs)* must be allocated to those programs using some reasonable basis. Costs incurred by the organization's administration and other support functions *(general and management costs)* might be allocated to all of the programs and activities of the organization (using some reasonable basis) for various reporting purposes.

Form 990 Allocations

IRS Form 990 and related forms require that costs be categorized as *program services, management and general,* or *fundraising;* within each category, the actual expense item is detailed. This information is also needed in more detail for organizations that prepare a schedule of functional expenses as supplemental information in their annual audit. This is a complicated yet critical topic for nonprofit organizations. This chapter introduces the concepts; your auditor can provide further guidance based on the organization's grant contracts and activities.

An example of a cost incurred for several programs would be the salary of a counselor who works part of the day with an after-school workshop and works the balance of the day in the teenage hotline program. Using the counselor's time records, it is easy to calculate the actual cost incurred by each program. The cost is allocated using the actual hours worked on each program.

Another example is the consumption of office supplies by the same two programs. In this case, the cost of performing an actual calculation far outweighs the benefit of knowing the office supply cost so precisely. Another method of allocating the cost will be used.

Senior management, central accounting, and the purchasing department are all examples of costs that might be allocated to all programs and activities. The allocation of these costs is done for the purpose of creating specialized reports for management or for a funding source.

A rule for effective cost allocations is to charge directly as many costs as possible. This makes it easier to adhere to OMB Circular A-122 (Cost Principles for Non-profit Organizations), which sets the rules for government grants and cost-reimbursement contracts. Directly charging expenses also reduces the amount of time and effort necessary to allocate costs. For example, have each program identify its office supply needs. Issue separate purchase orders to the vendor for each program. Require the vendor to invoice each program's purchase order separately. Using procedures to help the accounting department to post transactions directly to the program, department, or other cost center is more accurate and efficient than developing and applying any allocation technique.

Your organization's chart of account structure provides you with accounts where you can post costs directly to individual programs, as well as expense accounts that belong to no single program or activity (often called *common* or *shared* expenses). These accounts will be allocated at the end of the accounting period using a method designed specifically for the expense type.

If your organization receives any local, state, or federal funding, you should carefully research the accounting and record-keeping requirements mandated by the funding source. Some funding sources place a cap on overhead expenses; other sources do not allow certain expenses. If an expense is over the limit or not allowed, the funding source will not pay for it, and the funds will have to come from an unrestricted source of funds for the activity. It is imperative that the financial and operational staff understand the contract with the funding source. (Resource F of this book contains a checklist that is useful when your organization receives government grant funds.)

Specific cost principles issued by the OMB (Circular No. A-122) define allowable and non-allowable costs for federally funded organizations. (The entire document is available online; Resource G of this book has excerpts of A-122 to provide some insight into those cost principles.) Many states adopt the rules in A-122 as the basis for their own regulations, with certain modifications unique to the state, which are usually more restrictive.

The grant document and contract you negotiate with the funding source will generally govern. With careful negotiation, it is possible to get reimbursement for a cost that A-122 says is normally non-allowable; it is also possible for a necessary cost to be disallowed because the grant documents did not specifically identify the cost.

Occasionally a funding source will allow a normally unallowable cost in a specific budget. Check with your grant contract officer for more information. The opposite is also possible. Costs normally allowed by agency ABC might be expressly prohibited by agency DEF. Always read your grant agreement (which is a contract) and thoroughly understand your grant requirements.

Another important set of rules is found in OMB Circular No. A-87 (Cost Principles for State, Local, and Indian Tribal Governments). Despite the title, this circular contains concepts that serve as guidance about acceptable methods of cost allocation for a wide range of agencies. A-87 contains information on developing cost allocation plans. (Obtain a copy of these documents from http://www.whitehouse.gov/omb.) it is important to become familiar with the rules that affect your organization. Various funding sources also have their own interpretations of these circulars; it is important to understand the rules as applied by your funding source.

Allocation Methods

The allocation method chosen for a given cost needs to be rational and consistently applied. Selecting a reasonable allocation base is the first step in the process. Some typical allocation bases are listed in Exhibit 11.1.

The key to allocating administrative and overhead costs successfully is having a rational and justifiable written cost allocation plan. This plan should be developed with two goals in mind:

1. To approximate the true cost of running the program or activity

2. To maximize cost reimbursement from the funding source (Funding sources are more likely to support allocated program costs if they are clearly shown to be an integral part of the program.)

The cost allocation plan should be in writing, and it should be reviewed once a year for any necessary modifications required by changes in circumstances, such as a change in funding sources or a move to a new location.

EXHIBIT 11.1   **Sample Cost Allocation Methods**

Cost/Expense	Base/Method
Fringe Benefits	Total Salaries
Rent and Utilities	Total Square Footage
Vehicle Costs	Total Miles Recorded in a Log Identifying the Driver, Mileage, Purpose, and Specific Program of Activity
Management Salaries	Specific Management Time by Program
Telephone Expense	Separate Phone Lines or (if available) Logs Created by Telephone System Software

Once the cost allocation plan has been devised, the bookkeeper's job is to distinguish between costs using an actual method of allocation, such as the counselor's salary example, and those costs that will be allocated using some other reasonable method.

Depending on the allocation method used for a transaction, the cost allocation can take place at the time the transaction is recorded or at some later date (normally at the end of the interim accounting period).

Actual Allocation

When posting a transaction, the costs that can be allocated using the actual method are posted to their respective account codes. In Exhibit 11.2, time records provide the method of calculating gross pay per program (hours worked on a program divided by the total hours worked).

Fixed Allocation Method

Costs that are allocated by a fixed percentage of the cost category are posted to the series of expense codes when the original transaction is recorded. In Exhibit 11.3, rent expense is allocated based on a written analysis of the square footage actually used by each program or activity.

EXHIBIT 11.2   Actual Allocation Example

Alice Smith, Counselor
Weekly Salary $600

PROGRAM	HOURS	PERCENT	ALLOCATED SALARY
After School Workshop	22	55%	$330
Teenage Hotline	18	45%	$270
Totals	40	100%	$600

EXHIBIT 11.3   Fixed Allocation Method Example

ABC Realty Invoice for Rent $6,000

PROGRAM/COST CENTER	PERCENT	ALLOCATED RENT
After School Workshop	40%	$2,400
Pre-School Program	45%	$2,700
General Administration	15%	$900
Totals	100%	$6,000

Other Allocation Methods

Costs that will be allocated using some method other than actual are typically posted to an expense code not associated with any program (a common or shared expense code), and the total of that expense code is then allocated at the end of an accounting period by way of a general journal entry. In Exhibit 11.4, the auditing fee expense is allocated by the ratio of a program's income to the total income for all programs.

Cost allocation decisions are closely linked to the budget process. As we describe in Chapter Thirteen, the preparation of program and organizationwide budgets is an essential tool in the management of a nonprofit. The allocation methods used to create the budgets should be the same as the allocation methods applied to actual costs.

No matter which allocation method is used for a cost, the method should be written down and applied uniformly to all similar accounting transactions. Documentation of the allocation plan should be updated to reflect any changes. Since allocation plans might be subject to funding source rules, it is important to review the allocation plan to check for funding source requirements and guidelines.

Indirect Cost Allocation

Some government funding sources require a formal indirect cost proposal be prepared and approved to receive specific monies designated as indirect costs. *Indirect costs* are those costs that cannot be easily allocated or assigned to a program. This topic seldom affects smaller nonprofit organizations. (OMB Circulars A-87 and A-122 contain more detailed information.) There are large variations in the use of these plans based on policies of local funding sources in various parts of the country. Discuss this topic with your auditor to find out the policy in your area and for your specific funding sources.

Summary

When your organization has multiple programs or activities, you need a series of methods to allocate any costs not directly assignable to a specific program or activity. The allocation method you use might be different for each cost; the method chosen should

EXHIBIT 11.4   **Example Allocation Based on a Ratio of Income**

Auditing Fee
for the Year Ended 12/31/x5 $9,885

PROGRAM	ANNUAL INCOME	PERCENT	ALLOCATED AUDIT FEE
After School Workshop	$161,000	38.20%	$3,776
Teenage Hotline	$53,000	12.57%	$1,243
Pre-School Program	$207,500	49.23%	$4,866
Totals	$421,500	100.00%	$9,885

be selected using some reasonable, justifiable basis, and it should be applied consistently from period to period and among similar cost categories. The financial management of the organization should ask the auditors to review the cost allocation plan to ensure it is in accordance with the standards the auditors will use in performing their audit.

The bookkeeper must be familiar with the allocation process and with the cost allocation plan, since the posting of transactions correctly depends upon the accurate use of the appropriate allocation method. Accounting software often has the ability to automate the cost allocation process for those costs that can be allocated with predetermined ratios.

This concludes our look at how you record transactions correctly the first time.

PART THREE

Putting It All Together

E arly in this book, we stated the primary goal for the bookkeeper:

> To capture each transaction one time in a way that is fully documented, completely traceable, and fully usable by every person within and outside the organization who has a stake in the organization.

We have examined the accounting and bookkeeping processes needed to accomplish this goal, and we have explored the methods and techniques that can be used to accomplish the goal efficiently and cost effectively.

In this section, we discuss how the information will be used. Financial statements, budgets, and cash flow forecasting all begin with accounting information. A well-designed and well-maintained accounting system produces timely and accurate information, which is the basis for financial reporting, budgeting, and cash flow forecasting. The following chapters provide some insight into how the information in the accounting books can be analyzed and used by financial management. In most organizations, one part of the bookkeeper's job is to assist in the preparation of the reports discussed in these three chapters. Even if the reporting function is handled by someone else, bookkeepers should understand the basic concepts of financial reporting, budgeting, and cash flow.

CHAPTER 12

Financial Statements

How do most people (within and outside the organization) use financial information? While the accounting data are available in many forms that can be used for a variety of purposes, the most recognizable format is the *financial statement*. Financial statements are prepared by the accounting department for use by interested parties. A Certified Public Accountant or a CPA firm will provide one of three levels of service:

1. *Audit*—the highest level of assurance, based on testing and analysis of transactions according to professional guidelines

2. *Review*—a lower level of assurance, based on analysis of account balances according to professional guidelines

3. *Compilation*—presents management's financial statements based on minimum amounts of inquiry

Level of Assurance

The opinion letter or report letter issued by the CPA that accompanies the financial statements will specify the level of assurance; it will also address any matters the CPA considers serious enough to call to the attention of the reader. The level of assurance provided by the CPA is determined by the management of the organization. Management's decision is often dictated by state statutes that mandate, depending on the size of the organization, one of the three levels of assurance just described. You need to check your own state's laws. Some states require no annual filings unless you are a private foundation, and other states require annual filings and varying levels of CPA attestation regarding financial statements if your organization has a certain amount of assets and income. In addition, federal, state, and county funding sources might require audits prepared according to auditing standards established by the GAO (the auditing arm of congress). These auditing standards are more complex than the generally accepted auditing standards (GAAS) promulgated by the American Institute of Certified Public Accountants (AICPA).

If you receive federal funding, your organization might be required to be audited in accordance with Government Auditing Standards (GAS), also known as Yellow

Book. If your federal funding exceeds $500,000 in total, or if state statute requires it, your organization might need to be audited in accordance with OMB Circular A-133 (Audits of States, Local Governments, and Non-Profit Organizations). A-133 adds an enormous amount of compliance testing to the audit process.

You need to make sure the auditor you engage is experienced in working with nonprofit organizations both in auditing and in taxation. In addition, special audit standards, disclosures, and/or special audit schedules might be dictated by your grant agreements.

Another factor in determining the level of assurance is that nonprofit organizations are especially vulnerable to bad publicity. Donors and funding sources, such as foundations and government agencies, do not like to give money to organizations that are making headlines because they were defrauded by a bookkeeper or an executive director or board member.

As we have described repeatedly, the method used to record transactions presents the user of the information with two views: (1) the snapshot view of the organization and (2) the history view of how the organization got to this point.

Financial Statement Providing the Snapshot View

The financial statement that presents the snapshot view is called the *statement of financial position* (commonly referred to as a *balance sheet*), a picture of the organization's assets and liabilities at a single point in time. The name comes from the fact that the total of assets will always equal the total of liabilities and net assets—the two totals balance (as we know based on our discussion of the accounting equation). Exhibit 12.1 is an example of a statement of financial position for a nonprofit organization, showing all three types of net assets for two years.

Working Capital

Working Capital is an important indicator of financial health that is calculated using the statement of financial position. It is defined as current assets minus current liabilities. *Current* is defined as those assets that can be converted into cash in one year and liabilities that need to be paid within one year. It is an important and valuable computation. Current assets normally include cash, accounts receivable, short-term investments, prepaid expenses, and inventory. Current liabilities include accounts payable, accrued expenses, and the portion of loans or capital equipment leases due within one year. The bookkeeper should be aware of the computation and compare it to the organization's annual cash inflow and cash outflow. For example if net cash outflow is $8,000 a month, and working capital is $24,000, then the organization could theoretically survive three months if no new working capital were created. Depending on your organization's size and composition of income, the right amount of working capital can vary. If the organization receives grants from reliable government sources,

EXHIBIT 12.1 **Sample Statement of Financial Position**

ABC NONPROFIT
STATEMENTS OF FINANCIAL POSITION
DECEMBER 31, 20x5 AND 20x4

ASSETS	20x5	20x4
Current Assets:		
Cash	$195,169	$37,589
Contributions Receivable	37,950	38,820
Accounts Receivable	115,797	148,124
Prepaid Expenses	61,425	27,818
Total Current Assets	410,341	252,351
Long-Term Investments—Unrestricted	0	65,934
Long-Term Investments—Permanently Restricted	834,680	1,000,000
Security Deposits	2,290	2,200
Promises to Give	316,075	95,281
Furniture and Equipment (At Cost)—Net of Accumulated Depreciation of $46,548 in 20X5 and $40,590 in 20X4	16,083	20,047
TOTAL ASSETS	**$1,579,469**	**$1,435,813**

LIABILITIES AND NET ASSETS		
Current Liabilities:		
Accounts Payable and Accrued Expenses	$56,324	$24,988
Vacation Pay	12,004	14,054
Refundable Advances	0	106,250
Total Current Liabilities	68,328	145,292
Net Assets:		
Unrestricted Net Assets:		
Operations	68,544	211,562
Fixed Assets	16,083	20,047
Total Unrestricted Net Assets	84,627	231,609
Temporarily Restricted Net Assets	426,514	58,912
Permanently Restricted Net Assets	1,000,000	1,000,000
Total Net Assets	1,511,141	1,290,521
TOTAL LIABILITIES AND NET ASSETS	**$1,579,469**	**$1,435,813**

then working capital is not a major concern if programs are being run according to their respective budgets. If the organization relies on donations for a big chunk of cash inflow, then you need more working capital, since donations can be affected by a number of factors, such as a bad economy; you cannot pay staff with unpaid pledges. In the example statement of financial position, working capital equals $342,013 as of December 31, 20x5, which is total current assets of $410,341 less current liabilities of $68,328.

Financial Statements Providing the History View

The history view is provided primarily by two financial statements: (1) the *statement of support, revenue, and expenses and changes in net assets* and (2) the *statement of cash flows*. Both of these financial statements tie into the balance sheet:

- The *statement of support, revenue, and expenses* and *changes in net assets* (often called an *income statement* or a *profit and loss statement* in the for-profit world) presents the summary of transactions for the accounting period that resulted in a change in net assets from the beginning of the period to the end of the period. The ending net assets total matches the net assets total on the balance sheet.
- The *statement of cash flows* presents the summary of transactions for the accounting period that resulted in a change in cash and cash equivalents from the beginning of the period to the end of the period. The ending cash and cash equivalents total matches the cash and cash equivalents total on the balance sheet.

Exhibit 12.2 shows an example of the statement of support, revenue and expenses and changes in net assets. Exhibit 12.3 shows an example of the statement of cash flows.

Other Financial Statements

We are also including a financial statement containing information similar to Part II of Form 990. Depending on your classification as a nonprofit organization, your auditor might need to include the *statement of functional expenses* as part of the supplementary information of your audit report. Even if your organization does not need to include this statement, we think it is an excellent report to prepare for internal purposes, and it is needed for proper preparation of Form 990. The statement of functional expenses (Exhibit 12.4), which reports the amount of money your organization spends on each major activity and fundraising and management costs, is valuable since donors and funding sources can see how their money is being utilized.

In addition to the traditional financial statements, there are many variations of ways to present and use the accounting information. Chapter Fourteen includes some examples of financial reports organizations have used to better monitor their finances.

EXHIBIT 12.2 Sample Statement of Support, Revenue, and Expense

ABC NONPROFIT
STATEMENT OF SUPPORT, REVENUE AND EXPENSES
FOR THE YEAR ENDED DECEMBER 31, 20x5
WITH SUMMARIZED COMPARATIVE TOTALS FOR THE YEAR ENDED DECEMBER 31, 20x4

	Unrestricted			Temporarily Restricted	Permanently Restricted	20x5 Total	20x4 Total
	Operations	Fixed Assets	Total				
SUPPORT AND REVENUE:							
Support:							
Contributions	$566,964	$ —	$566,964	$396,514	$ —	$963,478	$530,214
Use of Contributed Facilities	105,000	—	105,000	—	—	105,000	105,000
Contributed Personnel	175,000	—	175,000	—	—	175,000	100,000
Contributed Professional Services	493,500	—	493,500	—	—	493,500	11,000
Total Support	1,340,464	—	1,340,464	396,514	—	1,736,978	746,214
Revenue:							
Conference Registration Fees	153,658	—	153,658	—	—	153,658	147,124
Publication Royalties	267,090	—	267,090	—	—	267,090	197,259
Investment Income	24,672	—	24,672	—	—	24,672	68,088
Unrealized Gains on Long-Term Investments	—	—	—	—	—	—	20,560
Other Income	5,863	—	5,863	—	—	5,863	16,061
Total Revenue	451,283	—	451,283	—	—	451,283	449,092
Net Assets Released from Restrictions	28,912	—	28,912	(28,912)	—	—	—
TOTAL SUPPORT AND REVENUE	1,820,659	—	1,820,659	367,602	—	2,188,261	1,195,306
EXPENSES:							
Program Activity and Development	1,671,244	4,392	1,675,636	—	—	1,675,636	905,786
General and Administrative	247,051	1,144	248,195	—	—	248,195	213,195
Fundraising	43,387	423	43,810	—	—	43,810	123,513
Total Expenses	1,961,682	5,959	1,967,641	—	—	1,967,641	1,242,494
Change in Net Assets	(141,023)	(5,959)	(146,982)	367,602	—	220,620	(47,188)
Net Assets, January 1,	211,562	20,047	231,609	58,912	1,000,000	1,290,521	1,337,709
Capital Acquisitions	(1,995)	1,995	—	—	—	—	—
Net Assets, December 31	$68,544	$16,083	$84,627	$426,514	$1,000,000	$1,511,141	$1,290,521

EXHIBIT 12.3   Sample Statement of Cash Flows

ABC NONPROFIT
STATEMENT OF CASH FLOWS
FOR THE YEAR ENDED DECEMBER 31, 20x5

Cash Flows from Operating Activities:

Change in Net Assets	$220,620
Adjustments to Reconcile Change in Net Assets	
to Net Cash (Used) for Operating Activities:	
Depreciation	5,959
Decrease in Contributions Receivable	870
Decrease in Accounts Receivable	32,327
(Increase) in Prepaid Expenses	(9,743)
(Increase) in Promises to Give	(244,658)
(Increase) in Security Deposits	(90)
Increase in Accounts Payable and Accrued Expenses	31,336
(Decrease) in Vacation Pay	(2,050)
(Decrease) in Refundable Advances	(98,318)
Net Cash (Used) for Operating Activities	(63,747)

Cash Flows from Investing Activities:

Sale of Investments	223,322
Purchase of Equipment	(1,995)
Net Cash Provided by Investing Activities	221,327
Net Increase in Cash	157,580
Cash—January 1, 20x5	37,589
Cash—December 31, 20x5	$195,169

Supplemental Data:

Interest Paid	0

EXHIBIT 12.4 Sample Statement of Functional Expenses

ABC NONPROFIT

SCHEDULE OF FUNCTIONAL EXPENSES

FOR THE YEAR ENDED DECEMBER 31, 20x5

WITH SUMMARIZED COMPARATIVE TOTALS FOR THE YEAR ENDED DECEMBER 31, 20x4

	Pre-School Program	Elderly Services	Teenage Hotline	Total Program Activity and Development	General and Administrative	Fundraising	20x5 Total	20x4 Total
Salaries	$131,246	$141,851	$58,331	$331,428	$101,210	$27,285	$459,923	$404,162
Payroll Taxes and Fringe Benefits	19,334	20,896	8,593	48,823	12,754	4,689	66,266	71,085
Non-staff Services	19,045	20,584	8,464	48,093	26,928	1,126	76,147	41,896
Professional Fees	254,500	275,066	113,111	642,677	54,129	–	696,806	91,409
Contributed Facilities Cost	30,095	32,528	13,376	75,999	22,805	6,196	105,000	105,000
Travel	45,118	48,764	20,053	113,935	1,373	3,576	118,884	81,594
Office Expense	7,053	7,624	3,135	17,812	8,810	299	26,921	25,852
Printing	32,034	34,622	14,237	80,893	–	–	80,893	66,677
Dues, Books, and Subscriptions	8,016	8,664	3,563	20,243	4,979	181	25,403	17,875
Conference Expenses	45,536	49,217	20,239	114,992	–	–	114,992	151,301
Awards	28,751	31,074	12,778	72,603	–	–	72,603	47,465
Editorial Expenses	22,422	24,235	9,966	56,623	–	–	56,623	41,296
Other Expenses	18,660	20,169	8,294	47,123	14,063	35	61,221	91,392
Total Expenses Before Depreciation	661,810	715,294	294,140	1,671,244	247,051	43,387	1,961,682	1,237,004
Depreciation	1,739	1,880	773	4,392	1,144	423	5,959	5,490
TOTAL EXPENSES—20x5	$663,549	$717,174	$294,913	$1,675,636	$248,195	$43,810	$1,967,641	
TOTAL EXPENSES—20x4	$358,691	$387,686	$159,409	$905,786	$213,195	$123,513		$1,242,494

Operating Budgets

Effective operating budgets are the first financial planning steps necessary after preparing your mission statement. Good budgets are the starting point in planning and managing your organization. Accurate and carefully prepared operating budgets must be developed for effective financial management. They must reflect reality based on the operational plans that resulted from the creation of your mission statement. *The Budget-Building Book for Nonprofits* (Dropkin and La Touche, 1998) provides specific instruction on how to develop budgeting processes that result in effective operating budgets. This chapter attempts to touch on key points raised in that book.

There are a lot of ideas identified in this chapter about budgeting. Depending on the size of your organization, you might only need to adopt some budget policies and use a small team to complete the entire budget. If you are a larger organization you might find you want to follow some of the more agency-wide ideas in the chapter. Budgeting, in our experience, is very different at various organizations. We hope you read the chapter carefully and then decide, based on your organization's size and needs, which strategies, policies, and team members to include in creating your budget. Remember, good budgets will make financial monitoring and reporting more effective. If we were asked to name the three foundations of good financial management, they would be (1) good budgeting, (2) good cash flow management, and (3) good bookkeeping.

Operating Budgets: Basic Concepts

Keep in mind while reading this chapter that the best operational budgeting is based on accrual-basis accounting. Using an accrual basis of accounting means that items are recorded as income for a fiscal period even though they were not actually received in that fiscal period—as long as they were earned during that period and legally belong to the organization. The money earned but not yet received is a receivable. Similarly, in an accrual-basis accounting system, items of expense are recorded in a fiscal period even when they are not actually paid during that fiscal period. Those items expensed but not yet paid are referred to as *accounts payable, accrued expenses,* or by other names, depending on the organization. We are writing this book for smaller organizations that we understand have limited time and resources to maintain financial records. The smallest nonprofit organizations might be able to operate on a cash basis, ignoring accrual accounting, although GAAP require your auditor at year end to report on an accrual basis. Computer accounting software is readily available to assist your organization. We recommend you keep your books and do your interim financial reports on the accrual system of accounting. It is well worth the extra effort.

Developing operating budgets is not a topic that can be adequately covered in one chapter. The following sections include:

- An overview of budgeting

- An introduction to some budget-building strategies

- An explanation of how to create a budgeting calendar

- A discussion of how to develop budgeting goals, guidelines, policies, and procedures

Overview of Budgeting

If we were limited to making only three overriding statements about the operational-budgeting process, they would be the following:

1. The budget must be based on a sound and clearly defined strategic plan.

2. The budgeting process must involve extensive collaboration.

3. The budget must be monitored on an ongoing basis.

In the area of collaboration, budgeting should be inclusive, bringing together the perspectives and interests of a wide variety of groups: the board, clients, management, staff, volunteers, prospective donors and income sources, and (when applicable) the general public. At the outset of the budget process, input from all relevant parties (stakeholders) should be sought. The approved budget should clearly and effectively communicate to the entire organization the priorities, goals, and operational plans that will advance the underlying strategic plan.

Budgeting as a dynamic process is also an important concept. Budgeting should not occur in a vacuum or for a limited period, producing a document that is never used effectively. Ongoing monitoring, data gathering and analysis, budget assumptions and revisions, and consideration of alternatives are needed.

Functions of Nonprofit Budgeting

Budgeting performs a number of important functions. Effective budgeting helps an organization to accomplish the following:

- Adjust plans, activities, and spending as needed

- Spend money cost-effectively

- Reach specific financial goals

- Prevent adverse audit findings

- Avoid incurring disallowed costs or other unnecessary expenses
- Act as a foundation for effective cash flow management

The clearer, more accurate, and better thought-out a budget is in the beginning, the more likely it is that the budget will successfully perform these functions.

Well-prepared budgets have other benefits too. They let everyone in the organization know:

- The goals to be achieved
- The work to be done to reach the goals
- The resources (people and things) needed to get the work done
- The resources available for getting the work done
- The timetable and deadlines for getting specific work done
- The individuals responsible and accountable for doing the required work

Additional functions that budgets serve for well-managed nonprofits include the following:

- Budgets provide the financial and operational guidance needed to successfully implement board policies and directives.
- Budgets allow management to measure and guide the nonprofit's immediate and long-term financial health and operational effectiveness.
- Budgets guide a nonprofit's acquisition and use of resources.
- Budgets anticipate expenses and identify income to pay for those expenses.
- Budgets are tools for controlling spending and avoiding deficits.
- Budgets help integrate all of the organization's activities.
- Budgets enable management to monitor actual income and expenses against those that were budgeted in order to assess the nonprofit's overall financial situation and to alter plans as needed.
- Budgets can serve as the basis for performance reviews and, in some cases, as compensation criteria.

Roles and Responsibilities in Nonprofit Budgeting

The roles people play in budgeting generally depend on a nonprofit's size, structure, and income sources. In general, budgets are best developed collaboratively, using the skills and knowledge of those involved at a number of levels. However, because creating a budget might involve sensitive or confidential issues, individuals involved in the budgeting process might need to be trained in their budget roles so they better understand what is expected of them.

The following descriptions identify the roles people in various positions in the organization might play in the budgeting process. Budgeting roles and responsibilities should be spelled out in written budgeting policies and procedures, which should be kept up to date and must be understood by those involved.

The Board of Directors. The board's role can vary according to its members' willingness and ability to commit time and effort to budgeting. Some boards are deeply involved and participate in planning the annual budget strategy and guidelines, draft budget analysis, and final approval. Other boards might rely more on management, effectively restricting the board's role in budgeting to budget review and approval. In addition, boards might designate a finance or budget committee with the specific responsibility of building the budget and monitoring performance against it.

Overall, the board is legally responsible for ensuring that budgets meet applicable laws and regulations, are fiscally sound, and further the nonprofit's tax-exempt purpose. Fulfilling this role generally involves the following:

- Developing and reviewing the nonprofit's mission statement and its specific goals and activities for achieving the mission
- Creating a statement of strategic program and service priorities to guide decisions about resource allocation during the budget process
- Establishing general budget policies, such as:

    Requirements for a balanced budget

    Policies on the use of cash reserves

    Decisions about salary increases, hiring, layoffs, new programs, capital projects, and major fundraising efforts or capital campaigns

- Reviewing and formally approving the budget
- Reviewing financial and narrative reports on budget implementation on a regular basis and planning for any needed corrective action

If possible, the board's review of budget reports should include a comparison against external or competitive benchmarks. For example, a child-care organization would want to ascertain how much it costs similar organizations to feed a child in day care for one week to determine the accuracy of this budgeted item.

The Executive Director or CEO. The executive director (ED) or CEO plays a sustained role in the budgeting process, usually being responsible for the following:

- Arranging and staffing any early strategic planning sessions with the board
- Preparing options and recommendations to guide budget development
- Ensuring that the budgeting schedule is met
- Reviewing draft budgets and making decisions regarding resource allocation
- Presenting the recommended budget to the board, explaining its provisions and possible consequences, and answering the board's questions

Depending on the size of the nonprofit and its staff, the ED or CEO might delegate many budgeting tasks to the CFO or other managers. However, the CEO always is responsible for ensuring that the budget is accurate, that it adheres to board policies, and that it is submitted on time for board review and approval. The ED or CEO is ultimately responsible for the organization's achievement of budgeted goals.

Once the budget has been approved, the ED or CEO is responsible for working with the CFO to implement it, which involves the following:

- Communicating the approved budget to management and communicating the approved budget to management and line staff so they understand it clearly

- Monitoring financial operations on an ongoing basis to compare actual income and expenses to those budgeted

- Identifying negative or positive deviations from the budget and determining what caused the variances

- Recommending or reviewing action plans to correct negative deviations and to capitalize on positive deviations.

Finally, the ED or CEO is responsible for communicating the results of financial monitoring and corrective action to the board and seeking its input and approval for needed fiscal or program changes.

The Finance Department. The representative or staff from the finance department will vary based on the size of the organization. In a large organization, the CFO plays a major and sustained role, often having day-to-day responsibility for coordinating budget development, implementation, and monitoring. In a smaller organization, the bookkeeper would play that role as the person most knowledgeable about the organization's financial records. Typically, the representative from the finance department (whatever the title) would perform the following tasks:

- Create a budget development calendar and ensure that deadlines are met

- Communicate budgeting policies and procedures to managers and line staff

- Establish a format for draft budgets

- Develop income and expense forecasts based on reviews of external economic and competitive trends when applicable

- Collaborate in setting expense and income targets in line with strategic plans for programs or units

- Evaluate draft budgets from program or unit managers for accuracy, reasonableness, adherence to applicable guidelines, and availability of anticipated resources

- Discuss draft budgets with the CEO and other managers as needed

- Make recommendations for reducing, increasing, or reallocating requested resources
- Prepare the budget document, in some cases helping present it to the board once the CEO's budget decisions are made

After the budget is approved, normally the bookkeeper is responsible for implementing financial reporting and monitoring, including preparing and analyzing budgeted versus actual income and expense reports for management and board use and overseeing any corrective actions needed.

Program, Unit, or Activity Managers. The proactive involvement of program, unit, or activity managers is essential to developing budgets that accurately reflect reality. Program managers are often the most knowledgeable on current program needs and the costs and effects of reducing or expanding operations. Program managers might also be able to supply the most relevant information when nonprofits are developing budgets for new programs or activities.

Ideally, program and unit managers are responsible for developing draft budgets for their areas, which can involve consulting other staff to evaluate current or new programs, operating costs, and staff and equipment needs. When it comes to carrying out budgets, program and unit managers often are in the best position to make decisions about resource allocation or recommend changes in activities to meet budgeted expense or income targets. All too frequently, organizations overlook the importance of input from program or unit managers and do not include them in the budgeting team.

Program or unit managers might also be responsible for assessing the costs of continuing or expanding current programs, as well as creating new programs or making modifications to conform to budget policies. In addition, they might meet with the bookkeeper and CEO to review draft budgets and explore options for change. This is a very important step in the budgeting process for future cash flow planning, as reviewing actual performance will give managers an opportunity to assess the accuracy of their ideas and modify cash flow planning accordingly.

After program and unit managers are informed about approved program budgets, they, in turn, inform staff about any budget or operational changes. They also review regular financial reports, monitor income and expenses, and help develop and implement corrective action plans for their specific areas of responsibility.

Other Possible Participants. Depending on the nature of the organization and its management style, a number of others might be involved in budgeting, including:

- Clerical support staff, who must prepare various documents and materials throughout the budgeting process and who need to understand the tasks required of them

- Consultants and outside specialists, such as independent auditors and accountants, architects, engineers, bond counsel, and specialists in program areas, who also need to know their roles and assignments

- Selected clients and volunteers, who often can provide beneficial ideas and input to improve budgets (and whose involvement or budget approval might be required by certain funding sources)

- Information systems staff, who might be called on to prepare special reports or otherwise analyze, provide, or integrate data

Budgeting Strategies

Effective budget development depends on having clearly defined strategies for the budgeting process. Nonprofits should clearly define their budget development strategies and communicate them to unit and program heads. This concept helps build wide support for budget decisions and avoids time-consuming conflicts and adjustments in the future. Unclear or uncontrolled budget development is likely to create implementation problems. The following subsections present four strategies that can help increase the accuracy and efficiency of budget development:

1. Setting annual organizational outcome goals from the top down to guide development of draft program and unit budgets

2. Setting annual income and expense targets from the top down to guide development of draft program and unit budgets

3. Requesting draft budgets from program and unit heads that show priorities for increased, decreased, and unchanged total budget amounts

4. Zero-based budgeting

The first two strategies favor top-down approaches to budget development and thus tend to limit program or unit heads' input. The second two strategies emphasize bottom-up approaches and thus tend to provide program and unit managers with more input. Each strategy has its own strengths and weaknesses, and elements of each can be combined to suit an organization's needs and style. The subsections that follow discuss each of these four strategies and provide worksheets to guide their planning and use.

Setting Annual Organizational Outcome Goals from the Top Down

This strategy calls for top management to consult with program and unit managers and appropriate staff before any initial draft budgets are developed.

Defining the overall organization's or specific programs' measurable outcome goals in advance provides a framework for managers and board members to make sure that (1) specific draft budgets and plans for the coming year actively support and further the established outcome goals and (2) that everyone involved has a clear understanding of what needs to be done.

Top management must assess what resources will be available for the next fiscal year based on the most recent income and expense figures and projections, as well as the outcome goals for the coming year. (The outcome goals might apply to the nonprofit as a whole or to individual programs or activities.)

To be effective, the outcome goals must be both specific and measurable. Many nonprofits require quantifiable performance measures or performance indicators that will demonstrate achievement of specific outcome goals. Quantifiable outcome goals have the added benefit of being useful as a basis for ongoing performance reporting. Following are examples of outcome goals and performance measures:

- Sample Outcome Goals

    Increase the number of weatherized owner-occupied housing units from 350 to 475 over a twelve-month period

    Reduce the average per-unit monthly heating cost by 5 percent

- Sample Performance Measures

    The actual number of housing units weatherized

    Actual reductions in monthly heating costs based on a comparison of heating bills for the same month of the year before and after services were provided

- Sample Outcome Goals

    Develop and implement a model employment skills training program by June 1st of the next fiscal year

    Provide training in the next twelve months to 250 low-income unemployed persons to improve their chances of job placement

    Place at least 65 percent of the target population in full-time jobs within two months of completing training

- Sample Performance Measures

    Implementation of the program by the specified date

    Number of clients enrolled in and completing training

    Number of clients employed two months after training

With this strategy, the specified outcome goals become the basis for program or unit managers to develop their draft budgets. Outcome goals and performance measures also contribute to the coming year's overall operating plan, providing a clear statement of what the overall organization intends to achieve and how results will be measured.

Use the worksheet in Exhibit 13.1 to plan when and how to carry out this top-down strategy.

1. List top management's initial ideas for the coming year's outcome goals to recommend to the board. (Consult the organization's written mission statement in developing them.)

2. List when and how top management will present their initial outcome-goal ideas to program and unit managers.

3. List when top management will discuss their outcome goals and get input from unit managers. (Gain input before deciding on final recommendations to the board, to get additional viewpoints, facilitate buy-in, and help unite people behind final decisions.)

4. After discussion with and input from unit heads, list top management's revised recommendations to the board for the coming year's organizational outcome goals. (State desired outcome goals clearly and specifically in order of priority.)

5. List the organization's final, board-approved outcome goals for the coming year. (Again, state them clearly and specifically in order of priority.)

These are some follow-through actions required of those managing the budgeting process:

- Management should include the year's board-approved goals in the package for developing draft budgets to be distributed to applicable unit heads.

- Unit heads must make sure their units' draft budgets include a brief narrative explaining how continuing activities, new initiatives, or proposed changes in their draft budgets will contribute to the nonprofit's overall goals for the coming year.

- In deciding on the final budget, top management and board members should use the narrative explanations in each draft budget to help assess the potential merits and contributions of each to the nonprofit's goals for the coming year.

Setting Annual Income and Expense Targets from the Top Down

Under this top-down budget development strategy, top management first sets expense and income targets for the coming year for the organization as a whole and each individual unit. In this way, units know in advance the income that is available (and the income they are expected to generate) during the coming year. Then each unit can develop a draft budget based on the income and expense targets.

Use the checklist in Exhibit 13.2 to plan when and how to carry out this top-down strategy.

Requesting Draft Budgets from Program and Unit Heads That Show Priorities

This strategy calls for each unit head to prepare three draft budgets for the coming year based on a range of percentage variations determined by top management and the board. There are three steps:

| EXHIBIT 13.2 | Worksheet for Setting Annual Top-Down Income and Expense Targets to Guide Development of Draft Program/Unit Budgets |

1. Top management forms a working group. [List the members of the working group, along with target dates for completion.]

2. The working group creates the following:

   a. Reasonably reliable projections of unavoidable (that is, a bare-bones estimate) expenses and desirable or hoped-for expense increases for the organization as a whole

   b. A projection of income fairly certain to be received and one of income likely to be received, again for the entire organization

3. The working group summarizes the fiscal position of the nonprofit as a whole for next year, using the group's expense and income projections as a basis.

4. The working group recommends expense and income targets for all programs, units and activities, based on estimated resources and expenses.

5. Top management reviews the working group's assumptions, calculations and targets, makes changes as appropriate, and submits them to the board. (Having the board approve income and expense targets can help avoid potential conflict among managers.)

6. Top management then clearly communicates board-approved income and expense targets to managers and unit heads in the package of information on developing draft budgets.

1. Top management decides what the percentage of variation should be between the three total draft budgets. For instance, one is unchanged from this year's total, one is 3 percent higher, and one is 3 percent lower. (In any given year, all three draft budgets might reflect differing rates of decreases, or increases, or whatever combination top management and the board call for.)

2. Each unit head prepares the three draft budgets to reflect the unit's priorities and includes a brief summary in each draft budget of the likely impact the specific changes will have on the unit's operations.

3. Top management and the board adjust each unit's draft budget up or down, depending on the most up-to-date understanding of the coming year's income and expenses, and informed by each unit's perspective on change.

The budget team should use the worksheet in Exhibit 13.3 to help plan, introduce, coordinate, and monitor the use of this approach.

Implementing Zero-Based Budgeting

Zero-based budgeting (ZBB) focuses on the thorough reevaluation of each of an organization's programs, units, and activities to determine if it should be continued (and, if so, how) and included in the next budget. The ZBB process requires that management justify the existence of every facet of the organization; essentially, ZBB has no built-in assumptions or automatically included items.

EXHIBIT 13.3	Worksheet for Program/Unit Heads to Prepare Three Draft Budgets

1. List the percentage variation from this year's unit budget total that top management decides each program or unit head must include in their three draft budgets for the coming year:

   A. A total of _____ percent more than this year's unit budget

   B. A total of _____ percent less than this year's unit budget

   C. The same total amount as this year's unit budget

Elements of Zero-Based Budgeting. Those using ZBB are starting the budgeting process from zero (as opposed to using prior budgetary figures to build on in creating the next budget). Another way to think of ZBB is that the process demands an answer to the question, If we were not already doing this, knowing what we know now, would we still choose to do it?

Managers must address more specific questions as well when beginning a ZBB process:

1. Should a given program, activity, or position be continued, or would other activities be more important or appropriate?

2. If the program, activity, or position is justified, should it continue operating in the same manner, or should it be modified?

3. If modified, how will it be modified, when, and by whom?

4. How much should the organization spend on the program, activity, or position being studied?

The next step in ZBB is to require every segment of the operating unit to do the following:

- Identify the major functions or activities it performs

- Answer the preceding four questions as they pertain to the operating unit

- Create alternatives or options based on the answers to the questions

- Project anticipated revenues and costs related to each option or alternative

Exploring and answering these questions can lead management to the following options:

- Abandon the specific unit, program, or activity, perhaps in favor of other, more effective options

- Change, strengthen, simplify, redirect, reorganize, outsource, or otherwise change the existing effort

- Make no changes

Possible Problems with Zero-Based Budgeting. ZBB can help nonprofits, particularly well-managed ones, improve their efficiency, effectiveness, and productivity. However, it is not a panacea, nor is it particularly easy. The following are potential difficulties that might arise while attempting ZBB:

- ZBB must have dependable, detailed cost information available from the accounting system (which is not always possible).

- ZBB often feels very threatening to both managers and staff because it involves evaluating, making comparisons, and deciding on desired changes.

- ZBB requires fairly detailed planning and cost calculations and can be made even more difficult and time-consuming if it is introduced organization-wide rather than piloted and phased in over time.

- In the real world it is difficult to decide to close a program or activity.

Despite these possible problems, ZBB obviously has many benefits, not the least of which is that it encourages managers to look at a broader range of options than they would if using incremental budgeting (strategies 1 through 3). Nevertheless, because of the potential difficulties, we recommend that organizations experiment with this technique before applying it in a full budgeting process. Using ZBB initially for just one or two programs will allow for a better understanding of its most beneficial application and its strengths and weaknesses.

Use the worksheet in Exhibit 13.4 to plan when and how to carry out this strategy.

EXHIBIT 13.4   **Worksheet for Zero-Based Budgeting**

The Zero-Based Budgeting Team should use this worksheet to help plan, introduce, coordinate, and monitor a zero-based budgeting approach. The responsible parties should complete the following steps:

1. List by whom, when, and how the ZBB approach will be explained to unit heads and others.
2. Identify the specific training that people in finance and other programs/units will get to understand and implement the ZBB approach.
3. List each of the organization's units, programs and activities that are to be reviewed and analyzed, along with the level of financial and other resources currently committed to and generated by each.
4. List which individuals in each unit, program, or activity will be sent the appropriate parts of the list for review, analysis, and option building.
5. Describe the various options or models that have emerged from each unit answering the question, If we were not already doing this, knowing what we now know, would we do it the same way?
6. List the anticipated income and costs for each model or option (use varying activity levels, when appropriate).
7. Describe whether each specific program, function, or activity should be eliminated, modified, or continued relatively unchanged.

Budgeting Calendars

The budgeting calendar shows the entire budget development cycle. Setting up a budgeting calendar includes the following steps:

1. Listing the major budget development tasks

2. Establishing the budgeting timetable, including specific deadlines for completing each task

3. Identifying the persons responsible for accomplishing each task

4. Obtaining input from the board and staff

5. Revising and distributing the finalized budgeting calendar

The budget development calendar should be reviewed each year and revised, based on last year's experience and any anticipated changes. The following subsections explain each step in creating a budgeting calendar.

Listing Major Budget Development Tasks. Major budget cycle tasks might vary depending on the size of a nonprofit and the overall budget development strategy it adopts. For instance, larger nonprofits might need lengthy data-gathering and planning processes that include multiple phases and tasks, such as the following:

- Developing guidelines for salary and price increases

- Preparing or updating income and expense estimates

- Reviewing and updating long-range financial and strategic plans

- Establishing income and expense goals for programs and departments

- Developing budget priorities, guidelines, and instructions for the coming year

Smaller nonprofits might require somewhat shorter planning processes and fewer phases and tasks. Regardless of the nonprofit's size, however, the CFO's (or bookkeeper's) first step is to think through the entire budget development cycle and clearly define what must be done.

Establishing Time Frames and Deadlines. Deciding when to begin and end the overall budget development process depends heavily on the size of the nonprofit and the complexity of the specific budget development strategy chosen.

Budgeting processes that involve active participation by program and unit managers should begin at least seven months before the budget must go into effect. Longer lead times give top management more time to prepare needed budgeting guidelines, materials, and instructions, and allow program and unit managers more time to develop draft budgets.

At the same time, however, long lead times also mean fewer months or quarters of current-year financial information are available to help project actual income and expenses into the coming year. Thus the need for accurate projections based on current financial data must be weighed against the need for a realistic time allotment for completing important budgeting steps.

Identifying Those Responsible for Each Task. Establish accountability for completing each budgeting task by identifying the individual responsible for ensuring completion of each required task by the deadline. This way, everyone knows who is supposed to do what in developing the budget.

Obtaining Input from the Board and Staff. Obtaining feedback from the board and staff on the draft budget cycle and calendar provides two benefits. First, members of the board and staff might identify aspects of the draft budget cycle and calendar that others might have overlooked in compiling these documents. Second, board and staff members might be able to recognize when deadlines are unrealistic from their individual or departmental perspective. Review by support and clerical staff can also be helpful, as they might be able to provide useful input and an accurate estimate of the time required to prepare and duplicate budget development instructions and materials.

Revising and Distributing the Finalized Budgeting Calendar. In revising and distributing the finalized budget calendar to the board and staff, it is critical that everyone involved in or affected by the budgeting process be clearly informed of the steps in the process, the budgeting schedule, and the expectation they are held to. Whenever the budgeting calendar is modified, the changes should be communicated in writing to the same people who received the first draft calendar.

Ideally, an organization's budgeting cycle will correspond to the natural cycle of its operations. This means that in determining the beginning and ending points of their budget cycles, organizations must take into account such factors as their fiscal year start date and the reporting requirements of funding sources and regulatory entities.

Budgeting Goals, Guidelines, Policies, and Procedures

Establishing budgeting goals, guidelines, policies, and procedures is essential to creating the overall context of budgeting for the coming year. To start this process, the board, CEO, and bookkeeper should review the nonprofit's mission, current fiscal status, and projected income and expenses for the coming year. Nonprofits with long-range financial plans usually also update them at this time, using current information to project fiscal and program trends likely to affect operations.

Based on their review and the specific budget development strategy they have chosen, the board, CEO, and bookkeeper then set organization-wide operating budget goals for income and expenses for the coming year. The goals they set will be used to help guide development of the coming year's organization-wide operating budget, as well as individual program and unit operating budgets. Note that in a smaller nonprofit, the organizational and program budgets might be one and the same.

Setting Guidelines for Operating Budgets

Often the board of directors, CEO, and bookkeeper all have input in establishing policies and guidelines for developing the coming year's budget, including matters related to the following:

- Specific program objectives and priorities

- Income and expense targets or limits

- Policies governing the creation of new programs or positions

- Guidelines for existing personnel costs, such as wage increases and fringe-benefit rates

Identifying Priorities in Operating Budgets

Effectively identifying priorities is contingent on a thorough understanding of an up-to-date and clearly defined mission statement. An accurate mission statement is necessary to guide programs—especially during planning and budgeting activities—because it summarizes an organization's basic purposes and primary reason for existence. A good mission statement can help your organization do several important things:

- Set clear organizational and program goals

- Make sure current and proposed programs and activities are appropriate

- Focus resources productively

- Help determine the specific activities and expenditures that should be maintained and the ones that should be reduced or eliminated

Reviewing the mission statement should be the first step in determining organizational or program priorities. The next step might include an examination of the following:

- Demographics of your service area

- Specific, realistic needs of your clients

- Actual response to your existing programs

Assessing existing programs (or any service gap or problem that becomes evident) using the criteria already described will provide important information to help identify priorities. For example, if it becomes clear that a certain program seems to meet community needs perfectly yet has an unexpectedly low rate of usage and little community support, a budget priority might be to conduct further research to determine the cause of this situation.

Setting Organization-Wide Operating-Budget Goals

The board, CEO, and bookkeeper work together to set total organization-wide operating income and expense goals:

- The total amount of income the organization as a whole expects to take in during the coming year

- The total amount the organization as a whole expects to spend to carry out all its activities during the coming year

Total operating income and total operating expenses should generally match. If organization-wide expense goals exceed income goals, meaning that anticipated expenses will exceed anticipated income, then the board, CEO, and bookkeeper should:

- Refigure total operating income and expense projections

- Be prepared to take corrective action later, such as cutting budgeted costs or generating additional income

- Formally decide to use funds from the organization's unrestricted funds to make up the difference

- Take the risk of operating at a deficit during the coming year (which is not recommended and is certainly not a sustainable strategy)

If organization-wide income projections exceed expense projections, meaning that estimated income is more than estimated expenses, then the board, CEO, and bookkeeper should:

- Adjust the total operating income and expense projections so they match

- Let the surplus stand as a hedge against unexpected costs during the coming year

- Designate the surplus for future use as needed

Setting Individual Program and Unit Operating-Budget Goals

The bookkeeper and CEO should work with managers of each individual program and unit to set program and unit income and expense projections for the coming year, based on the organization-wide income and expense projections. In turn, each program and unit manager should use individual program or unit income and expense projections to guide planning for the nature, staffing, and outcome goals of the specific program or unit (and for the line item detail in the program or unit operating budget). Total anticipated operating income and expenses for each individual program or unit should match. If they do not match, plans for alternative income generation must be developed, or expenses must be cut. Developing the discipline and knowledge to perform these steps can make a big difference in the future health of your organization.

Projecting income and expenses is easier, and the results more accurate and understandable, if written policies and procedures exist to provide program and unit managers with necessary guidance. The following are recommendations for establishing effective budgeting policies and procedures:

- Suggestions for Establishing Basic Budgeting Policies and Procedures

  Identify the specific steps, responsibilities, and timetables in the budgeting cycle and the budgeting calendar.

  Identify those responsible for preparing and disseminating the budgeting package to be used in preparing budget estimates.

  Identify the contents and format of the overall budgeting package to be used in preparing draft budgets and the format to be used in preparing draft budgets themselves.

  Identify the number of actual draft budgets to be prepared by program and unit managers. Options include a draft budget showing estimated increases in income or expenses, one showing no change, one showing estimated decreases in income or expenses, or any combination of these.

  Identify those responsible for preparing draft budgets and approving them.

  Identify processes for modifying in-house and funding-source budgets.

- Suggestions for Establishing Basic Income Projection Policies and Procedures

  Identify those responsible for estimating and approving proposed changes in income.

  Identify the percentage of change to existing income for program and unit managers to use in preparing draft budgets. Options include a percentage increase, no change, a percentage decrease, or any combination of these. Be sure to communicate in advance with all current and potential funding sources regarding any possible changes in funding or eligibility for specific funds.

  Identify those responsible for estimating and approving the certainty of receiving anticipated income from individual funding sources.

  Identify the level of certainty needed to include anticipated funds in the category of projected income in preparing draft program and unit budgets.

- Suggestions for Establishing Basic Expense Projection Policies and Procedures

  Identify those responsible for estimating and approving proposed changes in expenses.

  Identify the percentage of change to existing salaries, wages, and fringe benefits to be used in preparing draft budgets. Options include a percentage increase, no change, a percentage decrease, or any combination of these.

  Identify the methods for making changes to existing expenses in preparing draft budgets. Options include estimating a percentage increase or decrease, determining actual increases or decreases (by checking leases and catalogues and negotiating with suppliers and vendors).

Identify the methods for determining the amount of any new expenses for the coming budget year. Options include determining actual amounts (by checking leases, union contracts, and contacting and negotiating with suppliers and vendors).

Summary

Your budget will be only as effective as your planning and management ability. Budgeting requires discipline and a true team effort. The most common error to be avoided is not allowing enough time for proper planning and preparation.

CHAPTER 14

Cash Flow Reporting, Forecasting, and Management

Effective budgeting must be in place in order to create effective, useful, and reliable cash flow forecasts. In Chapter Thirteen, we discussed budgeting and its strategic importance and impact on an organization. *The Cash Flow Management Book for Nonprofits* (Jossey-Bass, 2001), by Murray Dropkin and Allyson Hayden, was written to help nonprofit organizations better understand the important topic of cash flow management.

This chapter is designed to help you, the bookkeeper, use the financial information you are generating to its best advantage in effectively managing cash flow. This chapter offers instructions and examples on how to develop cash flow forecasts.

Fundamentals of Cash Flow Forecasting

One of the fundamental differences between developing cash flow forecasts and operating budgets is in the accounting basis that is used for each. *Accrual-basis accounting,* which recognizes all income as it is earned (whether received or not) and all expenses as they are incurred (whether paid or not), should be used in operating-budget development. Cash flow forecasts, however, are constructed using *cash-basis accounting,* which includes only the money that is physically received and paid out. Therefore, the first step in using the organization's operating budget to develop cash flow forecasts is to eliminate the effect of accruals. This step will require two main actions: cash-basis accounting for cash inflows and cash-basis accounting for cash outflows.

Cash-Basis Accounting for Cash Inflows

For cash-basis purposes, only money that will be received and deposited by the organization in the period of the forecast should be recognized as cash inflow. For example, assume an organization holds a fundraising event for which 80 percent of the event's total expected proceeds is paid at the door as admission fees, and 20 percent consists of promises to make contributions that will not be received until the next fiscal period. The cash flow forecast for the period during which the event is held should only include the cash that will actually be received during that period. Contributions that were promised and will be received during a future fiscal period will be included in the cash flow forecast for the period during which they are actually received. This means that accrual-basis financial reporting would include all monies earned at the special event, and the cash flow forecast would include all monies received at the event. Another analogy might be useful: when you pay for a gift at the checkout counter at the bookstore with currency, you are on a cash basis reducing your available cash. When you use a credit card to purchase the gift, you have not paid out any cash, but you have created a debt you owe to the credit card company for the amount of the purchase. The total economic effect is identical. You spent cash in the first example, and incurred debt in the second example.

Calculating the cash inflow side of a cash flow forecast presents the challenge of recognizing as cash inflow only items that will be collected during the reporting period. To make the forecast as accurate as possible, the organization should examine cash collection rates for prior events. Organizations may also compare their accounts receivable balance with prior-year balances. Prior collection patterns and current characteristics will help in estimating the likely percentage of collection. These two components— immediately realizable cash and collection of receivables—will normally represent most of the cash inflow that should be recognized in the cash flow forecast. Obviously, there will be situations in which organizations will have other sources of cash inflow that should be included in forecasts. For example, in developing cash flow forecasts, proceeds from a bank loan were recognized as cash inflow in the cash flow forecast covering the fiscal period during which the loan was received.

Cash-Basis Accounting for Cash Outflows

The outflow component of the cash flow forecast will only include cash paid out by the organization for expenses and any cash payments (expenditures) made to pay down accounts payable or other liabilities. Depreciation and amortization expenses will not be included in forecasted cash outflows because they do not represent actual payments of cash.

A brief example will help illustrate some differences between cash-basis accounting and accrual-basis accounting. Suppose that an organization has an accrual-basis operating budget with expenses totaling $575,000. This figure includes a calculation of amortization- and depreciation-related expenses of $45,000. During the budget period, the organization will pay down $25,000 of debt. Accounts payable will increase by $15,000. These data would be treated in a cash flow forecast as follows:

• The $25,000 used to pay down a loan is a cash outflow that would not be included in an operating budget but that would be included in a cash flow forecast. Paying down a previously incurred liability is not an expense; it is simply a reduction in a liability. However, because money is actually paid out, this amount must be shown as an outflow on the cash flow forecast.

• The $45,000 allocated to amortization and depreciation is not a cash transaction and therefore would not be included in the cash flow forecast as an outflow. Amortization and depreciation are non-cash expenses that spread the cost of acquiring an asset over a certain period of time. Money paid to acquire an asset in a prior fiscal period has no impact on the current period's cash flow. The current period has amortization and depreciation expenses, but the cash outflow occurred in a prior period.

• The $15,000 increase in accounts payable indicates that the organization financed $15,000 of its operations by incurring additional accounts payable. But because this amount was not actually paid during the forecast period, it should not be included as a cash outflow in the cash flow forecast.

Exhibit 14.1 shows how the expenditures shown in the accrual-basis operating budget would be converted to the appropriate cash-basis expense figure to use in a cash flow forecast.

The aforementioned analysis only identifies the total outflow of cash. Next we must identify timing issues relating to cash flow. As is evident from the example just given, cash flow forecasts are summaries of the actual cash transactions for a given fiscal period. Money deposited and money paid out are the only transactions that will be included in cash flow forecasts. Keeping this concept in mind will make converting information from accrual-basis operating budgets into information applicable to cash-basis cash flow forecasting a relatively simple task for smaller organizations.

Cash Flow Forecasting Based on the Operating Budget

The process of creating cash flow budgets from the operating budget will involve reviewing and characterizing each line item in the operating budget. Identifying, analyzing, and determining how each line item of the operating budget affects cash flow and the month affected will provide additional necessary information for cash flow forecast development. The steps in this process are described in the following subsections.

Reviewing the Operating Budget

The first step in developing an accurate cash flow forecast is to review the organizational operating budget and assess the cash flow effect of each line item. To do this for your organization, you must figure out how each income or expense item will affect

EXHIBIT 14.1	Summary of Conversion from Operating Budget to Cash Flow Forecast

Total Expenses Per Operating Budget (Accrual Basis)	$575,000
Add Repayment of Prior Debt (Outflow)	25,000
	$600,000
Subtract Increase in Accounts Payable (No Outflow)	(15,000)
Subtract Depreciation and Amortization (No Outflow)	(45,000)
Net Cash Outflows Identified for Cash Flow Forecast	**$540,000**

cash inflow or outflow. For example, rent expense must normally be paid on time, or the organization will face legal action; thus rent expense will be a fairly straightforward cash outflow. Some operating-budget items may be paid over a longer period of time by negotiating with vendors. Organizations that choose to finance such items will have to consider the effect of doing so in the cash outflow component of their cash flow forecasts. Decisions regarding renting versus purchasing equipment and buying real property outright versus obtaining a mortgage will have impacts on cash flow. Conversely, budgeted non-cash items like depreciation and amortization have no effect on the cash flow forecast and will be eliminated in the conversion of items from the operating budget for use in the cash flow forecast. One exception relates to government grant programs. These grant programs sometimes allow the grantee to charge a specific budgeted amount to the grant. As a result, the organization's cash inflow would go up since a portion of the depreciation or usage charge is being funded as a cost of operating the program. Be aware of such contractual terms and take advantage of them when you can.

After each line item in the operating budget has been analyzed, and the cash flow effect and timing have been determined, the organization may begin to prepare the cash flow forecast.

Adjusting the Operating Budget to Create the Cash Flow Forecast

The second step in this process is modifying the information in the operating budget so that it can be incorporated into the cash flow forecast. The best way to approach this is to set up a worksheet such as the one shown in Exhibit 14.2. The column farthest to the left will contain the operating-budget line items. The next column will contain the expense amounts from the operating budget. The third column will show any cash-related adjustments to the operating-budget amounts. The fourth column will indicate the cash flow effect of the operating-budget line item.

When there is a direct relationship between the operating-budget item and the cash flow forecast item, there will be no adjustment necessary to incorporate the amount into the cash flow forecast. Line items that have a cash flow effect may require adjustments to operating-budget amounts in order to include them with accuracy in cash flow forecasts. For example, if your organization is acquiring new furniture at a cost of $50,000, and you are leasing it over five years, cash flow will be affected for the five-year period (as opposed to paying for the furniture in one payment, which would only affect cash flow for the period in which the payment was made).

Prior experience and future expectations will determine the adjustments your organization will have to make to include operating-budget amounts in cash flow forecasts. Items such as rent, utilities, and salaries should all have a direct effect on cash flow and will usually not require an adjustment.

Supplies, maintenance, and equipment purchases and similar line items may vary in their effect on cash flow, based on financing plans. Items such as depreciation and amortization will have to be flagged for elimination from the cash flow forecast unless reimbursable in some fashion from grant income as discussed previously.

EXHIBIT 14.2 Worksheet to Prepare an Annual Cash Forecast

UNIVERSAL NONPROFIT
WORKSHEET TO PREPARE AN ANNUAL CASH FORECAST
FOR FISCAL YEAR 20x5

BUDGET CATEGORY	ACCRUAL BUDGET	ADJUSTMENTS	EXPLANATION	CASH OUTFLOW
Personnel	$1,153,163	$(53,163)	Accrued Compensation	$1,100,000
Consultants and Professional Services	107,022	(82,022)	Deferred Payment Arrangement	25,000
Materials and Supplies	114,613		No Adjustment	114,613
Facility Costs	119,014		No Adjustment	119,014
Specific Assistance to Clients	89,873		No Adjustment	89,873
Other Costs	74,977		No Adjustment	74,977
Total Operating Costs	1,658,662			1,523,477
Capital Equipment	60,000	(46,000)	Equipment Financed	14,000
Totals	**$1,718,662**	**$(181,185)**		**$1,537,477**

Reviewing and Approving the Cash Flow Forecast

The annual cash flow forecast should be reviewed, and the beginning cash balance should be added to the net cash flow (cash inflow less cash outflow) to determine what the forecasted year-ending cash balance will be. Adjustments may have to be made to the planned cash payments for the year if the cash balances are too low. For example, your organization might decide to put off the purchase of a new computer system to conserve cash.

Short-Term Cash Flow Forecasting

Short-term cash flow forecasts should be designed to meet your organization's needs. Annual cash flow forecasts can be broken into whatever time periods will be most useful. Different sizes and types of organizations will benefit from different frequencies of cash flow forecasting. For example, in the case of a foundation with most of its assets in long-term investments, cash flow forecasts on an annual basis may be all that is necessary. If your organization receives diverse types of funding, such as funding from many special events or contribution sources, your cash forecasting will be much more complicated and challenging and should be done more frequently. Organizations interested in preparing daily, weekly, quarterly, or annual cash flow forecasts should see Exhibits 14.3, 14.4, 14.5, and 14.6, respectively, for examples.

In cash flow forecasts the cash inflow and cash outflow items should be put into the time period they are expected to be received or paid out. For example, periodic items such as rent are distributed throughout the year. Personnel expenses might fluctuate if there is seasonal demand for the services the organization provides. In addition, cash flow forecasts should show both the beginning and ending cash balances. Each of these components of the forecast is essential to managing cash flow. They will help the organization monitor the cash balance and assist management in identifying excessive balances or potential overdrafts.

Cash balances may vary widely during different fiscal periods as a result of seasonal volume fluctuations, weather, contribution patterns, and other factors. This is why preparing cash flow reports on a frequent basis is very helpful to ongoing cash flow management. As stated previously, however, your organization will need to assess its unique cash flow management needs to determine the frequency and detail of cash flow reporting that will be most beneficial. There is no rule of thumb in this regard. Our recommendation is that most organizations should, at minimum, prepare quarterly cash flow forecasts, such as the one shown in Exhibit 14.5.

The final step in cash flow forecast development is thorough review of the forecasts by both financial managers (bookkeepers) and operations managers. The timing and amounts of the cash flows should be examined and critiqued. If the draft cash flow forecasts pass this review, the documents may be finalized, and any corrective action plans may be implemented.

EXHIBIT 14.3 **Daily Cash Flow Forecast**

UNIVERSAL NONPROFIT
DAILY CASH FLOW FORECAST
FOR WEEK ENDED

		MONDAY	TUESDAY	WEDNESDAY	THURSDAY	FRIDAY	TOTALS
OPENING CASH BALANCE:		$270,649	$262,612	$256,590	$246,038	$239,260	$270,649
CASH INFLOWS:							
	Revenue 1	$7,186	$4,312	$10,780	$5,390	$8,264	$35,932
	Revenue 2	3,054	1,832	4,581	2,290	3,512	15,269
	Revenue 3	2,335	1,401	3,503	1,751	2,686	11,676
	Revenue 4	1,796	1,078	2,695	1,347	2,066	8,982
	Revenue 5	1,437	862	2,156	1,078	1,652	7,185
	Revenue 6	1,257	754	1,886	943	1,446	6,286
	Revenue 7	898	539	1,347	673	1,033	4,490
TOTAL CASH INFLOW		$17,963	$10,778	$26,948	$13,472	$20,659	$89,820
TOTAL CASH AVAILABLE		$288,612	$273,390	$283,538	$259,510	$259,919	$360,469
CASH OUTFLOWS:							
	Payroll	$—	$—	$—	$—	$—	$—
	Payroll Taxes	—	—	—	—	—	—
	Health Insurance	—	—	—	—	—	—
	Consultants	9,000	5,400	13,500	6,750	10,350	45,000
	Rent	—	—	—	—	—	—
	Other Costs	14,000	8,400	21,000	10,500	16,100	70,000
	Capital Purchases	—	—	—	—	—	—
	Loan Repayments	3,000	3,000	3,000	3,000	3,000	15,000
TOTAL CASH OUTFLOW		$26,000	$16,800	$37,500	$20,250	$29,450	$130,000
CLOSING CASH BALANCE		$262,612	$256,590	$246,038	$239,260	$230,469	$230,469

Periodic Review of the Cash Flow Forecast

In addition to review of the draft cash flow forecast by financial and operations managers, proper cash flow forecasting will require organizations to perform regular periodic reviews of forecasts. Actual cash flow will almost never be exactly as anticipated, and the differences between the reality and the projections must be assessed, evaluated, and incorporated into future forecasts. An analysis of the sources and uses of cash should be conducted on a regular basis to identify variances. This analysis should include an examination of changes in working capital (current assets less current liabilities), asset acquisitions and other capital expenditures, and the effects of any financing on cash flow forecasts. These processes will provide your organization with a clear picture of the true current cash flow status. It might also help organizations assess how accurate their projection methodologies are and will reveal the precise nature of potential future cash flow problems.

Periodic reviews should also involve recasting shorter-term cash flow forecasts to determine whether or not the annual forecast remains accurate and reliable. Those reviewing cash flow forecasts must assess if variances will impact future cash projections. If it becomes apparent that future cash projections are no longer valid, the organization must take action to secure new sources of cash or cut projects that draw on the organization's cash. Management can take specific actions, such as delaying an equipment purchase, making a request to current donors for additional funds, or restructuring operations. Monitoring overall economic and market conditions is critical. For example, after the events of September 11, 2001, some organizations found donations severely affected, as donors retargeted contributions to September 11–related charities or issues. As oil prices break new records on a regular basis, some nonprofits will be affected. Nonprofits with large fleets of vehicles are feeling a cash flow pinch due to unexpected gasoline costs. Housing organizations are being hit with large insurance, heating oil, and utility costs. Cash flow is a very lively topic and always needs careful attention.

Cash flow forecast preparation might present an excellent opportunity for organizations to improve cash flow management. Cash flow forecasts reflecting monthly or weekly cash outflow and inflow can give important insights into the operating plan of the organization and the way that plan is affecting cash flow. However, the most important insight that a cash flow forecast provides is the level of cash available at any given time during the forecast period.

Corrective Actions for Forecasted Cash Shortages

The organization can pursue several corrective actions when a cash shortage is forecasted. However, the first action that should be taken is to identify what will cause the projected cash deficit. Perhaps an equipment purchase was unwisely planned during a period of low cash inflow. When cash balances are low, nonessential purchases should be delayed to conserve cash. However, if greater operating expenses or falling support causes the projected cash shortage, the problem is more serious. The organization must identify the direct cause of the deficiency when forecasted cash shortages are due to operational problems. The organization must also investigate and analyze

EXHIBIT 14.4   Weekly Cash Flow Forecast

UNIVERSAL NONPROFIT
WEEKLY CASH FLOW FORECAST
FOR 13 WEEKS ENDED

	WEEK 1	WEEK 2	WEEK 3	WEEK 4	WEEK 5	WEEK 6
OPENING CASH BALANCE:	$270,649	$230,469	$66,969	$47,080	$(121,256)	$130,574
CASH INFLOWS:						
Revenue 1	35,932	34,600	29,600	54,267	152,733	40,600
Revenue 2	15,269	14,705	12,580	23,063	64,911	17,255
Revenue 3	11,676	11,245	9,620	17,636	49,638	13,195
Revenue 4	8,982	8,650	7,400	13,566	38,183	10,150
Revenue 5	7,185	6,920	5,920	10,853	30,546	8,120
Revenue 6	6,286	6,055	5,180	9,496	26,728	7,105
Revenue 7	4,490	4,325	3,700	6,783	19,091	5,075
TOTAL CASH INFLOW	$89,820	$86,500	$74,000	$135,664	$381,830	$101,500
TOTAL CASH AVAILABLE	$360,469	$316,969	$140,969	$182,744	$260,574	$232,074
CASH OUTFLOWS:						
Payroll	$—	$170,100	$—	$170,100	$—	$170,100
Payroll Taxes	—	21,150	—	21,150	—	21,150
Health Insurance	—	—	—	34,000	—	—
Employee Benefits	—	33,750	—	33,750	—	33,750
Consultants	45,000	—	35,000	—	35,000	—
Rent	—	—	—	20,000	—	—
Other Costs	70,000	25,000	40,000	25,000	80,000	25,000
Capital Purchases	—	—	—	—	—	—
Loan Repayments	15,000	—	18,889	—	15,000	—
TOTAL CASH OUTFLOW	$130,000	$250,000	$93,889	$304,000	$130,000	$250,000
CLOSING CASH BALANCE:	$230,469	$66,969	$47,080	$(121,256)	$130,574	$(17,926)

cost drivers (objects or actions that drive costs above an expected amount) so that corrective action may be taken. Such analyses include reviewing materials and processes to determine whether any savings can be attained by using different materials or changing policies and procedures. A line of credit or an interim loan would be an acceptable solution for a short-term cash flow shortage. (Before borrowing money, the organization must prove to the lender that they have the capacity to repay the amount borrowed plus interest.) However, without a corrective plan of action, the cash flow problem will return at a later date. The organization might also want to go to significant donors to ask for cash ahead of a normally scheduled date to ease the impact of a cash

Week 7	Week 8	Week 9	Week 10	Week 11	Week 12	Week 13	Totals
$(17,926)	$256,074	$44,404	$222,345	$32,175	$77,839	$28,669	$270,649
161,600	52,933	108,733	41,933	54,267	101,933	72,427	941,558
68,680	22,496	46,211	17,821	23,063	43,321	30,781	400,156
52,520	17,203	35,338	13,628	17,636	33,128	23,538	306,001
40,400	13,233	27,183	10,483	13,566	25,483	18,106	235,385
32,320	10,586	21,746	8,386	10,853	20,386	14,485	188,306
28,280	9,263	19,028	7,338	9,496	17,838	12,674	164,767
20,200	6,616	13,591	5,241	6,783	12,741	9,053	117,689
$404,000	$132,330	$271,830	$104,830	$135,664	$254,830	$181,064	$2,353,862
$386,074	$388,404	$316,234	$327,175	$167,839	$332,669	$209,733	$2,624,511
$—	$200,340	$—	$204,120	$—	$170,100	$90,405	$1,175,265
—	24,910	—	25,380	—	21,150	11,240	146,130
—	34,000	—	—	—	34,000	8,500	110,500
—	39,750	—	40,500	—	33,750	17,937	233,187
35,000	—	35,000	—	35,000	—	18,333	238,333
—	20,000	—	—	—	20,000	5,000	65,000
80,000	25,000	40,000	25,000	40,000	25,000	41,666	541,666
—	—	—	—	—	—	—	—
15,000	—	18,889	—	15,000	—	8,148	105,926
$130,000	$344,000	$93,889	$295,000	$90,000	$304,000	$201,229	$2,616,007
$256,074	$44,404	$222,345	$32,175	$77,839	$28,669	$8,504	$8,504

flow problem. The organization must attempt to obtain advances and increase cash balances through any reasonable means while implementing adjustments to eliminate future cash flow problems.

Cash Flow Reporting, Monitoring, and Analysis

The key to maintaining your organization's cash flow financial health is having the capacity to respond to changes in the environment. The nonprofit operating environment is dynamic, owing to both internal and external factors. Organizations must be

EXHIBIT
14.5 **Quarterly Cash Flow Forecast**

UNIVERSAL NONPROFIT

QUARTERLY CASH FLOW FORECAST

FISCAL YEAR 20x5

	FIRST QUARTER	SECOND QUARTER	THIRD QUARTER	FOURTH QUARTER	TOTAL
OPENING CASH BALANCE:	$270,649	$8,504	$(114,984)	$(135,469)	$270,649
CASH INFLOWS:					
Revenue 1	$941,558	$912,592	$962,785	$1,001,296	$3,818,231
Revenue 2	400,156	361,994	358,374	379,876	1,500,400
Revenue 3	306,001	285,293	290,999	285,645	1,167,938
Revenue 4	235,385	215,111	225,866	232,642	909,004
Revenue 5	188,306	179,041	188,889	185,111	741,347
Revenue 6	164,767	148,295	154,968	160,392	628,422
Revenue 7	117,689	111,358	114,698	118,139	461,884
TOTAL CASH INFLOW	$2,353,862	$2,213,684	$2,296,579	$2,363,101	$9,227,226
TOTAL CASH AVAILABLE	$2,624,511	$2,222,188	$2,181,595	$2,227,632	$9,497,875
CASH OUTFLOWS:					
Payroll	$1,175,265	$1,067,750	$1,080,655	$1,060,765	$4,384,435
Payroll Taxes	146,130	127,630	130,567	121,637	525,964
Health Insurance	110,500	97,650	100,475	93,767	402,392
Employee Benefits	233,187	206,975	210,625	197,650	848,437
Consultants	238,333	175,000	165,000	135,750	714,083
Rent	65,000	60,000	62,500	62,500	250,000
Other Costs	541,666	487,500	467,575	425,750	1,922,491
Capital Purchases	—	15,000	—	25,000	40,000
Loan Repayments	105,926	99,667	99,667	101,567	406,827
TOTAL CASH OUTFLOW	$2,616,007	$2,337,172	$2,317,064	$2,224,386	$9,494,629
CLOSING CASH BALANCE	$8,504	$(114,984)	$(135,469)	$3,246	$3,246

able to recognize when it will be necessary to modify financial plans, budgets, and cash flow forecasts in response to the environment and to circumstances within the organization. Having formal mechanisms in place for such monitoring and modification will allow your organization to adapt to changes quickly and efficiently.

The most important aspect of monitoring an organization's financial health is being able to identify problems early in the cash flow financial cycle. The earlier your organization can identify areas of operations that will require attention or intervention, the more likely it is to correct problems before they cause substantial financial

EXHIBIT 14.6 Annual Cash Flow Forecast

UNIVERSAL NONPROFIT
ANNUAL CASH FLOW FORECAST
FOR YEAR ENDED DECEMBER 31

	20x5	20x6	20x7	20x8	20x9	Five-Year Recap
OPENING CASH BALANCE:	$270,649	$3,246	$(193,080)	$84,967	$264,779	$270,649
CASH INFLOWS:						
Revenue 1	$3,818,231	$3,727,081	$3,675,425	$3,550,750	$3,675,985	$18,447,472
Revenue 2	1,500,400	1,440,238	1,410,155	1,375,500	1,260,555	6,986,848
Revenue 3	1,167,938	1,149,503	1,172,493	1,160,575	1,100,660	5,751,169
Revenue 4	909,004	881,995	865,665	825,785	795,235	4,277,684
Revenue 5	741,347	748,676	715,675	685,985	650,785	3,542,468
Revenue 6	628,422	600,364	580,685	550,685	535,155	2,895,311
Revenue 7	461,884	464,159	460,557	455,758	430,125	2,272,483
TOTAL CASH INFLOW	$9,227,226	$9,012,016	$8,880,655	$8,605,038	$8,448,500	$44,173,435
TOTAL CASH AVAILABLE	$9,497,875	$9,015,262	$8,687,575	$8,690,005	$8,713,279	$44,444,084
CASH OUTFLOWS:						
Payroll	$4,384,435	$4,186,679	$4,061,078	$4,020,468	$4,030,499	$20,683,159
Payroll Taxes	525,964	397,734	385,802	381,944	382,897	2,074,341
Health Insurance	402,392	382,075	370,612	359,494	348,709	1,863,282
Employee Benefits	848,437	797,280	765,388	734,773	705,382	3,851,260
Consultants	714,083	647,047	601,754	559,631	520,457	3,042,972
Rent	250,000	226,625	209,628	193,906	179,363	1,059,522
Other Costs	1,922,491	2,150,322	1,825,675	1,749,335	1,723,095	9,370,918
Capital Purchases	40,000	45,000	36,996	150,000	100,000	371,996
Loan Repayments	406,827	375,580	345,675	275,675	225,675	1,629,432
TOTAL CASH OUTFLOW	$9,494,629	$9,208,342	$8,602,608	$8,425,226	$8,216,077	$43,946,882
CLOSING CASH BALANCE	$3,246	$(193,080)	$84,967	$264,779	$497,202	$497,202

consequences. In order to do this effectively, data collection, analysis, and reporting must be maintained at a high level of accuracy and consistency. Those responsible for monitoring cash flow must receive the required information in a timely, clear, and complete manner. This section of the chapter focuses on the report-monitoring aspect of cash flow management and includes information on how management can use reports to recognize and isolate potential threats to financial health.

Effective cash flow management requires vigilance and flexibility: vigilance in being ever mindful of current and developing situations that might require corrective action and flexibility in being able to modify plans accordingly. Unfortunately, some finance professionals and bookkeepers believe it is an admission of failure to redo a budget or cash flow forecast at the halfway point in a fiscal year. In reality, there is nothing farther from the truth. Revising budgets and cash flow forecasts in response to changing circumstances is essential to effective overall financial and cash flow management. Cash is not a theoretical concept. If your organization does not have cash available, it will go out of business. If your organization fails to meet a payroll because of its cash flow problems, staff morale and confidence in the organization will be seriously harmed. If your organization does not effectively manage cash and fails to pay rent, causing your landlord to start eviction proceedings, it will be hard to run your day-care or counseling center. If your office equipment supplier shows up at your headquarters in the middle of the workday to repossess your copier (this can actually happen), your organization will be severely inconvenienced. Forecasting cash flow must receive serious attention from top management.

The cash flow forecasts we have been discussing in this chapter will only be valuable to the extent that they are used. The following sections discuss some ways these tools may be used as part of an effective report-monitoring package.

Cash Receipts and Disbursements Reports

One of the most effective reports for monitoring cash flow forecasts is based on the cash receipts and cash disbursements model. This is a simple model in which input depends on history and reasonable expectations about the future.

The first step in creating a cash receipts and disbursements report is to list all your sources of cash by category. The categories you use might be very specific or very broad, depending on your organization's needs and preferences. Common categories include program service revenue, grants and contracts, and interest income. At the bottom of this section of the report, leave room for the sum of cash from all sources.

The next section of the report, the cash disbursements section, shows how cash is used. This section should be placed below the cash receipts section and should include all cash disbursements, listing them by category. Common categories for cash disbursements are rent, insurance, salaries, capital expenditures, and loan repayments. As with the cash inflow section, leave room at the bottom of this section to show the total of all disbursements.

The very bottom of the report should show net cash received or disbursed. The beginning cash balance should be placed above the cash receipts section, and the ending cash balance should be placed below the cash disbursements section. This will produce an ending cash balance that either will or will not be within an acceptable range. If current or future cash balances are below required levels, it is the organization's responsibility and duty to take corrective action to resolve the cash shortfalls.

Variance Reports

Variance reports can also assist your organization in identifying where problems may exist. A variance report compares forecasted cash flow with actual cash flow. The difference between the forecasted and actual numbers is the *variance*. Obviously, all significant variances should be investigated and explained. The variance report, like any tool, can be both under- and overused. If the report is not generated or is ignored, significant problems might go unidentified and will not be addressed in a timely manner. However, if the report is overused, valuable time and resources might be wasted on researching immaterial variances. Those responsible for cash flow monitoring must carefully select and use variance reports in the appropriate context. Universal Nonprofit's experience, as described in the following example, illustrates appropriate and beneficial use of variance reports.

Universal Nonprofit was having significant cash flow problems. Actual cash flow had been significantly lower than forecasted. We discovered that a larger-than-anticipated amount of money was being spent on personnel. Further investigation revealed that several departments in the organization were using per-diem staff hired from agencies that supplied temporary staff. The organization took this action because, as a result of recruitment problems, it had a shortage of full-time staff. Paying for the higher-priced temporary staff was leading to greater-than-expected personnel costs. Once management identified the problem through reviewing its variance reports, corrective action could be taken. Universal Nonprofit addressed the problem by launching an intensive and well-planned recruitment effort to hire full-time staff. During the following budget-planning meeting, Universal Nonprofit redesigned its approach to professional staffing, cutting its personnel costs by 15 percent.

Three types of variance reports are the most useful in providing information for cash flow monitoring and modification purposes. These reports help an organization recognize problems in operations and in the forecasting process. The three reports are the following:

- Forecasted-versus-actual cash flow report
- Analysis of key cash flow variances report
- Historical cash flow variances report

Forecasted-Versus-Actual Cash Flow Report. The *forecasted-versus-actual cash flow report* will compare the forecasted cash flow with actual cash flow. The difference between the forecasted and actual amounts is the variance. When it is a material amount, the variance should be examined to determine its cause. In this report, materiality is a factor to pay attention to. It is a challenging concept, because a number of factors will influence the amount at which a variance is material for your particular organization. If your working capital is weak, and you only have enough working capital to exist for two months, your materiality factor is going to be different from that of an organization with a twelve-month reserve of working capital. A good rule of thumb is to use 3 percent variance as a starting point for materiality, with 5 percent variance as a trigger for concern. In the beginning of a fiscal year, a larger variance might be better tolerated than it will be later in a fiscal year because there will still be time to correct the problem.

A forecasted-versus-actual cash flow report is an excellent tool for an organization to use in order to determine where cash flow problems exist. It is best used in conjunction with the other cash flow report mentioned earlier. See Exhibit 14.7 for an example of a forecasted-versus-actual cash flow report.

EXHIBIT 14.7	Forecasted-Versus-Actual Cash Flow Report

UNIVERSAL NONPROFIT
FORECASTED-VERSUS-ACTUAL CASH FLOW REPORT
FISCAL YEAR 20x5

	CASH FLOW FORECAST	CASH FLOW ACTUAL	DOLLAR VARIANCE	PERCENT VARIANCE
CASH INFLOWS:				
Program Revenue	$175,000	$157,550	$(17,450)	−9.97%
Grants and Contracts	575,000	550,000	(25,000)	−4.35%
Contributions	75,000	95,000	20,000	26.67%
TOTAL CASH INFLOWS	$825,000	$802,550	$(22,450)	−2.72%
CASH OUTFLOWS:				
Personnel Costs	$475,000	$481,250	$6,250	1.32%
Supplies	115,000	105,125	(9,875)	−8.59%
Insurance	45,000	43,500	(1,500)	−3.33%
Communications	17,500	16,730	(770)	−4.40%
Space Costs	150,000	152,500	2,500	1.67%
TOTAL CASH OUTFLOWS	$802,500	$799,105	$(3,395)	−0.42%
NET CASH FLOW	$22,500	$3,445	$(19,055)	−84.69%

Analysis of Key Cash Flow Variances Report. The *analysis of key cash flow variances report* is similar to the forecasted-versus-actual report but goes into greater detail to investigate the significant variances. This report is divided into three parts. The left-hand column shows the forecasted cash flow; the second column shows the actual cash flow; and the third column is reserved for identifying significant variances and providing explanations for those variances. The purpose of the report is to make three determinations regarding each variance:

1. What caused the variance

2. Whether the cause of the variance was internal or external

3. How the variance will affect future cash flow forecasts, budgets, and operations

When the variance and its causes are identified, the organization must implement a corrective action plan to rectify the problem. If the source of the problem is external, an evaluation must be performed on the external factors that caused the variance, to identify any future problems. When external factors are causing ongoing problems, restructuring might be necessary to ensure the organization remains competitive in the future. For example, if a government program in which your organization participates is suddenly eliminated, your organization will have to determine how it will need to modify operations in response to this change. See Exhibit 14.8 for an example of a key variances report.

Historical Cash Flow Variances Report. The purpose of the *historical cash flow variance analysis report* is to analyze the effectiveness of the cash flow forecasting model. This report compares the forecasted amounts with actual amounts on monthly, quarterly, and annual bases and identifies items that have been consistently forecasted incorrectly. By using this report, your organization can improve its forecasting model in order to set more realistic goals and objectives. Your organization must make sure that it clearly identifies who is responsible for the analysis of cash flow and who is responsible for supervising implementation of the corrective action plan. See Exhibit 14.9 for an example of a historical cash flow variance analysis report. As the bookkeeper, you need to discuss with colleagues which reports help them the most. Sometimes the staff wants a more detailed report than do the board members. You need to understand what your internal customers want as information. Then a compromise might have to be reached since you need time to do the payroll and pay bills and perform the other tasks assigned to you. It sometimes takes a while before the right balance is achieved regarding the required level of financial reporting.

Summary

Effective cash flow management requires the constant vigilance of all members of the organization. Adequate cash flow is critical to survival.

EXHIBIT 14.8 Analysis of Key Cash Flow Variances Report

UNIVERSAL NONPROFIT
ANALYSIS OF KEY CASH FLOW VARIANCES REPORT
FISCAL YEAR 20x5

	Budgeted	Actual	Variance	Variance Percentage	Is the Variance Significant?	Explanation
CASH INFLOWS:						
Program Revenue	$175,000	$157,550	$(17,450)	−9.97%	Yes	Forced to close for a week due to severe weather.
Grants and Contracts	575,000	550,000	(25,000)	−4.35%	Yes	One funding source ceased operations.
Contributions	75,000	95,000	20,000	26.67%	Yes	Additional donations solicited to help offset lost grant.
TOTAL CASH INFLOWS	$825,000	$802,550	$(22,450)	−2.72%	Yes	See Above
CASH OUTFLOWS:						
Personnel Costs	$475,000	$481,250	$6,250	1.32%	No	N/A
Supplies	115,000	105,125	(9,875)	−8.59%	Yes	Delayed purchases.
Insurance	45,000	43,500	(1,500)	−3.33%	No	Negotiated a less expensive premium.
Communications	17,500	16,730	(770)	−4.40%	No	Monitored usage more effectively.
Space Costs	150,000	152,500	2,500	1.67%	No	N/A
TOTAL CASH OUTFLOWS	$802,500	$799,105	$(3,395)	−0.42%	No	
NET CASH FLOW	$22,500	$3,445	$(19,055)			

EXHIBIT 14.9 Historical Cash Flow Variances Analysis

UNIVERSAL NONPROFIT
HISTORICAL CASH FLOW VARIANCES ANALYSIS
FISCAL YEAR 20x5

	Month of December 20x5			Quarter Ended 12/31/x5			Fiscal Year Ended 12/31/x5		
	Budgeted	Actual	Variance	Budgeted	Actual	Variance	Budgeted	Actual	Variance
CASH INFLOWS:									
Program Revenue	$27,500	$27,900	$400	$87,587	$89,280	$1,693	$175,000	$157,550	$(17,450)
Grants & Contracts	—	—	—	75,000	68,450	(6,550)	575,000	550,000	(25,000)
Contributions	15,000	15,750	750	47,775	50,400	2,625	75,000	95,000	20,000
TOTAL CASH INFLOWS	$42,500	$43,650	$1,150	$210,362	$208,130	$(2,232)	$825,000	$802,550	$(22,450)
CASH OUTFLOWS:									
Personnel Costs	$25,000	$23,735	$(1,265)	$95,000	$107,730	$12,730	$475,000	$481,250	$6,250
Supplies	5,000	4,350	(650)	17,500	14,000	(3,500)	115,000	105,125	(9,875)
Insurance	750	800	50	2,250	2,400	150	45,000	43,500	(1,500)
Communications	500	515	15	1,500	1,575	75	17,500	16,730	(770)
Space Costs	10,500	10,750	250	31,500	33,000	1,500	150,000	152,500	2,500
TOTAL CASH OUTFLOWS	$41,750	$40,150	$(1,600)	$147,750	$158,705	$10,955	$802,500	$799,105	$(3,395)
NET CASH FLOW	$750	$3,500	$2,750	$62,612	$49,425	$(13,187)	$22,500	$3,445	$(19,055)

Conclusion

I f you are reading this book, you share our enthusiasm and respect for the nonprofit sector. You might be a bookkeeper, board member, employee, volunteer, consultant, or a representative of an organization that funds nonprofit organizations. Those of us who have worked with and observed the nonprofit sector understand the vital role nonprofit organizations play in our society. They represent a major economic and social force. The employees, board members, and volunteers associated with nonprofit organizations make an enormous contribution to making our world a better place.

It is our belief that timely, accurate, and clear financial information helps ensure the survival and success of your nonprofit organization. In our work with nonprofits, we have seen organizations with poor bookkeeping and financial reporting fail to survive despite offering needed services. As described throughout this book, the typical nonprofit is under intense review from the various stakeholders associated with it. Successful nonprofit organizations focus on controlling their funds to become financially stronger, enabling them to fulfill their missions.

This book has focused on bookkeeping and accounting, budgeting, cash flow forecasting and management, and reporting. You must install the best accounting system for your organization based on its size, mix of funding sources, and overall operations. Your board and executive staff must model superior leadership, a collaborative culture, and overall support to build and maintain the best financial records. If your organization follows these concepts, your organization will have an enormous advantage over other organizations that fail to follow the principles of good financial record keeping:

- First, the organization should prepare accurate budgets based on its mission, goals, and plans.

- Second, the organization should prepare accurate and timely financial reports and compare the actual results to the budget. When material variances are identified by the financial reports, an effective corrective action plan should be prepared and implemented rapidly.

- Last, accurate cash flow reports and forecasts must be kept up to date and monitored by finance staff and top management to ensure the organization never fails to make a payroll or pay an important bill.

You need all three of these elements to ensure the success of your organization.

These five recommendations are important to your organization's continued success:

1. Communication/collaboration
2. Innovation in budgeting
3. Emphasis on cash flow
4. Continuous training
5. Professional financial consulting

Communication/Collaboration

To be successful, the organization must use effective communication and collaboration skills in budgeting, effective cash flow planning, and bookkeeping. Communication and collaboration are integral aspects of successful financial management. The earlier and more intensively you involve all relevant parties in your financial processes, the more effective the result will be.

The most effective method to improve financial performance is to have a weekly meeting with a fixed agenda between key staff in bookkeeping, finance, fundraising, and management. In a small organization, this might be a two-person meeting, and in larger organizations it might involve many participants. Regardless of the agenda, one purpose of the meeting should be to inform all participants of the big picture. For example, the person in charge of fundraising should inform bookkeeping about future fundraising activities; the bookkeeper can then plan for the additional resources (time and money) that will be required as a result of the fundraising campaign. At each meeting, participants should discuss any procedural problems that have surfaced; resolution of these problems will help to fine tune the entire organization.

It is important that financial reports, such as "budget-versus-actual reports and cash flow forecasts, be discussed among and between the participants. For example, if the cash flow forecast indicates a problem in making a payroll in three months, then management must get that information in writing and take the action necessary to ensure that the payroll is met.

Here is one of the most important lessons to learn from this book:

Management and bookkeeping must meet frequently and communicate in writing.

Innovation in Budgeting

Innovation is a word we frequently hear in this millennium. One truly great innovative idea, opportunity budgeting, was first described by Peter F. Drucker in *Managing in Turbulent Times* (HarperCollins, 1980). Briefly, *opportunity budgeting* is the process by which organizations build into their budgets funds not earmarked for a particular use but identified for use when an opportunity presents itself. Opportunity budgeting provides the structure and the ability to be innovative and to react to changes in the environment.

A second idea, based on a similar concept, is that organizations put a contingency line item in a budget of 5 to 10 percent. This provides the organization with the flexibility to react to changing financial results. If income is below the amount budgeted, the contingency allowance gives the organization a safety net. If income and expenses meet the budgeted figures, then the organization has a surplus that it can use in future periods or for other purposes. This strategy is not usable if the budget you are preparing is for a cost reimbursement grant, since such monies are only earned when spent.

Emphasis on Cash Flow

There is an old saying: "Cash Is King." Failure to remember this adage can lead to bankruptcy. Cash is the most liquid, portable asset of the organization; well-designed and well-implemented internal control procedures are essential. People do not steal journal entries; they steal cash. In addition to safeguarding the asset, it is vital to properly plan for expenditures and to forecast the organization's cash flow position. Financial statements showing a surplus are no consolation if the organization runs out of cash.

Continuous Training

Organizations must have the systems and structures in place for training staff on an ongoing basis. There are good reasons to provide ongoing training to staff, board members, and volunteers:

- It creates an environment in which learning and increasing effectiveness are valued.

- It provides staff with skills and information for improving financial operations.

Professional Financial Consulting

This book was written for bookkeepers and other parties interested in the nuts and bolts of accumulating, analyzing, and recording the transactions of a nonprofit organization. The more complex aspects of nonprofit financial management, auditing, and tax reporting are left to other books. While this book addresses the basics, it is important for your organization to engage an experienced accountant or Certified Public Accountant (CPA) to assist your bookkeeping and accounting staff when needed. The CPA firm or individual CPA is a resource to answer questions on bookkeeping and other, often complex, issues (including internal controls, the application for tax exemption, maintaining tax exempt status, UBIT, sales taxes, and cost allocation plans). Whether it is required by state law or not, it is worthwhile for the nonprofit organization to engage a CPA firm to perform an annual audit in accordance with GAAP, GAAS, and with any additional audit standards required by your funding sources.

It is essential for you to recognize when expert consultation is necessary. If you are searching for assistance, here are a few suggestions:

- Ask a nonprofit organization you think is well run for a recommendation.

- Contact your state CPA society. In many states the society has a specific committee composed of CPAs most interested in working with nonprofit organizations.

- Ask a funding source for a recommendation—they see many financial statements and they might indicate a special confidence in a firm or two.

- Visit the website set up to support this book for more ideas and resources.

Spend the time and resources to find the right financial consultant, with the type of experience you need, and your organization will have a greater opportunity to be successful.

PART FOUR

Resources

This section provides you with additional resources on the subject of nonprofit organizations and bookkeeping. Visit the Web site for this book at http://www. josseybass.com/go/bookkeepingfornonprofits for additional information, worksheets, updates, and other resources.

Resource A is a list of guidelines on the subject of good financial management.

Resource B contains guidance about setting up your paper and computer files.

Resource C discusses alternative record keeping approaches, including manual ledger, computer service bureaus, computer software applications, and Web-based accounting systems.

Resource D is an introduction to managing your computer system's security and data protection.

Resource E is a brief overview of the process of organizing a nonprofit, applying for recognition of exempt status, and the tax reporting issues facing nonprofit organizations.

Resource F contains a checklist designed to assist bookkeepers in preparing for the special challenges of a government grant. Many of the concepts identified in the checklist are useful for effective management of any type of grant.

Resource G contains excerpts of OMB Circular A-122. This circular establishes principles for determining costs of grants, contracts, and other agreements between the federal government and nonprofit organizations; the bookkeeper must become familiar with the concepts in A-122. (The full document is available on the web at http://www.whitehouse.gov/omb; the excerpts presented in this book provide a brief look at the document that discusses cost principles.)

Resource H is a list of interesting Web sites. The information at these sites provides invaluable help for bookkeepers and other nonprofit staff members.

Resource I is a useful bibliography.

A Good Financial Management

These rules are designed to provide a framework for an organization to properly plan, budget, keep good books, control cash flow, and institute financial monitoring. They are not rules in any legal sense; they are guidelines for the organization to follow as it works toward fulfilling its mission and goals.

Written Financial Policies and Procedures

The organization needs written financial policies and procedures that address how the organization keeps its books. These policies relate to all aspects of financial management, including bookkeeping, budgeting, cash flow, and financial reporting and monitoring. Such policies and procedures should be updated at least annually.

Dissemination of Policies and Procedures

The financial policies need to be widely disseminated among all levels of staff, volunteers, clients, and board members. Everyone has some financial responsibility to the organization. For example, a staff member needs to understand the importance of keeping good time records to substantiate time worked so accurate payrolls can be prepared. That same staff person might be counseling a client and thereby generating a billable service, payable by the federal government. This staff person must make sure that the client's chart is properly filled in to substantiate the services rendered. Auditors will review such records, which are needed to substantiate billings and services provided to the organization's clients. The supervisory staff needs to understand its role within the financial system.

Effective Hiring, Training, and Accountability

The organization must hire competent personnel and give them the proper resources to perform their record-keeping roles. Effective performance management and accountability controls need to be built into the system. There should be a clear organization chart that delineates responsibilities within the finance department and within the entire organization. People need to know what authority they have or do not have to purchase materials. The policies need to identify who is delegated with what authority. For example, the policy must specify who can sign a check on behalf of the organization and which dollar amounts of checks need two signatures.

Effective Communication

The accounting department must be given the information and respect needed to function properly. The staff in accounting must know when a special event is planned so they can assist in designing any special financial procedures needed for the event. For example, accounting must bill special event sponsors for their participation. Accounting must also check with the insurance broker to verify that the organization is properly insured for the special event activity.

Proper Internal Control

The financial policies need to reflect the proper internal control procedures that protect the organization's assets from theft and to ensure accurate financial reports. Good internal controls should be designed to consist of a series of checks and balances, preventing one individual from having total control of an activity within the organization. For example, one person should not deposit funds, record them in the books, write checks, and then do the bank reconciliation. Internal control procedures must always be in force; no one in the organization is exempt from adhering to these procedures. This is not a reflection on the personnel of the organization; it is a reflection on the realities faced by all organizations.

Accurate and Timely Budgets

Budgets need to be prepared accurately by a collaborative team of staff, volunteers, board members, consultants, clients, and anyone else able to supply useful data. Budgets need to be truthful representations of effective overall planning. They should cover all aspects of the operations. They need to be correlated with the actual staffing plans the organization has for an activity. Most frequently missed is the need to update budgets when circumstances or plans change. The second most frequently missed budget item is setting up a proper amount for contingencies in a budget. In the new millennium, uncertainties are becoming more difficult to plan for. One effective strategy is to budget monies for situations or needs that might have arisen from unforeseen circumstances.

Financial Monitoring and Oversight

Financial monitoring involves proper design of policies and procedures, effective training, and proper oversight. The oversight must consist of the preparation of regular financial monitoring reports tailored to the organization's operations. These reports must compare actual financial performance to budgets. In addition, cash flow forecasts must be prepared on a regular basis to ensure proper cash management. Variances in either of these reports beyond a specific amount must be explained, and when necessary, a corrective action plan must be instituted. A good rule to follow is that a variance of 5 percent or more requires careful research and perhaps remedial action.

Compliance Requirements of Grants

For-profit organizations must adhere to compliance rules to make sure they follow applicable laws and regulations such as OSHA and ADA. Nonprofit organizations need to follow the aforementioned rules plus any regulations and restrictions that are part of a grant contract with a private organization, foundation, federal, state, county, or city funding sources. It is essential that the bookkeeping and finance staff thoroughly understand grant rules. For example, government grants invariably require grantees to follow various versions of the Davis Bacon Law, which mandates that contractors paid with public dollars must pay workers at comparable pay scales to union workers. Grant compliance can be very complicated and requires the bookkeeping staff to have in-depth knowledge of the grant contract.

Client Eligibility

The eligibility criteria defined in a grant or government contract identifies the characteristics the grantor or funding source wants the recipient of the services to have. For example, specific income eligibility and other rules relate to which people can receive money under the Women, Infants, and Children program (WIC), a thirty-year-old program to improve the nutrition of eligible women, infants, and children. A nonprofit organization receiving funds for such an activity must maintain documentation that only eligible participants receive the designated assistance and services. If the agency fails to adhere to WIC guidelines, the nonprofit could conceivably fail in fulfilling the grant contract and therefore have to return any funds spent improperly or otherwise make restitution. In some instances organizations have less responsibility, since clients come to the organization with identification indicating they are eligible as certified by another entity. Frequently the certifying entity is a governmental unit. In most organizations, the bookkeeper or finance department is not directly responsible for compliance and eligibility issues unrelated to financial transactions. However, since a failure to comply with the complex set of requirements relating to these issues could be very damaging for the organization, it is very important that accounting know the rules and what is really going on at the organization. *Damaging* in this context means that the organization might have to return funds spent for services to ineligible clients. Even if the funding source does not try to collect these funds, one definite result will be the cessation of the award of any future contracts of this type. It is imperative that joint planning and monitoring meetings take place with program, accounting, and executive staff to make sure a clear assignment of compliance responsibilities takes place.

Adequate Insurance

The organization must consult with experienced insurance professionals to purchase and monitor adequate insurance coverage for the various complex risks associated with the operation of nonprofit organizations. Malpractice, directors and officers, bonding, and a wide gamut of liability, theft, valuable papers, accounts receivable, and business interruption coverage should be discussed with experienced insurance professionals and adequate coverage obtained.

Annual Audit, Tax Returns, and Information Filings

The organization should be audited annually in accordance with the audit standards applicable to its funding sources and state law by a CPA firm experienced in auditing similarly funded organizations. This firm also should be retained to prepare all required tax returns and information filings.

Careful study of these rules will encourage and mandate effective communication on a regular basis between all areas of a nonprofit organization.

Setting Up Your Files

The physical organization of your paperwork and computer files is critical to meeting the goal we have for your bookkeeping system: that each transaction is fully documented, completely traceable, and fully usable. If you can't find a document, the system fails to meet the goal.

The entire topic of record confidentiality has become a national concern. Privacy statutes have made the need for protecting information related to staff and clients very important. In addition, laws such as the Health Insurance Portability and Accounting Act (HIPAA) have made poor or improper record keeping a very dangerous and potentially costly situation.

In this resource, we'll suggest some ways to organize your files. The techniques we describe have been used by thousands of organizations; they provide a good starting point for designing your system. How many of these ideas you implement will depend on the size of your organization and your own experience and evaluation of the situation.

Large organizations sometimes maintain a formal central depository for all important permanent files such as contracts, insurance policies, and leases. Some larger organizations hire trained librarians to maintain their most important files and to train other staff on proper indexing and filing techniques. Smaller organizations should delegate one person to act as a file supervisor to make sure all files are removed from open areas and properly secured at the end of each day. This is an important activity to protect clients and staff.

Paper Files

A typical nonprofit organization has to organize many different types of documents, including the following categories:

- General correspondence
- Funding source proposals, grant awards, contracts, and agreements
- Committee and board reports
- Reference materials
- Accounting records

Organizing the accounting records is an important component of any bookkeeper's job. As we have written repeatedly, each transaction and financial event must be traceable. With properly organized and maintained paperwork, the ability to trace a transaction back to the source document is greatly enhanced.

The types of accounting records maintained by an organization vary, but the following list discusses the most common document types:

• *Cash receipts*—a photocopy of the check and remittance advice for each receipt, when available, is filed with a copy of the cash receipts summary for each bank deposit. The cash receipts summary includes the date of the deposit, the source of the receipt, the amount of the receipt, and a posting reference. The source of the receipt could be a funding source, a client of the organization, or any other source of funds. In a fee-for-service organization, it is sometimes advisable to use one cash receipts summary and bank deposit for client payments and a separate summary and bank deposit for all other receipts on the same day. The posting reference describes the reason for the receipt; this could be a funding source reference, accounts receivable invoice number, or a general ledger account code reference and description. The Cash Receipts summary, copies of each check, and a copy of the bank deposit slip are all filed together in chronological order in a monthly folder.

• *Invoices*—when the organization prepares an invoice for services rendered to a client, such as in a fee for service situation, one copy of the invoice is filed chronologically, and another copy of the invoice is filed by client name. Any supporting documents are filed in the client's folder. A new set of client folders is started with each new fiscal year. Depending on the activity being invoiced, other copies of the invoice might be printed and forwarded to the appropriate department or program in the organization. A daily invoice register is created and filed in chronological order. If your organization bills for services related to any federal, state, or managed care program, such files might be subject to annual and more frequent audits. Billings not properly documented both at the patient or client file level and at the accounting level can lead to serious loss of revenue and penalties. In addition, recent privacy regulations attached to HIPAA create severe penalties for failing to protect client records properly from public disclosure. It is also important to make sure all patient or client files are being kept according to standards specified by the funding source, HMO, or entity paying for the services. Good files are not just an internal management goal but are also needed to protect the organization against severe penalties.

• *Cash disbursements*—a copy of the remittance advice (or, if one is not available, a photocopy of the check) is stapled to the invoices being paid and is filed by vendor name. Most computer software supports the printing of a three-part 8½ × 11-inch check, where the top section is a remittance advice listing the payment details, the middle section is the actual check, and the bottom section is a copy of the remittance advice. The top two sections are sent to the vendor, and the bottom section forms the top page of the paid invoice packet. Attached to each invoice are the supporting documents: purchase order, receiving document, and approval forms. The vendor files are kept alphabetically; a new set of files is started with each new fiscal year. A cash disbursements journal or daily check register is created and filed in chronological order.

• *Unpaid vendor invoices*—here we need two sets of files. As these documents are received, they are filed alphabetically by vendor in a file of unprocessed vendor invoices. This same file contains other documents from the vendor invoice packet, such as receiving documents, packing lists, and copies of the purchase order. Once these documents are processed, the vendor invoice is posted and filed alphabetically by vendor in the processed vendor invoice file. Processing the vendor invoice packet includes the matching of invoice, purchase order, receiving document, packing list, and approval forms. Having two sets of unpaid vendor invoice files organizes the process and helps prevent the inadvertent posting and payment of a vendor invoice prior to approval. A purchase journal, which includes the details of each posted vendor invoice, is created daily and filed in chronological order. The documents in the processed vendor invoice files match the accounts payable open items report, while the documents in the unprocessed vendor invoice files represent potential items for accrual, as well as work still to be done.

• *Purchase orders*—these documents are normally created on multi-part forms and distributed to the appropriate departments. One copy is filed numerically, and a second copy is filed by vendor name; both of these files are located in the purchasing department if the organization has one; otherwise they are located in the accounting department. A copy of the PO is sent to accounts payable, where it is filed in the unprocessed vendor invoice file that we described above. A copy is sent to the receiving department, and another copy is sent to the person with budgetary responsibility for approvals. This budgetary person may be the bookkeeper or another staff person designated by management. Other copies are often used for various purposes.

• *Insurance policies, leases, and contracts*—copies of these documents are filed by individual program. Depending on the nature of the document, they should be filed in a permanent folder or a fiscal year folder. Documents that span fiscal years are filed in the permanent folder. A new set of annual folders is started with each new fiscal year. Please remember that it is a good rule to never throw out an insurance policy; they should be part of your permanent files even though most policies now only cover events that occurred during the insurance period.

• *Bank statements and bank reconciliations*—these documents are filed in chronological order.

• *Monthly accounting reports*—summaries of cash receipts, A/R invoicing, accounts receivable open items, cash disbursements, purchase journals, accounts payable open items, general journals, general ledgers, and trial balances are created each month and are filed chronologically.

• *Employee records*—a separate folder is maintained for each employee, containing all documents related to the employment of the individual. This folder is usually divided into various compartments, holding documents from the application and hiring process, annual reviews, sick, holiday and vacation logs, health benefit documents, pension documents, and other types of correspondence. The employee folders are filed alphabetically in two sections: one for active employees and another for inactive employees.

• *Payroll records*—these reports are filed chronologically and are maintained on a calendar year basis.

• *Payroll tax records*—the depository advices and copies of all payroll tax returns are filed by calendar quarter.

• *Financial reports, budgets, board reports, and minutes*—these documents are filed chronologically by category.

• *Permanent file*—this should include audits, incorporation papers, personnel policies, corporate by-laws, board reports, and other documents that span calendar and fiscal periods.

All of the files should be maintained in secure file cabinets that are locked after business hours. Key documents should be kept in a fireproof safe.

Paper documents are only useful when they can be easily located. When devising a filing structure, you have to anticipate the possible scenarios when a document is needed. You might know the date when the client was invoiced but not the client name; having a copy of the invoice filed by date helps you locate the document. You might know the client name but not know the invoice number; copies of the invoices filed alphabetically help you locate the document. Alternate ways to find the same document make the goal of transaction traceability easy to achieve.

CHECKLIST B.1   **Insurance Coverage Checklist**

☐ Has an experienced insurance broker assessed the organization's risks and exposures?

☐ Is all mandatory coverage in place (for example, workers' compensation insurance, disability insurance)?

Is the organization adequately covered for the following risks?

  ☐ Fire and comprehensive (property)

  ☐ Theft

  ☐ Vehicle

  ☐ General liability

  ☐ Fidelity bonding

  ☐ Business interruption

  ☐ Errors and omissions (malpractice)

  ☐ Sexual harassment

  ☐ Valuable papers

  ☐ Special coverage for other exposures

Record Retention Rules

Federal, state, and other record retention rules vary. For example, payroll-related records should be retained for at least seven years. Some grants specify a five-year rule for record retention, beginning after the audit for the period has been prepared. Federal tax reporting normally requires supporting records and documents for three years after the date a return is filed. If the IRS performs an audit of a return, they might ask for an extension of time in order to complete the audit. Different rules may apply to pension plan records; this issue needs careful oversight and planning. Discuss these matters with your auditor, accountant, or attorney for guidance based on your location and your contractual activities.

Record retention rules also apply to computer records. It is advisable to print out and retain reports from computer software rather than relying solely on copies of the data maintained in a digital format. Damage to the media, changes to standard media formats, and changing computer software versions may limit your ability to use digitally based records. Accounting records stored on an eight-inch floppy disk are useless when current computer hardware lacks an eight-inch disk drive.

Computer Files

The computer system in any organization is used for a wide variety of tasks by many different users. We will discuss security, passwords, backups, and other technical topics in Resource D; in this resource, we focus on the physical layout of the computer files and documents you create and use every day.

No single file structure is right for everyone; so much depends on the individual requirements of your staff. In the next section, we'll take a look at ABC Nonprofit, a fictional organization designed to illustrate the process of analyzing and implementing a computer file structure.

Implementing a File Structure: ABC Nonprofit

ABC Nonprofit has a local area network in its headquarters, consisting of five personal computers used by the following individuals:

1. Accounting manager

2. Bookkeeper

3. Accounts payable clerk

4. Receptionist

5. Office manager

ABC Nonprofit uses many computer applications; the three applications we will discuss are the Fund-Account accounting package, Microsoft Word, and Microsoft Excel. ABC's local area network is based on the *peer-to-peer model;* there is no separate computer that serves as a file server.

Our first step is to survey the computer usage and requirements of the staff members. The survey of the staff reveals the computer activity shown in Exhibit B.1.

Survey of Staff's Computer Activity

APPLICATION	ACCOUNTING MANAGER	BOOKKEEPER	A/P CLERK	RECEPTIONIST	OFFICE MANAGER
Fund-Account	Heavy	Heavy	Heavy	None	None
Excel	Heavy	Heavy	Light	Light	Light
Word	Light	Heavy	Light	Heavy	Light

Based on estimated computer activity of the five staff members, we have determined the office manager's machine has the largest amount of spare computing power. The office manager is given the most powerful computer; this PC will handle requests from other computers on the network, it will service the office manager's processing needs, and it will be used to produce a daily backup of the shared information.

When Fund-Account is installed, the software asks you to choose the location for the data files. ABC installed the Fund-Account files in a folder called *FundAccount* on the office manager's computer. Since the office manager is not going to use Fund-Account, the application software is not installed on her machine. Fund-Account is installed on the computers used by these individuals: the accounting manager, the bookkeeper, and the accounts payable clerk. In each case, Fund-Account looks for the data files on the office manager's machine; all users of the accounting software are accessing the same data.

Each of the five staff members uses Word and Excel. By default, these applications are set to save documents to the "My Documents" folder on the local hard disk. While that location is fine for documents that will not be used by another user, most documents created in ABC's offices are shared, at one time or another, by other staff members. ABC has adopted the following technique:

- General purpose documents are stored on the file server (the office manager's machine).

- Private or confidential documents are stored in the local *My Documents* folder.

We will create a folder on the office manager's hard drive called *ABC*; this folder, and any folders created within this folder, are shared by the staff members. Access to the individual sub-folders is controlled with passwords.

In the ABC folder, we will create the following sub-folders:

- Users

    AcctMgr

    Bookkeeper

    APClerk

    Reception

    OffMgr

- Accounting2004

  Misc

  GL

  AR

  AP

  Payroll

- General

  Correspondence

  Reference

  Board

- Programs2004

  Program1

  Proposals

  Grants

  Contracts

  Agreements

  Program2

  Proposals

  Grants

  Contracts

  Agreements

Some of these folders have restricted access based on the type of information and confidentiality requirements, and other folders are openly shared by the staff members. Each fiscal year, new folders are created when appropriate; for example, a new folder called *Programs2005* (and all sub-folders) is added for the new fiscal year.

The structure of this design lends itself to easily finding a computer document, and it also facilitates the backup process. Copying both the *FundAccount* folder and the *ABC* folder on the office manager's PC to another media captures all of the Fund-Account, Word, and Excel documents created by the staff.

Using the Web for File Storage

The low cost of Web site hosting packages makes it possible for every organization to have a Web site. Aside from the promotional and educational advantages of publishing a site, hosting packages offer you an additional resource: off-site disk storage. It is a simple task to create a password-protected folder on your Web site's server to store documents, both for safekeeping and to provide access to selected individuals. The documents are not accessible to the casual Web site visitor, but they can be easily downloaded by individuals who possess the exact link to the document as well as the password to give them access. This is a great way to distribute a large document; you simply e-mail the link and password to the intended recipients, and they can retrieve the document at a time and place convenient for them.

Intranet

An easy way to publish documents for members of your local area network (LAN) is to save the document as an HTML file to a folder that everyone has access to (Microsoft Office products offer the HTML file type as one of your choices when saving a document). A true Intranet has a Web server attached to your LAN, which will serve up the HTML files upon request. Your organization could set up a Web server for the LAN, but it isn't necessary. Members of your staff can simply point their Web browser at the HTML files to view them as Web pages. This is an effective way to distribute employee manuals, policies, procedures, and event announcements.

Summary

The design and implementation of your file structure is critical to having a fully documented, completely traceable, and fully usable accounting system. By examining the types of transactions and documents you need to file and by visualizing the scenarios where you will need to locate documents, you can maintain your files in a logical and efficient manner.

RESOURCE C Alternative Recordkeeping Approaches

Every organization implements their recordkeeping system based on their needs, skill level, and budget. In this resource, we'll examine several of the options available. Our goal is to discuss some recordkeeping approaches, which we hope you will find useful.

Manual Ledgers

Manually posted accounting systems have been used for hundreds of years, but the increasing availability of technology has eliminated manual systems from serious consideration for nearly every organization. The concepts it employs are valid and instructive, so it has been largely relegated to the classroom. Individual procedures in any accounting system will continue to be done manually, but today the majority of accounting procedures, the posting of the general ledger, and the generation of reports are all commonly done by computer.

Service Bureaus

In the era before personal computers became affordable, the only way for a small organization to automate its accounting system was to use a service bureau. Designed to process data prepared by the organization and generate reports from that data, service bureaus handled transactions in batches. This predecessor to more modern methods was and still is used for activities such as payroll. Service bureaus never had great success in maintaining a full set of books for most clients, since such systems lack the real-time posting and retrieval of information required for effective financial management.

Payroll service bureaus, which still play a dominant role in this particular area of recordkeeping, are recommended for all nonprofit organizations. Payroll service bureaus are commonly used by organizations of all sizes because the constantly changing payroll tax laws and filing requirements are difficult and expensive for individual organizations to manage. The payroll service bureau can directly deposit paycheck amounts into the employees' bank accounts, and many organizations have the payroll service remit all withholding and payroll taxes directly to the taxing authorities. In addition, many payroll service bureaus offer other services in the areas of human resources and fringe benefits, including the tracking of sick, holiday, and vacation time. One recent trend is the electronic transfer of payroll data from the organization to the payroll service, which can save time and reduce processing errors.

Before selecting a payroll service company, make sure it offers the range of services, security, and backup facilities required by your organization. Continue to monitor and review the payroll and payroll tax reporting functions to ensure that the payroll service bureau is performing according to the contract.

Software and Hardware

It is difficult to make a decision about hardware without considering the software you intend to use. The brand of computer is often less important than the flavor of software it is capable of running. Everyone has a preference, but this topic largely centers on the computer's Operating System (OS). Typically you will have a choice of machines running these OSs:

- Windows
- Linux
- Apple OS

While other systems exist, most small and medium-sized organizations will select computers from one or more of these OS families.

Windows dominates the market; therefore it has the largest variety of software applications available in the marketplace. Linux is becoming more popular, but so far much of its popularity has been in the server arena; its desktop applications are not as numerous or as widely used as a similar Windows title. Apple OS runs only on Apple Computers; it has a dedicated group of supporters and users, and it excels in the graphic arts arena.

Accounting Software

There are many popular accounting software packages available for small- and medium-sized organizations, including these market leaders:

- Blackbaud Financial Edge
- Fund EZ
- Great Plains Accounting
- MAS 90
- MIP Fund Accounting (Best Software)
- Peachtree Accounting
- QuickBooks Pro

Selecting the right software for your organization involves many factors, including the design of your chart of accounts (see Chapter Three) and the structure of your organization. It is important that you understand the capabilities of the software and how closely the software matches your organization's needs. Most software has alternative methods of recording transactions. For example, one method of recording a disbursement will present you with the image of a check; another method of recording that transaction will present you with a table in the form of a check register. Here are some questions to consider when you are selecting your accounting software:

- Is the chart of accounts structure adequate for your current and future needs?

- Does the software include a job costing component that can be utilized to track program and department activity?

- Is a multi-user version available (all but the smallest organizations will need to have more than one user at a time able to access and update the accounting records)?

- What is the maximum number of concurrent users?

- Is there a limit on the number of records allowed (vendors, general ledger accounts, and so on)?

- Does the accounting period structure in the software match your organization's accounting period structure?

- Are the standard reports informative?

- Can you create custom reports?

- Can data be exported for further analysis?

- Can you close accounting periods to prevent further entries?

- Can you close individual software modules (A/R, A/P, Payroll) independently of one another and independently from the general ledger?

- Is there a safeguard against the deletion of previously posted transactions?

- Is a budget module available?

- Is a cash forecasting module available?

- Is an audit trail produced for all transactions that indicates who posted the transaction and when it was posted?

Off-the-shelf accounting packages do an adequate job, but customization of the features is seldom an option. You need to select the package that most closely fits the needs of your organization. You can then use the techniques in this book to record the transactions accurately as they occur.

Interim reporting capabilities are essential for a nonprofit organization. Grant funding sources require reports based on the period covered by the grant. Not all grants match the organization's year end, and not all grants are twelve months in duration. The accounting software you select must be flexible in selecting the reporting period.

Most accounting software also provides added flexibility by allowing you to export the data into a spreadsheet format.

Here is an important caveat: computer users often become comfortable with word processing and spreadsheet software. These applications are extremely powerful, and many users become proficient at entering and manipulating information with them. It is tempting to attempt to post your books using your spreadsheet application: you already know how it works, you already own it. . . . *Don't do it.* At its best, accounting done with a spreadsheet program is simply a manual system with pretty formatting and automatic addition of amounts. True accounting software packages do much more than simply add up amounts and produce printouts of the data entered. For example, properly designed accounting software requires the user to make an entry to correct an error or change a previously entered item. After the correcting entry, both entries remain visible in the records, so an audit trail exists for anyone reviewing records. Proper internal controls do not exist in spreadsheets or word processors; changes can be made at any time without traceability. For this and for many other reasons, you should never attempt to maintain your organization's financial records using a spreadsheet or word processing application. Certain low-end accounting software packages (often designed to maintain a personal or small business checkbook) allow the erasure of prior entries and also neglect the requirement to maintain an audit trail for every posting. Such accounting systems fail to meet minimum standards and should be avoided.

As we've seen in previous chapters, your word processing and spreadsheet programs are essential tools that you use when analyzing and documenting accounting information. The proper use of the right accounting software will help your bookkeeping system meet the goal we introduced in our opening chapter: To capture each transaction one time in a way that is fully documented, completely traceable, and fully usable by every person within and outside the organization who has a stake in the organization.

Concurrent Users

The accounting package you choose for your organization should be designed for concurrent users or offer an upgrade path to a version that supports concurrent users. Even small organizations will at one time or another need to give two or more staff members access to the accounting system at the same time. This feature is frequently labeled *multi-user capability,* and you should consider the long-term impact of selecting any accounting package that does not offer it. Attempting to use a software package not designed to have concurrent users in a multi-user environment will lead to corrupt data and an unreliable recordkeeping system.

Single PC

The smallest organizations can afford to purchase a personal computer (PC). The advantages are too numerous to list here. We've discussed the accounting packages that are available, but it is important to note that your computer should be capable of handling the following tasks (at a minimum):

- Accounting

- Word processing

- Spreadsheets

- E-mail

Local Area Network

A Local Area Network (LAN) is a group of individual computers located in a single geographic location, tied together to enable them to share resources such as files and printers. There are many variations available, but most LANs fall into one of three categories:

1. Peer-to-peer

2. File server and peer-to-peer

3. Client/server

In a peer-to-peer network, individual computers are connected together in a workgroup. Each computer in the LAN has resources, such as disk drives, file folders, and printers, which can be shared with other computers in the workgroup. This is an economical way of maximizing your investment in equipment, and it works well in a small office with just a few computers. Security is somewhat limited; resources can be shared as *read only,* and access can be limited by establishing passwords. One disadvantage of a peer-to-peer network is that resources are not available unless the owner (computer) of the resource is powered on and connected to the LAN. Another disadvantage is that the performance of a computer that is sharing a resource could decline as it services requests from other computers in the workgroup.

Using a separate computer to act as a file server in a peer-to-peer network improves the flexibility and performance of the LAN. This is essentially a peer-to-peer network with a single computer devoted to making resources available to members of the LAN. The file server is always on and available, and all of its attention is devoted to handling requests from the workgroup.

A true client/server network has a computer dedicated to storing and manipulating data on the network. Clients, which are other members of the LAN, send a request to the server, at which point the server actually processes the request. In a peer-to-peer network, the file server will allow another computer to use a file; the service it provides is minimal—just enough to give access to the data. In a client/server environment, the client will issue a request, and the server will carry it out—actually taking over some of the processing. This is a common set-up for larger organizations, where powerful back-end systems are implemented. Smaller organizations often start out with the less costly LANs discussed earlier.

Wide Area Network

Connecting computer systems over more than one geographic area is the task of a wide area network (WAN). If you use a broadband connection, such as a cable modem, when you connect to the Internet, you are using a form of a WAN. It is possible to connect the remote locations of your organization together in a WAN, but the details are beyond the scope of this book.

ASP Model

Since the late 1990s, there has been a trend toward using an Application Service Provider (ASP) to implement computer applications. ASPs offer everything from generic applications such as word processors and spreadsheet programs to complex financial integrated systems. The theory is that ASPs will obtain the latest version of the application and deploy it on large servers at their location; organizations will pay rent to the ASP to be able to use the application over some type of communication line.

The ASP model offers several advantages:

- Your organization can employ fewer information technology staff members.

- You avoid the higher up-front costs of purchasing a server, purchasing the application software, and deploying everything.

- You can get up and running more quickly because the ASP has already deployed the application.

- Your data is securely hosted in another location.

- Because your connection is often handled by a Web browser, the operating system you run on your local machine does not have to match the OS running on the ASP server.

- If you need to record financial transactions at multiple locations, such as writing checks or recording the collection of money, it is relatively easy to use the ASP model to post those transactions in real time. The cost is often much less than the installation of a WAN. (You might want to hire an experienced system consultant to help guide your decisions in this area.)

One of the big appeals of the ASP model is that it avoids the high cost and frequency of upgrading an application you have purchased and installed yourself. Under your Service Level Agreement, you are usually entitled to use the latest version of the application that is available; you are renting the application, and the ASP is responsible for maintaining the software.

Disadvantages of the ASP model include:

- There is usually little chance of customizing the application, since the software has been deployed to service many different organizations.

- The overall cost of ownership might be higher than purchasing and deploying the application software in-house.

- Your access to your data is dependent on two critical components: the ASP's server and the communication line.

The ASP's inability to guarantee access to your information is the biggest potential problem with the ASP model. Servers can be vulnerable to Denial-of-Service (DoS) attacks, where malicious individuals bombard a server with requests in an effort to overwhelm the server's capacity to respond. The communication line used to connect to the ASP is also subject to periods of downtime and unacceptably slow performance. Despite everyone's best efforts, it is unreasonable to expect access 100 percent of the time.

It is tempting, when faced with a high-priced new version of your software, to try to eliminate the need to purchase and deploy your own copy. Given the fact that the ASP model is still relatively new, it makes sense to proceed cautiously. If your staff are constantly using word processing and spreadsheet applications, the possible interruption of connection to the ASP would bring their activities to a halt. It makes sense to avoid the ASP model in this case.

One area where it often makes sense to use the ASP model is for the payroll application. The complexities of payroll taxes and payroll-related regulations often make it a good choice for using an outside service. Many payroll service companies now offer an ASP version, providing you with the ability to set your own data entry schedule, enabling you to update information directly, and giving you the freedom to print reports as needed. Payroll (under the ASP model) is an example of taking a function that is commonly performed by an outside service bureau and making it more flexible.

Off-Site Data Depository

The prevalence of the Web has made it easy and affordable for all organizations to have their own Web sites. Aside from the promotional benefits derived from an Internet presence, many Web site hosting packages give your organization a cost-effective method of storing data off site. This is useful for several reasons:

- Copies of your data stored on a remote Web server can be used as a backup in the event of a disaster at your physical location.

- Authorized individuals can retrieve selected data when traveling.

Most Web site hosting packages provide a large amount of storage space, much larger than the typical Web site requires. By setting up a separate folder, with appropriate permissions and passwords, your organization can copy files to the Web host. These files would not be available to the general public; the files' location is secured and hidden from a visitor to your site. Many organizations utilize this method to distribute draft documents and preliminary reports.

Summary

When planning your accounting system, be sure to consider these topics:

- Number of staff members requiring access
- Number of computers to be connected to the workgroup
- Availability of IT staff and/or consultants
- Budget
- Physical layout of your staff's work space
- Availability of a broadband (high-speed Internet access) connection
- Number of employees
- Number of vendors and suppliers
- Number of funding sources
- Number of programs, departments and cost centers
- Chart of accounts account number structure
- Number of accounts in the chart of accounts
- Accounting periods in the business cycle
- Support options provided by the accounting software
- Support options provided by the hardware vendors

Many other factors are involved in the selection process. We have tried to give you the overview you will need to tackle the task intelligently.

Managing Your Computer System: Security, Backups, and Other Considerations

One of the most valuable assets owned by any organization is not listed on a financial statement; it cannot be found in a general ledger account or in any other single accounting record. This valuable asset is *the information contained in the accounting system.* When measured by the amount of time it took to create and organize the information, its value is enormous. When you discover that much of that information is irreplaceable, its value cannot be measured.

Safeguarding your accounting system has always been important. In the past, the major concerns were the physical security of the location of the system and the mechanical functioning of the equipment. The threats included the theft of computer equipment, fire in the facility, and hard disk crashes. Today those same concerns exist, but they have been joined by a wide variety of new threats: viruses, spyware, theft of information, and theft of services.

Technology changes rapidly. It is important to keep abreast of the latest trends and security issues. The topics discussed here provide a starting point for the organization as it attempts to deal with this ever-changing and often complex task.

The Cost of Inaction

When considering the pros and cons of implementing and enforcing any security or data backup policy, it often crystallizes the issue to envision the worst-case scenario. What is the cost to re-enter every transaction for the last week, if the decision is made to skip the backup, and disaster strikes? Every measure taken to safeguard the accounting system is a form of insurance; you hope that you never need it, but you are thankful you have it when the worst case happens.

Security

Computer security has become increasingly more complex with each new technological development. The rise in connectivity has added valuable new capabilities and advantages. At the same time, computers are no longer isolated and invulnerable to threats from outside of the facility.

Internet Security

The advantages of the Internet have been well documented. Even the smallest organization can afford an always-on connection to the World Wide Web and to an e-mail server. E-mail has replaced the fax machine as the least expensive and most convenient method of sending and receiving documents. Web sites offer nearly unlimited resources for research and other uses (see the discussion in Resource C).

A connection to the Internet is also a point of vulnerability. Data are transmitted in two directions over the connection; any communication requires both the sending and receiving of information. Incoming data pose a potential threat. There are important steps to take in order to prevent someone outside of the facility from entering the computer system without permission and damaging or stealing the information.

Firewalls

While a computer is connected to the Internet, other computers on the Internet could potentially attempt to gain access over the connection; they are looking for open ports. Internet ports provide a mechanism for many different types of communications (such as Web browsing, e-mail, file sharing, networking, remote control programs, viruses, and so on) to use simultaneously the Internet connection on a PC. An open port is similar to an open door; it is a potential way to get inside. Unfortunately, the default factory configuration for PCs leaves a number of ports—specifically, those used for file sharing and networking—dangerously open.

A *firewall* is either a hardware device or a software program designed to monitor the traffic passing through a computer system. Firewalls use a set of rules that analyze the source of the data, the destination of the data, the port numbers used to transmit the data, and other components in order to determine whether or not to block the data transmission. Properly configured firewalls effectively block access to open ports by unauthorized applications. Any data that fail to meet the established criteria are discarded.

Hardware implementations of a firewall are commonly available when you purchase a *router*. These will stop all unauthorized inbound traffic originating from the Internet. In any local area network sharing a single high-speed Internet connection (such as a cable modem or DSL), a hardware router with firewall protection should be considered absolutely essential. A single hardware router will protect all PCs behind it from unsolicited inbound attacks.

However, it is important to note that a hardware firewall (particularly inexpensive routers with limited firewall abilities) doesn't necessarily stop all unauthorized activity. Once a malicious program is loaded on a PC behind the hardware firewall (via e-mail or other means), it might appear to the hardware firewall as an authorized program. At that point, the infected PC is originating outbound traffic, some of which may subsequently invite or authorize a computer outside the firewall to accept the invitation. This process is very similar to Web browsing or retrieving e-mail: when you click on a link or open your e-mail, you are inviting the external computer hosting the Web page or your e-mail account to send that page or message back through the firewall to your computer. The only difference between legitimate applications (such as a Web browser or e-mail program) and malicious programs is the port number used. Properly configuring hardware firewalls for maximum protection sometimes requires knowledge of these port numbers.

Software firewalls are also available from a variety of sources, but these are designed to protect only the PC it is loaded on. However, they do offer an added level of security; by default they analyze all outbound traffic as well as inbound and require that you specifically authorize every program requesting such Internet access. They will alert you by way of a pop-up message if some mysterious new program is suddenly requesting access to the Internet.

Virus Scanners

The biggest outside threat to any computer system comes from a computer virus. A *virus* is a piece of computer software that embeds itself into a system and then attempts to fulfill its mission, much to the detriment of its host. Viruses attempt to replicate themselves and spread the infection to other computer hosts. Many viruses have other missions as well, such as the destruction of data on the host system, sending spam from the host computer, or the acquisition of private information from the host.

Viruses are spread when an infected file is opened or executed on a previously uninfected computer. Infected files come into a computer system in a variety of ways:

- Opening an e-mail attachment

- Downloading software from the Web

- Opening an infected file from another computer on the local area network (LAN)

- Sharing an infected file on a floppy disk

    Exploiting weaknesses in the operating system (this requires no action on the user's part) directly over the Internet on a computer without firewall protection

Effective protection against virus infection comes from a combination of four things: (1) a rule against opening files from unknown sources; (2) use of a software or hardware firewall; (3) downloading and installing operating system security patches; and (4) the implementation and usage of an up-to-date virus scanner. *Operating system security patches* repair vulnerabilities that can otherwise be exploited by virus writers to penetrate your system. Virus scanners are software programs that run constantly and examine every file opened on a computer. The file's contents are compared to a virus definition library, and any matches produce a warning. Out-of-date virus software is not an effective defense; new viruses are discovered every day, and the virus scanner can only detect virus patterns it knows about. Most virus scanning software is available on a subscription basis; updates are available online and can be installed quickly and easily every day.

File Sharing, Passwords, and User Privileges

Nearly every local area network is designed to allow some file sharing capability. In an accounting system, authorized network users require access to the accounting data files; by definition, this common access means they are sharing the data.

Since data that are available to be shared are visible from other connected computers, the possibility exists that the data could be visible and accessible from a computer connected through the Internet. If possible, store the data to be shared on a machine that is not directly connected to the Internet. For any machine with an Internet connection, turn off the file-sharing capability for all folders with sensitive information. Better yet, machines directly connected to the Internet should have file sharing disabled altogether. In a network environment, there is usually very little need for end-user workstations to have file sharing enabled in the first place; that function is best handled by the file server.

Set up passwords and user privileges for all computers on the LAN. Change the passwords often for every user. Passwords should be a combination of alphanumeric characters; try not to use names, dates, or common words that are more easily guessed. Enforce a rule that passwords should not be written down and attached to the keyboard or monitor for easy reference. Use screen saver security utilities that will automatically require the entry of a password after a certain period of inactivity.

Spyware, Malware, and Adware

Although programs in these categories rarely represent a direct threat to accounting system security, they are so prevalent, hard to remove, and easily prevented that they deserve mention here. Such programs can literally hijack your Web browser: they can force your home page to be changed to a Web site you have no interest in, track which Web sites you visit, insert offensive Web sites into your list of bookmarks, and cause a barrage of pop-up advertisements whether you are actively surfing the Web or not. Users are enticed into downloading and installing these pests because they are disguised as, or bundled with, purportedly useful programs such as screensavers, free games, weather trackers, download enhancers, peer-to-peer file sharing, search toolbars, and so on. Once embedded into a system, such programs can slow down your system, disable Internet access, track keystrokes, and disable the Web browser's security settings allowing other pest programs (or worse) to install themselves subsequently without even asking permission.

If your browser already exhibits some or all of these behaviors, avoid the temptation to download and install pop-up blockers. They won't work, because they are addressing the symptom, not the problem. Your best approach is first to uninstall any such programs offering an uninstall option, download and use any of a number of programs to remove most of the remaining ones, and then review any and all programs that automatically run when you start your computer. You will also need to reset the browser's security levels and home page.

Simple preventative measures work better. Educate all Internet users never to accept any offer to download and install any free software of any kind, no matter how fun or useful it seems.

Physical Security

If you have just one PC or more than one computer linked together in a local area network (LAN), you need to make sure physical security is adequate. Unfortunately, physical theft of computers, based on their relatively small size and usefulness, is an epidemic in some organizations. Machines should be locked down with security cables when necessary. Servers should always be maintained in secure areas of your organization.

Other Security Considerations

Create and enforce a computer usage policy for the organization. The policy should address at least the following concerns:

- Installing software
- Security rules regarding password usage and maintenance
- E-mail attachment usage
- Downloading files
- Logging off and logging on
- Web site browsing restrictions
- Use of disks from outside sources
- Backup methods and rules

Common sense is one of the main weapons against computer security threats; the implementation of a comprehensive computer usage policy helps to make sure everyone uses common sense.

System Backup

Making regular backups of the computer system is essential protection against physical disaster, mechanical failure, malicious actions, and simple human error. The backup process includes the making of a copy of the system's data and transporting the copy to another physical location. The backup methodology offers many choices; selection of the appropriate choices depends on the organization, the computer system, and the circumstances at the time of the backup.

Incremental or Complete?

Backups can be made of information that has changed since the time of the previous backup, or backups can include all information on a computer system. The incremental option assumes that a valid, complete backup exists; in the event of a failure, the complete backup would be restored first, and then subsequent incremental backups would be restored by date order. Depending on the volume of information, the organization could elect to create a complete backup every time. The incremental backup strategy is more cost effective with large quantities of data.

File by File or Image?

Backup software offers a choice between creating a file-by-file backup and creating an image of the disk. In a file-by-file backup, each individual file can be accessed independently. Image backups are generally useful only when creating a complete backup. Modern compression techniques can be applied in either case. The file-by-file method is generally more flexible.

Generational Strategy

All backups are created on some type of media. There are many choices available, but each medium is a physical product subject to imperfections and a limited useful life. To minimize the risk of media failure, implement a strategy of maintaining multiple generations of backups. With this strategy, every backup is a new generation of data. Assuming that each backup is a complete set of files, today's backup is the son, yesterday's backup is the father, the day before yesterday's backup is the grandfather, and so on. Keep five or six generations in the backup archive before re-using the media. Backups created on media that cannot be re-used should be retained as long as space permits.

Media

Backup data can be recorded on several types of media: CD-R, CD-RW, DVD-R, DVD-RW, DVD+R, DVD+RW, Tape, and a separate hard disk are among the choices. The various formats of CD and DVD reflect the ability to reuse the media; the *RW* designation means the disk can be erased and re-written. Media are inexpensive enough; when using CD or DVD technology, use the write-once variety, and keep the backup in the archive. Tape is designed to be re-used; implement a generational strategy when using tape. Copying data to a separate hard drive is another possibility; unless the drive is portable and can be easily taken off-site, this type of backup media is of limited value.

Off-Site Repository

Backups should be stored in a secure, separate physical location. In the event of a fire or other disaster, a backup that is stored in the same building as the computer system provides absolutely no protection. Off-site storage via an Internet storage provider is becoming more common and should be investigated as an alternative method of storing backup data.

RAID (Redundant Array of Independent Disks)

One computer design that has recently become more affordable is *RAID* technology. RAID comes in several levels; Level 1 provides complete duplication of a hard disk on a matching second hard disk. This is also called *disk mirroring*. In Level 1, the duplicate disk write is made simultaneously with the original disk write. This protects the operation from disk failure, but it does not eliminate the need for regular, systematic backups.

UPS

Install an *Uninterruptible Power Supply* throughout the network. Even in locations with a reliable electrical supply, data can be lost during blackouts, brownouts, and large spikes in the voltage supplied. When the power goes out, UPS devices provide enough power to complete a single task and shut the system down properly; they also have the ability to clip harmful spikes to prevent damage to the equipment.

Software Audit

Every computer in the organization should be subject to a software audit on a periodic basis. The software installed on each computer is inventoried and the software licenses for all applications are documented. Application software that has been installed without a license exposes the organization to liability; corrective action should be taken to acquire the proper number of licenses for the users in the organization. A strict policy against installing software on a computer without proper approval should be enforced.

Insurance Coverage

Insurance coverage for computer hardware, software, and media is a complicated topic. Discuss your computer insurance needs with a knowledgeable insurance representative. In some cases computer equipment needs to be specifically identified on an insurance policy instead of just being listed as general equipment. In addition, many insurance policies only insure the cost of the physical media used for backups and not the value of the information contained on the media. Remove all backup media from the premises. The same insurance limitation applies to paper records. You can purchase valuable papers coverage; this is sometimes advisable despite the added cost if your paper files cannot be safeguarded in any other way.

Summary

Accounting information is valuable. A great deal of time and effort goes into the accumulation, recording, and analysis of the data. Safeguarding this valuable asset is easily accomplished if the organization develops and implements the necessary policies and procedures.

Organization and Tax Issues of Tax-Exempt Organizations

The differences in bookkeeping between for-profit and nonprofit organizations have been highlighted throughout this book. In this section, we will briefly explore the requirements of establishing an exempt organization and applying for and maintaining the tax-exempt status.

A great resource is the material prepared by the Internal Revenue Service on this topic. The IRS does an amazing job in its instructions and materials related to tax-exempt organizations. The portion of the IRS Web site devoted to charities and nonprofits is excellent.

The following publications are of particular interest:

- IRS Publication 557 (Tax Exempt Status for Your Organization)

- IRS Publication 598 (Tax on Unrelated Business Income of Exempt Organizations)

New IRS publications are issued, and older publications are updated on a regular basis. Visit the IRS Web site (www.irs.gov) often; you can also register for an e-mail notification service to inform you when new material is available on the site.

We encourage you to look at some of the taxation books published by John Wiley & Sons. Jody Blazek's books make the complex subject of tax-exempt taxation as clear as possible. Bruce Hopkins's books are also excellent.

You must rely on your CPA or tax attorney if you have a tax question or issue. The area of nonprofit taxation is complex; in addition to the federal laws, there are some challenging variations in certain states and within states at the local level. Complicating the issue is the fact that there are at least three different types of private foundations, several different categories of public charities (with their own set of rules), and over twenty additional classifications of tax-exempt organizations. Add in the variations in state laws governing exempt organizations and the sales and use tax rules—you have quite a lot of material.

The following is designed to give an overview of some federal tax rules in the tax-exempt world. The majority of tax-exempt organizations incorporate; there are other legal forms that an attorney can discuss with you (the overview below assumes the corporate form). Once you have decided on the organization's legal form, use an attorney and CPA experienced in applying for tax exemption. Small organizations with limited funds can find help with the incorporation and application processes from a number of organizations staffed by volunteer attorneys and CPAs. Contact your state's CPA society and ask to speak to the chairperson of the committee working with nonprofit organizations. A Web search of local resources in most areas of the country will yield additional assistance—a useful search phrase is *nonprofit support center.*

Overview

Engage an attorney to incorporate the proposed organization under the applicable state law. Some states, such as New York, have a number of different state tax-exempt corporate categories; the category selected depends on the charitable purpose. The next step is to apply for federal approval of the organization's exempt status. File IRS Form 1023 or IRS Form 1024 (which form to use is determined by the category of operations and the classification desired). The forms and instructions are available at http://www.irs.gov. The instructions will explain which form to use and how to proceed depending on your mission, goals, and planned activities.

The Internal Revenue Service reviews the application, asks some clarifying questions, and, if satisfied with your answers, issues a *determination letter,* which indicates your organization's responsibilities going forward. It is important to read the determination letter carefully. If your determination letter indicates it is a *final determination letter,* you have completed the process (as long as you adhere to the laws and regulations and meet the various related tests). Normally, the IRS will issue a determination letter requiring you to show, after an initial period of operation, that your actual operations did adhere to the plans you included in your application. Whether or not the letter is final, donors may rely on the determination letter as proof that they contributed to an exempt organization.

The filing of specific annual reporting forms depends on the size (measured in total support and revenue received each year) and type of exempt entity you are. Small nonprofit organizations might not have to file an annual return; others must file a short form (990EZ) or a regular annual return (990); private foundations file a 990PF. If the organization's unrelated business income exceeds a certain threshold you might need to file a 990T and pay estimated unrelated business income taxes (UBIT). Refer to the instructions for each form to see which rule applies to your organization.

The 990 series of forms can be complex, since you are not only reporting income and expense, but you are also documenting the organization's continued qualification to be considered exempt (based on the services provided) and, in many circumstances, your sources of income. For organizations that qualify as a public charity, another complicated compliance issue is the composition of income; certain ratios of public monies and contributor monies in relationship to total income must be maintained to ensure continuance of exempt status as a publicly supported charity versus a private foundation.

Obtaining and maintaining the organization's tax-exempt status is complicated. You should use the resources listed in this book to seek more knowledge in this area and engage experienced professional help for your organization. The organization's auditor should prepare the required forms for the IRS. Some smaller organizations prepare their own forms to save money. While funds are always a limited resource, especially in a small nonprofit organization, doing the form yourself could endanger the ability of your organization to maintain its exempt status.

Checklist: Financial Monitoring of Government Grants

G rants, particularly from governmental sources, usually have far more complex financial management requirements than grants from non-governmental sources. This checklist is designed to help bookkeepers better prepare for the challenges of a government grant. This checklist should be reviewed collaboratively with a program staff person to ensure proper interpretation of grant requirements.

Action Steps

A. Review Official Funding Approval Notification and Grant Documents:

1. Review the award notice/contract carefully to ensure understanding of all conditions of award. Do not assume prior grant conditions are the same as the new grant. Grant conditions change based on legislation, regulation, and directives from governmental officials.

2. Compare staff identified in budget to actual staff hired to ensure all positions filled are in budget. Some positions might require specific licenses, educational requirements, and/or degrees.

B. Facilities, Equipment, and Supplies:

1. Follow all bidding requirements, procurement policies, and procedures mandated by grant.

2. Identify amount of funds available.

3. Compare purchase orders to items in budget.

C. Develop Evaluation Designs and Materials:

1. Identify funding source evaluation requirements.

2. Identify in-house evaluation requirements.

3. Assign evaluation data-gathering/analysis responsibilities.

4. Familiarize staff with program and financial evaluation requirements, procedures, forms, and responsibilities.

D. Recordkeeping and Reporting:

1. Identify funding source reporting requirements.

2. Identify in-house reporting requirements.

3. Assign data-gathering and reporting responsibilities.

4. Create/revise record-keeping forms, procedures, and responsibilities as needed.

5. Integrate data-collection and reporting requirements with any existing database capabilities.

6. Familiarize staff with record-keeping and reporting forms, procedures, and responsibilities.

7. Begin data collection and analysis.

8. Prepare and submit required monthly in-house reports.

9. Prepare/submit funding-source reports and others as required.

E. Program Monitoring and Control:

1. Program/unit head and bookkeeper meet regularly with in-house supervisor to monitor progress against program/unit work plan and specific program/unit goals.

2. Identify, plan, and take corrective action as needed.

3. Request any needed program/activity modifications in writing, including extension, if allowed and needed.

F. Budget Monitoring and Control:

1. Prepare internal operating program/unit budget.

2. Disseminate operating budget as appropriate.

3. Program/unit head communicates regularly with finance regarding expenses, budget, and finances.

4. Identify, plan, and take corrective action as required.

5. Request budget modifications in writing as needed.

6. Request carryover of funds, if allowed and needed.

G. Program and Financial Evaluation:

1. Begin evaluation data collection and analysis.

2. Prepare and submit required in-house evaluations.

3. Prepare and submit interim and final funding-source evaluations as required.

Excerpts from OMB Circular A-122

G rants are a major source of support for many nonprofit organizations. Many grants have specific requirements and restrictions; as we discussed earlier in the book, federally funded organizations are subject to the cost definitions in OMB Circular No. A-122. In addition, many states, counties, and cities have adopted A-122, applying it to programs they fund. A-122 is a lengthy document that is modified periodically; the entire text is available at this Web site: http://www.whitehouse.gov/omb/circulars/a122/a122.html.

Spend some time reading and studying the entire document; it provides information that is essential to the management of grant contracts.

What follows are excerpts from that document; a quick look at the topics covered will reveal why this document is so important for so many nonprofit organizations.

Your actual grant budget and contract govern your relationship with a particular funding source. Not withstanding the language and guidance in A-122, costs not allowable in A-122 might be allowable if your grant documents specifically allow them. Costs considered allowable in A-122 might be disallowed if they are not specifically identified in your grant documents.

United States OMB Circular No. A-122 (Excerpted)
Revised

SUBJECT: Cost Principles for Non-Profit Organizations

1. Purpose. This Circular establishes principles for determining costs of grants, contracts and other agreements with non-profit organizations. It does not apply to colleges and universities . . . state, local and federally-recognized Indian tribal governments . . . or hospitals. The principles are designed to provide that the Federal Government bear its fair share of costs except where restricted or prohibited by law. The principles do not attempt to prescribe the extent of cost sharing or matching on grants, contracts, or other agreements . . .

2. Supersession. This Circular supersedes cost principles issued by individual agencies for non-profit organizations.

3. Applicability. . . .These principles shall be used by all Federal agencies in determining the costs of work performed by non-profit organizations under grants,

cooperative agreements, cost reimbursement contracts, and other contracts in which costs are used in pricing, administration, or settlement. All of these instruments are hereafter referred to as awards. The principles do not apply to awards under which an organization is not required to account to the Federal Government for actual costs incurred.

ATTACHMENT A

Circular No. A-122

GENERAL PRINCIPLES

Table of Contents

A. Basic Considerations

ATTACHMENT A

Circular No. A-122

GENERAL PRINCIPLES . . .

A. Basic Considerations . . .

2. Factors affecting allowability of costs. To be allowable under an award, costs must meet the following general criteria:

a. Be reasonable for the performance of the award and be allocable thereto under these principles.

b. Conform to any limitations or exclusions set forth in these principles or in the award as to types or amount of cost items.

c. Be consistent with policies and procedures that apply uniformly to both federally-financed and other activities of the organization.

d. Be accorded consistent treatment.

e. Be determined in accordance with generally accepted accounting principles (GAAP).

f. Not be included as a cost or used to meet cost sharing or matching requirements of any other federally-financed program in either the current or a prior period.

g. Be adequately documented . . .

ATTACHMENT B

Circular No. A-122

SELECTED ITEMS OF COST

[Note: The 'selected items of cost' section defines each cost item; see the actual defi- nition in A-122 to determine if the cost is allowable or non-allowable. In addition, grantees need to be aware that specific grants negotiated by your organization and approved by the funding source can contradict A-122. If a contract officer can be convinced that your program needs to spend money on an item normally not allow- able in A-122, be sure to get the exception in writing and approved by the proper level of official.]

Table of Contents

33. Page charges in professional journals
34. Participant support costs
35. Patent costs
36. Pension plans
37. Plant security costs
38. Pre-award costs
39. Professional service costs
40. Profits and losses on disposition of depreciable property or other capital assets
41. Publication and printing costs
42. Rearrangement and alteration costs
43. Reconversion costs
44. Recruiting costs
45. Relocation costs
46. Rental costs
47. Royalties and other costs for use of patents and copyrights
48. Selling and marketing
49. Severance pay
50. Specialized service facilities
51. Taxes
52. Termination costs
53. Training and education costs . . .
54. Transportation costs
55. Travel costs
56. Trustees . . .

H Web Site Resources

The following is a list of useful Web sites for bookkeepers and other readers interested in nonprofit organization management, finances, fundraising, and many other topics. (Web site addresses occasionally change; these links are valid as of March 2005.)

The first site you should visit is http://www.josseybass.com/go/bookkeepingfor nonprofits, the Web site for *Bookkeeping for Nonprofits*. The site has updated information and additional resources you will find valuable.

Other useful sites:

- http://www.allianceonline.org—the Alliance for Nonprofit Management

- http://www.charitychannel.com

- http://www.dropkin.com—Murray Dropkin's Web site, devoted to nonprofit financial consulting

- http://www.fordfound.org—the Ford Foundation

- http://www.foundations.org—a directory of charitable grant-makers

- http://www.guidestar.org—the National Database of Nonprofit Organizations

- http://www.irs.gov—the Internal Revenue Service

- http://www.josseybass.com—Jossey-Bass publishes many excellent books for nonprofit organizations

- http://www.l2li.org—the Leader to Leader Institute site (formerly the Drucker Foundation Web site)

- http://www.muridae.com/nporegulation—federal and state regulations for nonprofits

- http://nccs.urban.org—the National Center for Charitable Statistics (this site has the link you will need to download the full UCOA plus many other resources)

- http://www.ncna.org—the National Council of Nonprofit Organizations

- http://nonprofit.about.com—general information from about.com

- http://www.nonprofitquarterly.org—electronic version of the periodical

- http://www.nonprofits.org—Internet Nonprofit Center
- http://www.philanthropy.com—electronic version of the periodical *The Chronicle of Philanthropy*
- http://www.whitehouse.gov/omb—the OMB Web site (this site has the full text of OMB circulars)

RESOURCE I Bibliography

Core Texts

The following texts were used in the writing of this book:

Dropkin, M., and Allyson Hayden. *The Cash Flow Management Book for Nonprofits.* San Francisco: Jossey-Bass, 2001.

Dropkin, M., and Bill LaTouche. *The Budget-Building Book for Nonprofits.* San Francisco: Jossey-Bass, 1998.

Sumariwalla, R. D., and Wilson C. Levis. *Unified Financial Reporting System for Not-for-Profit Organizations: A Comprehensive Guide to Unifying GAAP, IRS Form 990 and Other Financial Reports Using a Unified Chart of Accounts.* San Francisco: Jossey-Bass, 2000.

Additional Texts

Additional texts that are very helpful to nonprofit organizations include the following:

Blazek, J. *IRS Form 990: Tax Preparation Guide for Nonprofits.* New York: John Wiley & Sons, 2004.

Blazek, J. *Tax Planning and Compliance for Tax-Exempt Organizations: Rules, Checklists, and Procedures.* New York: John Wiley & Sons, 2004.

Carmichael, D., Murray Dropkin, and Meryl Reed. *PPC's Guide to Audits of Nonprofit Organizations.* Fort Worth, Tex.: Practitioners Publishing Company, 2004.

Drucker, P. F. *Management Challenges for the 21st Century.* HarperBusiness, 2001.

Drucker, P. F. *Managing the Non-Profit Organization: Principles and Practices.* New York: HarperBusiness, 1992.

Hopkins, B. *The Law of Tax-Exempt Organizations.* New York: John Wiley & Sons, 2003.

Ruppel, W. *Not-for-Profit Accounting Made Easy.* New York: John Wiley & Sons, 2002.

Fundraising

Few small nonprofit organizations spend significant amounts of money on fundraising. A document from the AICPA SOP 98–2, titled *Accounting for Costs of Activities of Not-for-Profit Organizations and State and Local Governmental Entities that Include Fundraising,*

235

is a valuable resource in this sometimes under-emphasized area. This document was issued after decades of discussion, and it contains wonderful examples in it to guide the implementation of its guidelines. Since the area of fundraising is under increasing scrutiny, it is more important than ever to maintain complete and accurate records of fundraising costs. SOP 98–2 contains guidelines for organizations that solicit donations; it is an essential resource for the bookkeeper faced with accounting for fundraising activity.